The Forbes
Scrapbook of

THOUGHTS
ON THE
BUSINESS
OF LIFE

The Forbes
Scrapbook of

THOUGHTS
ON THE
BUSINESS
OF
LIFE

TRIUMPH BOOKS, INC.
Chicago

Library of Congress Catalog Number: 92-050111

International Standard Book Number: 1-880141-10-8

This 1992 trade edition is published and distributed by
Triumph Books, Chicago, by arrangement with Forbes Inc.

Triumph Books, Inc.
1436 West Randolph Street
Chicago, IL 60607

Printed in the United States of America

FOREWORD

My father wrote the introduction included in this new edition of "Thoughts on the Business of Life" for the first edition, published twenty-six years ago.

There is nothing that I can add to it.

It says in his inimitable, wonderful way exactly why this book exists.

The continuous demand by thousands for this volume is just another proof that Dad was so right in his belief that for men who matter life's intangibles have more meaning than the tangibles.

MALCOLM FORBES

INTRODUCTION

The moving motive in establishing FORBES Magazine, in 1917, was ardent desire to promulgate humaneness in business, then woefully lacking.

Too many individual and corporate employers were merely mercenarily-minded, obsessed only with determination to roll up profits regardless of the suicidal consequences of their shortsighted conduct.

They were without consciousness of their civic, social, patriotic responsibilities.

This writer warned, a third-of-a-century ago, that unless employers altered their tactics, unless they exhibited more consideration for their workers, the time would come when "Politicians will step in and do the job in a way that employers will not like."

That has happened with a vengeance!

Every issue of FORBES, since its inception, has appeared under the masthead: " With all thy getting, get understanding."

Not only so, but we have devoted, all through the years, a full page to " Thoughts on the Business of Life," reflections by ancient and modern sages calculated to inspire a philosophic mode of life, broad sympathies, charity towards all.

Having assiduously sought all these years to pursue this objective, I would — having already passed the Biblical span of three-score-years-and-ten — pass on contented if I could conscientiously feel that we have rendered at least a little service to our day and generation, that we have done something towards bequeathing a better world for my four sons and an increasing number of grandchildren.

This volume is a humble contribution to furthering human, humane Understanding.

I'm convinced, despite all the woes, wars, strife, bloodshed afflicting mankind at this moment, that Robert Burns was truly prophetic when he wrote:

> " It's comin' yet for a' that,
> That Man to Man, the world o'er,
> Shall brothers be for a' that."

I have faith that the time will eventually come when employees and employers, as well as all mankind, will realize that they serve themselves best when they serve others most.

— B. C. FORBES

P.S. Very cordial acknowledgment is hereby tendered my two long-time, faithful, assiduous associates, George Wolf and Gertrude Weiner, for their enthusiastic labors in the production of this volume.

The Forbes
Scrapbook of

THOUGHTS ON THE BUSINESS OF LIFE

THE FORBES SCRAPBOOK OF THOUGHTS ON THE BUSINESS OF LIFE

If we work marble, it will perish; if we work upon brass, time will efface it; if we rear temples, they will crumble into dust; but if we work upon immortal minds and instill into them just principles, we are then engraving upon tablets which no time will efface, but will brighten and brighten to all eternity. — *Daniel Webster*

The past, the present and the future are really one — they are *today*. — *Stowe*

Our vast progress in transportation, past and future, is only a symbol of the progress that is possible by constantly striving toward new horizons in every human activity. Who can say what new horizons lie before us if we can but maintain the initiative and develop the imagination to penetrate them — new economic horizons, new horizons in the art of government, new social horizons, new horizons expanding in all directions, to the end that greater degrees of well-being may be enjoyed by every one, everywhere. — *Alfred P. Sloan, Jr.*

The man who will use his skill and constructive imagination to see how much he can give for a dollar, instead of how little he can give for a dollar, is bound to succeed. — *Henry Ford*

No man is born into the world whose work is not born
with him. There is always work, and tools to work with, for
those who will, and blessed are the horny hands of toil.
The busy world shoves angrily aside the man who stands
with arms akimbo until occasion tells him what to do; and
he who waits to have his task marked out shall die and
leave his errand unfulfilled.   — *James Russell Lowell*

Everywhere in life the true question is, not what we have
gained, but what we do.   — *Carlyle*

Within us all there are wells of thought and dynamos of
energy which are not suspected until emergencies arise.
Then oftentimes we find that it is comparatively simple to
double or treble our former capacities and to amaze ourselves by the results achieved. Quotas, when set up for us
by others, are challenges which goad us on to surpass ourselves. The outstanding leaders of every age are those
who set up their own quotas and constantly exceed them.
                    — *Thomas J. Watson*

Too many people are thinking of security instead of opportunity. They seem more afraid of life than death.
                    — *James F. Byrnes*

If a thing is old, it is a sign that it was fit to live. Old
families, old customs, old styles survive because they are fit
to survive. The guarantee of continuity is quality. Sub-
merge the good in a flood of the new, and the good will come
back to join the good which the new brings with it. Old-
fashioned hospitality, old-fashioned politeness, old-fashioned
honor in business had qualities of survival. These will
come back.   — *Capt. Edward V. Rickenbacker*

Through unity of action we can be a veritable colossus in support of peace. No one can defeat us unless we first defeat ourselves. Every one of us must be guided by this truth. — *Dwight D. Eisenhower*

If you want to succeed you should strike out on new paths rather than travel the worn paths of accepted success.
— *John D. Rockefeller*

The nature of men and of organized society dictates the maintenance in every field of action of the highest and purest standards of justice and of right dealing. . . . By justice the lawyer generally means the prompt, fair, and open application of impartial rules; but we call ours a Christian civilization, and a Christian conception of justice must be much higher. It must include sympathy and help-fulness and a willingness to forego self-interest in order to promote the welfare, happiness, and contentment of others and of the community as a whole. — *Woodrow Wilson*

Science belongs to no one country. — *Louis Pasteur*

Whatever task you undertake, do it with all your heart and soul. Always be courteous, never be discouraged. Be-ware of him who promises something for nothing. Do not blame anybody for your mistakes and failures. Do not look for approval except the consciousness of doing your best. — *Bernard M. Baruch*

There will always be a Frontier where there is an open mind and a willing hand. — *Charles F. Kettering*

Don't be misled into believing that somehow the world
owes you a living. The boy who believes that his parents,
or the government, or any one else owes him his livelihood
and that he can collect it without labor will wake up one
day and find himself working for another boy who did not
have that belief and, therefore, earned the right to have
others work for him.   *— David Sarnoff*

I steer my bark with hope in the head, leaving fear astern.
                              — Thomas Jefferson

What I am concerned about in this fast-moving world in
a time of crises, both in foreign and domestic affairs, is not
so much a program as a spirit of approach, not so much a
mind as a heart. A program lives today and dies tomorrow.
A mind, if it be open, may change with each new day, but
the spirit and the heart are as unchanging as the tides.
                              — Owen D. Young

The right of commanding is no longer an advantage
transmitted by nature; like an inheritance, it is the fruit
of labors, the price of courage.   *— Voltaire*

What an exciting super-tomorrow it will be! Americans
are today making the greatest scientific developments in our
history. That is a promise of new levels of employment,
industrial activity and human happiness.
                              — Clarence Francis

In no direction that we turn do we find ease or comfort.
If we are honest and if we have the will to win we find only
danger, hard work and iron resolution.
                              — Wendell L. Willkie

Essential characteristics of a gentleman: The will to put himself in the place of others; the horror of forcing others into positions from which he would himself recoil; the power to do what seems to him to be right, without considering what others may say or think. — *John Galsworthy*

Though conditions have grown puzzling in their complexity, though changes have been vast, yet we may remain absolutely sure of one thing; that now as ever in the past, and as it will ever be in the future, there can be no substitute for elemental virtues, for the elemental qualities to which we allude when we speak of a man, not only as a good man, but as emphatically a man. We can build up the standard of individual citizenship and individual well-being, we can raise the national standard and make it what it can and shall be made, only by each of us steadfastly keeping in mind that there can be no substitute for the world-old commonplace qualities of truth, justice, and courage, thrift, industry, common sense and genuine sympathy with the fellow feelings of others. — *Theodore Roosevelt*

Keep true, never be ashamed of doing right; decide on what you think is right, and stick to it. — *George Eliot*

In business, as most of it is constituted today, a man becomes valuable only as he recognizes the relation of his work to that of all his associates. One worker more or less makes little difference to most big organizations, and any man may be replaced. It is the cumulative effort that counts. — *W. Alton Jones*

It is less important to redistribute wealth than it is to redistribute opportunity. — *Arthur H. Vandenberg*

I think luck is the sense to recognize an opportunity and the ability to take advantage of it. Every one has bad breaks, but every one also has opportunities. The man who can smile at his breaks and grab his chances gets on.

— *Samuel Goldwyn*

Recently, in my opinion, there has been too much talk about the Common Man. It has been dinned into us that this is the Century of the Common Man. The idea seems to be that the Common Man has come into his own at last. But I have never been able to find out who this is. In fact, most Americans will get mad and fight if you try calling them common. . . . I have never met a father and mother who did not want their children to grow up to be uncommon men and women. May it always be so. For the future of America rests not in mediocrity, but in the constant renewal of leadership in every phase of our national life.

— *Herbert Hoover*

Keeping a little ahead of conditions is one of the secrets of business; the trailer seldom goes far.

— *Charles M. Schwab*

All the money in the world is no use to a man or his country if he spends it as fast as he makes it. All he has left is his bills and the reputation for being a fool.

— *Kipling*

The humanities and science are not in inherent conflict but have become separated in the twentieth century. Now their essential unity must be re-emphasized, so that twentieth-century multiplicity may become twentieth-century unity.

— *Lewis Mumford*

Do it the hard way! Think ahead of your job. Then nothing in the world can keep the job ahead from reaching out for you. Do it better than it need be done. Next time doing it will be child's play. Let no one or anything stand between you and the difficult task, let nothing deny you this rich chance to gain strength by adversity, confidence by mastery, success by deserving it. Do it better each time. Do it better than anyone else can do it. I know this sounds old-fashioned. It is, but it has built the world.

— *Harlow H. Curtice*

Our country's honor calls upon us for a vigorous and manly exertion; and if we now shamefully fail, we shall become infamous to the whole world.

— *George Washington*

The war years count double. Things and people not actively in use age twice as fast. — *Arnold Bennett*

They that deny a God destroy man's nobility; for certainly man is of kin to the beasts by his body; and, if he be not kin to God by his spirit, he is a base and ignoble creature.

— *Bacon*

The opportunity for the average workman to rise to the management positions in industry was never better than it is today. These opportunities will continue to grow in the next decade. If the average intelligent and honest workman supplements his practical work experience with study of the general problems of business he will find privileged opportunities and promotion awaiting him.

— *Henry H. Heimann*

One should never put on one's best trousers to go out to
fight for freedom.   — *Henrik Ibsen*

Never say, " I don't think." The only think that makes
you a higher order of animal is the ability to think.
                              — *Henry H. Buckley*

It is the privilege of posterity to set matters right between
those antagonists who, by their rivalry for greatness,
divided a whole age.   — *Addison*

When, against one's will, one is high pressured into making a hurried decision, the best answer is always " No,"
because " No " is more easily changed to " Yes," than
" Yes " is changed to " No."   — *Charles E. Nielson*

Men heap together the mistakes of their lives, and create
a monster they call Destiny.   — *John Oliver Hobbes*

Fundamentally, the force that rules the world is conduct,
whether it be moral or immoral. If it is moral, at least
there may be hope for the world. If immoral, there is not
only no hope, but no prospect of anything but destruction
of all that has been accomplished during the last 5,000
years.   — *Dr. Nicholas Murray Butler*

Salvation and justice are not to be found in revolution,
but in evolution through concord. Violence has ever
achieved only destruction, not construction; the kindling
of passions, not their pacification; the accumulation of hate
and destruction, not the reconciliation of the contending
parties; and it has reduced men and parties to the difficult
task of building slowly after sad experience on the ruins of
discord.   — *Pope Pius XII*

We often pray for purity, unselfishness, for the highest qualities of character, and forget that these things cannot be given, but must be earned. *— Lyman Abbott*

The important thing is to know how to take all things quietly. *— Michael Faraday*

Facts are to the mind what food is to the body. On the due digestion of the former depend the strength and wisdom of the one, just as vigor and health depend on the other. The wisest in council, the ablest in debate, and the most agreeable companion in the commerce of human life, is that man who has assimilated to his understanding the greatest number of facts. *— Burke*

All the strength and force of man comes from his faith in things unseen. He who believes is strong; he who doubts is weak. Strong convictions precede great actions. *— J. F. Clarke*

One must be poor to know the luxury of giving. *— George Eliot*

The first thing to learn in intercourse with others is non-interference with their own particular ways of being happy, provided those ways do not assume to interfere by violence with ours. *— William James*

Every industrious man, in every lawful calling, is a useful man. And one principal reason why men are so often useless is that they neglect their own profession or calling, and divide and shift their attention among a multiplicity of objects and pursuits. *— Emerson*

Prayer is a force as real as terrestrial gravity. As a physician, I have seen men, after all other therapy had failed, lifted out of disease and melancholy by the serene effort of prayer. Only in prayer do we achieve that complete and harmonious assembly of body, mind and spirit which gives the frail human reed its unshakable strength.

— Dr. Alexis Carrel

You can't be asleep in business — at the ends of the arms of Morpheus are the hands of the receiver.

— Frank Romer

It's so much easier to do good than to be good.

— B. C. Forbes

We do not need more men. We do not need more money. We do not need more materials. What we do need is something to give a man a new spirit. . . . The problem of today is the people of today. It is people that make the times and not the times that make people. The trouble is with man himself.   *— Paul Garrett*

When a teacher of the future comes to point out to the youth of America how the highest rewards of intellect and devotion can be gained, he may say to them, not by subtlety and intrigue; not by wirepulling and demagoguery; not by the arts of popularity; not by skill and shiftiness in following expediency; but by being firm in devotion to the principles of manhood and the application of morals and the courage of righteousness in the public life of our country; by being a man without guile and without fear, without selfishness, and with devotion to duty, devotion to his country.   *— Elihu Root*

The big salaries in business always go to those who have what it takes to get things done. That is true not only of those executives who guide the destinies of a business, but it is true of those upon whom those executives must depend for results. — *J. C. Aspley*

The young man who has not wept is a savage, and the old man who will not laugh is a fool. — *Santayana*

There can be no such thing as a necessary evil. For, if a thing is really necessary, it cannot be an evil and if it is an evil, it is not necessary. — *Tiorio*

The most unproductive, empty, fruitless fellow in the world is the man with a barren heart. Happiness can never reach him, for nothing good and lasting can lodge in his heart. It is solid as a billiard ball. Contrast this man with his barren heart with the human that plays the game of life fairly and honestly and is willing to make others happy by his own sacrifices. — *F. D. Van Amburgh*

If we are not responsible for the thoughts that pass our doors, we are at least responsible for those we admit and entertain. — *Charles B. Newcomb*

Whatever may happen, every kind of fortune is to be overcome by bearing it. — *Virgil*

Whenever you are angry, be assured that it is not only a present evil, but that you have increased a habit. — *Epictetus*

You, yourself, have got to see that there is no just inter-
pretation of life except in terms of life's best things. No
pleasure philosophy, no sensuality, no place nor power, no
material success can for a moment give such inner satisfaction as the sense of living for good purposes, for maintenance of integrity, for the preservation of self-approval.

— Minot Simons

A war fitness conference some time ago declared that the
highest form of recreation is to go to church. The word
recreation should be written re-creation. More real rest
can be gained from an hour and a quarter of worship under
these circumstances than by eighteen holes of golf.

— Norman Vincent Peale, D.D.

Habit must play a larger place in our religious life. We
worship when we feel like it, we pray when we feel like it.
We read the Bible when we feel like it. Leaving our religious exercises to the promptings of impulse, we become
creatures of impulse rather than soldiers of Christ. An army
made up of creatures of impulse would be only a mob. So
is a church.   *— Ralph W. Sockman, D.D.*

Aside from the strictly moral standpoint, honesty is —
not only the best policy, but the only possible policy from
the standpoint of business relations. The fulfillment of the
pledged word is of equal necessity to the conduct of all business. If we expect and demand virtue and honor in others,
the flame of both must burn brightly within ourselves and
shed their light to illuminate the erstwhile dark corners of
distrust and dishonesty. . . . The truthful answer rests
for the most part within ourselves, for like begets like.
Honesty begets honesty; trust, trust; and so on through
the whole category of desirable practices that must govern
and control the world's affairs.   *— James F. Bell*

Well done is better than well said.

— Benjamin Franklin

The war for freedom will never really be won because the price of freedom is constant vigilance over ourselves and over our Government. *— Eleanor Roosevelt*

If you want to know how rich you really are, find out what would be left of you tomorrow if you should lose every dollar you own tonight? *— Wm. J. H. Boetcker*

It seems to me that the thing that makes the theater worthwhile is the fact that it attracts so many people with ideas who are constantly trying to share them with the public. Real art is illumination. It gives a man an idea he never had before or lights up ideas that were formless or only lurking in the shadows of his mind. It adds stature to life. *— Brooks Atkinson*

The criterion by which these people judge their action is a simple one. If in any part of the world the Communist Party, by no matter what means, is in power, that is democracy. If anywhere the Communists fail, then, however fair the conditions, it is regarded as Fascism.

— Clement Attlee

Salesmanship consists of transfering a conviction by a seller to a buyer. *— Paul G. Hoffman*

Sunshine is delicious, rain is refreshing, wind braces up, snow is exhilarating; there is no such thing as bad weather, only different kinds of good weather. *— Ruskin*

Surely, life is more than eating and drinking, more than buying and selling, more than getting and spending, more than the cultivation of the mind and a healthy body. It is the widening of our horizon, the broadening of our vision, the reaching out to eternal realities, the discipline of self until we can truly say, " I live, yet not I but Christ liveth in me."   — *E. Clowes Chorley, D.D.*

To the natural philosopher, there is no natural object unimportant or trifling. From the least of Nature's works he may learn the greatest lessons.   — *Sir John Herschel*

One of the most amazing things ever said on this earth is Jesus's statement: " He that is greatest among you shall be your servant." Nobody has one chance in a billion of being thought really great after a century has passed except those who have been the servants of all. That strange realist from Bethlehem knew that.

— *Harry Emerson Fosdick, D.D.*

Lack of something to feel important about is almost the greatest tragedy a man may have.

— *Dr. Arthur E. Morgan*

Be charitable in your thoughts, in your speech and in your actions. Be charitable in your judgments, in your attitudes and in your prayers. Think charitably of your friends, your neighbors, your relatives and even your enemies. And if there be those whom you can help in a material way, do so in a quiet, friendly, neighborly way, as if it were the most common and everyday experience for you. Tongues of men and angels, gifts of prophecy and all mysteries and all knowledge are as nothing without charity.

— *Cardinal Hayes*

Our best friends and our worst enemies are our thoughts.
A thought can do us more good than a doctor or a banker or
a faithful friend. It can also do us more harm than a brick.

— *Dr. Frank Crane*

Let goodness go with the doing. — *Marcus Aurelius*

It is a tragedy when the mind, soul and heart are in
slavery in a way of life which refuses to recognize that
people have rights before God. It is a war which makes hate
a badge of honor, slavery the keystone to prosperity. Not
to resist would make one an accomplice to crime. Resistance
was part of the program of Jesus. We must resist oppression
and tyranny. We have to end it no matter what it costs.

— *Joseph R. Sizoo, D.D.*

The sense of humor is the oil of life's engine. Without it,
the machinery creaks and groans. No lot is so hard, no aspect of things is so grim, but it relaxes before a hearty laugh.

— *G. S. Merriam*

Reason, too late perhaps, may convince you of the folly
of misspending time. — *George Washington*

One of the most devastating experiences in human life is
disillusionment. Of course there are some illusions the disillusionment of which is healthy. It takes two things to
bowl over a tree — a heavy wind outside and decay inside.
Much of the moral wreckage is caused by inner cynicism
— a disgust with life's futility, an inability to see sense in
it. A person in that mood is an easy mark for the next high
wind. — *Art Sisson*

If you count all your assets you always show a profit.
                                        — *Robert Quillen*

" Safety first " has been the motto of the human race for
half a million years; but it has never been the motto of
leaders. A leader must face danger. He must take the
risk and the blame, and the brunt of the storm.
                                        — *Herbert N. Casson*

The young man who has the combination of the learning
of books with the learning which comes of doing things with
the hands need not worry about getting along in the world
today, or at any time.   — *William S. Knudsen*

Despise not any man, and do not spurn anything; for
there is no man that has not his hour, nor is there anything
that has not its place.   — *Rabbi Ben Azai*

Reaction is not a secondary concern for a democracy. It
is a primary concern, for the kind of recreation a people
make for themselves determines the kind of people they
become and the kind of society they build.
                                        — *Harry A. Overstreet*

Think all you speak, but speak not all you think.
Thoughts are your own; your words are so no more.
                                        — *Patrick Delany*

No enjoyment, however inconsiderable, is confined to the
present moment. A man is the happier for life from having
made once an agreeable tour, or lived for any length of
time with pleasant people, or enjoyed any considerable interval of innocent pleasure.   — *Sydney Smith*

There must appear a spiritual and moral leadership rising above economic and political situations. Governments in both their domestic and foreign policies appeal for popular support by promises of material gain. We cannot make peace by mere appeal to greed. We must give the peoples of the world something to live for as well as something to live on. — *John Haynes Holmes*

I don't like to lose, and that isn't so much because it is just a football game, but because defeat means the failure to reach your objective. I don't want a football player who doesn't take defeat to heart, who laughs it off with the thought, " Oh, well, there's another Saturday." The trouble in American life today, in business as well as in sports, is that too many people are afraid of competition. The result is that in some circles people have come to sneer at success if it costs hard work and training and sacrifice. — *Knute Rockne*

Good temper, like a sunny day, sheds a ray of brightness over everything; it is the sweetener of toil and the soother of disquietude! — *Washington Irving*

The most insignificant people are the most apt to sneer at others. They are safe from reprisals, and have no hope of rising in their own esteem but by lowering their neighbors. — *Hazlitt*

Let him who expects one class of society to prosper in the highest degree, while the other is in distress, try whether one side of his face can smile while the other is pinched. — *Fuller*

He who rules must humor full as much as he commands. — *George Eliot*

Nobility of birth does not always insure a corresponding unity of mind; if it did, it would always act as a stimulus to noble actions; but it sometimes acts as a clog rather than a spur.   — *Colton*

Conceal thy domestic ills.   — *Thales*

If any man is rich and powerful he comes under the law of God by which the higher branches must take the burnings of the sun, and shade those that are lower; by which the tall trees must protect the weak plants beneath them.

— *Henry Ward Beecher*

The gates of thought, — how slow and late they discover themselves! Yet when they appear, we see that they were always there, always open.   — *Emerson*

The young man who would succeed must identify his interests with those of his employer and exercise the same diligence in matters entrusted to him as he would in his own affairs. Back of all the gifts the candidate for success may possess must be a willing capacity for hard work. . . . Youth today is not considered a handicap in selecting men for responsible jobs, as it was twenty years ago. . . . In almost any field today in which a youngster has an intelligent interest, the road to the top is open as it never was before. But the one way to the top is by persistent, intelligent, hard work.   — *A. T. Mercier*

We ought always to deal justly, not only with those who are just to us, but likewise to those who endeavor to injure us; and this, for fear lest by rendering them evil for evil, we should fall into the same vice.   — *Hierocles*

Whoever serves his country well has no need of ancestors.

— *Voltaire*

What helps luck is a habit of watching for opportunities, of having a patient, but restless mind, of sacrificing one's ease or vanity, of uniting a love of detail to foresight, and of passing through hard times bravely and cheerfully.

— *Victor Cherbuliez*

A man's name is not like a mantle which merely hangs about him, and which one perchance may safely twitch and pull, but a perfectly fitting garment, which, like the skin, has grown over him, at which one cannot rake and scrape without injuring the man himself.   — *Goethe*

Hardship, unbelief, suffering and poverty have not stopped our soldiery from rendering their service to God and man. The Salvation Army is a great empire, an empire without a frontier made up of a tangle of races, tongues and colors such as never before in all history gathered together under one flag.   — *Gen. Evangeline Booth*

As long as men and nations are aware of their divine origin, that human beings are a reflection of the source of all life, then it follows that it is the beholden duty of man to increase goodness, beauty, truth and peace in the world. But when men and nations deny the relationship of man to the divine, then the soil is fertile for the growth of hatred, injustice, strife and war.   — *Joseph Zeitlin*

The spirit of man is more important than mere physical strength, and the spiritual fiber of a nation than its wealth.

— *Dwight D. Eisenhower*

There is no problem of human nature which is insoluble.
— *Ralph J. Bunche*

Economic and military power can be developed under
the spur of laws and appropriations. But moral power does
not derive from any act of Congress. It depends on the
relations of a people to their God. It is the churches to
which we must look to develop the resources for the great
moral offensive that is required to make human rights
secure, and to win a just and lasting peace.
— *John Foster Dulles*

This world and life of ours are filled with inequalities.
The worst possible use to make of this fact, however, is
to allow resentments to possess us. All of us have imagined
limitations, but we have also the privilege of pushing them
aside, and spreading our lives out! We never know any of
our limitations until we put ourselves to the test. There
are always " growing pains " working within us.
— *George Matthew Adams*

A nation's character is the sum of its splendid deeds; they
constitute one common patrimony, the nation's inheritance.
They awe foreign powers, they arouse and animate our
own people.   — *Henry Clay*

As you cherish the things most worthwhile in your
family life, cherish the things most worthwhile in your
company.   — *Wm. B. Given, Jr.*

Books worth reading once are worth reading twice; and
what is most important of all, the masterpieces of literature
are worth reading a thousand times.   — *John Morley*

Citizenship comes first today in our crowded world.
. . . No man can enjoy the privileges of education and
thereafter with a clear conscience break his contract with
society. To respect that contract is to be mature, to
strengthen it is to be a good citizen, to do more than your
share under it is to be noble. — *Isaiah Bowman*

Speaking much is a sign of vanity; for he that is lavish
in words is a niggard in deed. — *Sir Walter Raleigh*

No one knows where he who invented the plow was born,
nor where he died; yet he has done more for humanity than
the whole race of heroes who have drenched the earth with
blood and whose deeds have been handed down with a precision proportionate only to the mischief they wrought.
— *Colton*

Words without actions are the assassins of idealism.
— *Herbert Hoover*

Knowledge is the eye of desire and can become the pilot
of the soul. — *Will Durant*

Prosperity is only an instrument to be used, not a deity to
be worshipped. — *Calvin Coolidge*

There are three things to aim at in public speaking: first
to get into your subject, then to get your subject into yourself, and lastly, to get your subject into your hearers.
— *Gregg*

Good humor is one of the best articles of dress one can
wear in society. — *Thackeray*

Although men are accused of not knowing their own weakness, yet perhaps few know their own strength. It is in men as in soils, where sometimes there is a vein of gold which the owner knows not of. — *Swift*

Possessions, outward success, publicity, luxury — to me these have always been contemptible. I believe that a simple and unassuming manner of life is best for every one, best both for the body and the mind. — *Albert Einstein*

Part of human nature resents change, loves equilibrium, while another part welcomes novelty, loves the excitement of disequilibrium. There is no formula for the resolution of this tug-of-war, but it is obvious that absolute surrender to either of them invites disaster.

— *J. Bartlet Brebner*

There is honor in labor. Work is the medicine of the soul. It is more: it is your very life, without which you would amount to little. — *Grenville Kleiser*

Those whom you can make like themselves better will, I promise you, like you very well. — *Lord Chesterfield*

It is great to have friends when one is young, but indeed it is still more so when you are getting old. When we are young, friends are, like everything else, a matter of course. In the old days we know what it means to have them. — *Edvard Grieg*

One of the strongest characteristics of genius is the power of lighting its own fire. — *John Foster*

More and more clearly every day, out of biology, anthropology, sociology, history, economic analysis, psychological insight, plain human decency and common sense, the necessary mandate of survival that we shall love all our neighbors as we do ourselves, is being confirmed and reaffirmed.

— Ordway Tead

Brotherhood is the very price and condition of man's survival.   *— Carlos P. Romulo*

The opportunity and the necessity for the Government's service to its people cannot be confined within rigid limits. The Constitution sets no such bounds. It is a living, vital institution whose function is to guide and not to curb necessary governmental powers.   *— Stanley F. Reed*

A man who has reformed himself has contributed his full share towards the reformation of his neighbor.

— Norman Douglas

The only things in which we can be said to have any property are our actions. Our thoughts may be bad, yet produce no poison; they may be good, yet produce no fruit. Our riches may be taken away by misfortune, our reputation by malice, our spirits by calamity, our health by disease, our friends by death. But our actions must follow us beyond the grave; with respect to them alone, we cannot say that we shall carry nothing with us when we die, neither that we shall go naked out of the world.   *— Colton*

You can't sit on the lid of progress. If you do, you will be blown to pieces.   *— Henry Kaiser*

The happiness of life is made up of minute fractions —
the little, soon forgotten charities of a kiss or smile, a kind
look, a heart-felt compliment, and the countless infinitesi-
mals of pleasurable and genial feeling.   — *Coleridge*

If some period be not fixed, either by the Constitution or
by practice, to the services of the First Magistrate, his
office, though nominally elective, will, in fact, be for life,
and that will soon degenerate into an inheritance.
                                          — *Thomas Jefferson*

Nothing relieves and ventilates the mind like a resolution.
                                          — *John Burroughs*

An executive cannot gradually dismiss details.   Business
is made up of details and I notice that the chief executive
who dismisses them is quite likely to dismiss his business.
    Success is the sum of detail.   It might perhaps be pleasing
to imagine oneself beyond detail and engaged only in great
things, but as I have often observed, if one attends only to
great things and lets the little things pass the great things
become little; that is, the business shrinks.
    It is not possible for an executive to hold himself aloof
from anything.   No business, no matter what its size, can
be called safe until it has been forced to learn economy and
rigidly to measure values of men and materials.
                                          — *Harvey S. Firestone*

Ridicule, the weapon of all others most feared by en-
thusiasts of every description, and which from its predomi-
nance over such minds, often checks what is absurd, and
fully as often smothers that which is noble.
                                          — *Walter Scott*

Beautiful forms and compositions are not made by chance, nor can they ever, in any material, be made at small expense. A composition for cheapness and not excellence of workmanship is the most frequent and certain cause of the rapid decay and entire destruction of arts and manufactures.

— *Josiah Wedgwood*

One pound of learning requires ten pounds of common-sense to apply it. — *Persian Proverb*

To save something each month develops self-control. This power frees one from fear and gives abiding courage.

— *Samuel Reyburn*

The greatest remedy for anger is delay. — *Seneca*

Few enterprises of great labor or hazard would be undertaken if we had not the power of magnifying the advantages we expect from them. — *Johnson*

The world is governed more by appearances than by realities, so that it is fully as necessary to seem to know something as to know it. — *Daniel Webster*

Nothing more impairs authority than a too frequent or indiscreet use of it. If thunder itself was to be continual, it would excite no more terror than the noise of a mill.

— *A. Kingston*

All business proceeds on beliefs, or judgments of probabilities, and not on certainties. — *Charles W. Eliot*

So long as new ideas are created, sales will continue to reach new highs.   — *Charles F. Kettering*

A man can do his best only by confidently seeking (and perpetually missing) an unattainable perfection.

— *Ralph Barton Perry*

Without consistency there is no moral strength.

— *Owen*

There is so much good in the worst of us, and so much bad in the best of us, that it behooves all of us not to talk about the rest of us.   — *Robert Louis Stevenson*

The prizes go to those who meet emergencies successfully. And the way to meet emergencies is to do each daily task the best we can; to act as though the eye of opportunity were always upon us. In the hundred-yard race the winner doesn't cross the tape line a dozen strides ahead of the field. He wins by inches. So we find it in ordinary business life. The big things that come our way are seldom the result of long thought or careful planning, but rather they are the fruit of seed planted in the daily routine of our work.

— *William Feather*

There comes a point in any organization where *too much* supervision means that supervisors spend too much time writing memorandums to one another, making needless telephone calls to one another, and the like, with no more *productive* work being accomplished in the aggregate, and possibly even less. We must strike the correct balance between *too much* supervision, and *too little* supervision.

— *Gustav Metzman*

Every attempt, by whatever authority, to fix a maximum of productive labor by a given worker in a given time is an unjust restriction upon his freedom and a limitation of his right to make the most of himself in order that he may rise in the scale of the social and economic order in which he lives. The notion that all human beings born into this world enter at birth into a definite social and economic classification, in which classification they must remain permanently through life, is wholly false and fatal to a progressive civilization. — *Dr. Nicholas Murray Butler*

Mediocrity requires aloofness to preserve its dignity.
— *Charles G. Dawes*

We should all be very careful when we say " no " to a suggested improvement or plan made by a subordinate. A " no " in most cases is final. We are usually more careful when we say " yes " because we know that our " yes " decisions will have to stand the test of performance or further approval. As a matter of fact, we should be more careful with our " noes " for the very reason that they do not have to stand the test of performance or further approval.
— *A. W. Robertson*

Of hobbies there are many, many, kinds. For example, money-making. But money-making is not exactly a hobby, for it will scarcely carry a boy along in continuous joy, comfort and pleasure — to say nothing of a full-grown man. Money comes, not because it is ridden as a hobby, but because a real hobby is ridden so cleverly and carefully that it oozes out money on the side! — *John Cotton Dana*

Indulge yourself in pleasures only in so far as they are necessary for the preservation of health. — *Spinoza*

There is no reader so parochial as the one who reads none but this morning's books. Books are not rolls, to be devoured only when they are hot and fresh. A good book retains its interior heat and will warm a generation yet unborn.
— *Clifton Fadiman*

The dignity of man is vindicated as much by the thinker and poet as by the statesman and soldier.
— *Dr. James B. Conant*

It is a fine thing to have ability, but the ability to discover ability in others is the true test.   — *Elbert Hubbard*

One of the best lessons that anyone can learn in life is how to use time wisely. Consider what can be done in ten minutes. If you need a little mental relaxation, you can sit down with a friend and play a game of cards. If you need some physical recreation, you can engage in a few exercises that will help tone up your body. Perhaps you have a friend who for weeks or months has been looking for a letter. Then there may be among your acquaintances someone whose friendship you would value highly and whose counsel would be profitable. Learn to use ten minutes intelligently. It will pay you huge dividends.
— *William A. Irwin*

Facts that are not frankly faced have a habit of stabbing us in the back.   — *Sir Harold Bowden*

To men and women who want to do things, there is nothing quite so driving as the force of an imprisoned ego. . . . All genius comes from this class.
— *Mary Roberts Rinehart*

It is not so important to be serious as it is to be serious about the important things.

— *Robert Maynard Hutchins*

We must drop the idea that change comes slowly. It does ordinarily — in part because we think it does. Today changes must come fast; and we must adjust our mental habits, so that we can accept comfortably the idea of stopping one thing and beginning another overnight. We must discard the idea that past routine, past ways of doing things, are probably the best ways. On the contrary, we must assume that there is probably a better way to do almost everything. We must stop assuming that a thing which has never been done before probably cannot be done at all.

— *Donald M. Nelson*

A character standard is far more important than even a gold standard. The success of all economic systems is still dependent upon both righteous leaders and righteous people. In the last analysis, our national future depends upon our national character — that is, whether it is spiritually or materially minded.

— *Roger Babson*

The worst cliques are those which consist of one man.

— *George Bernard Shaw*

Justice remains the greatest power on earth. To that tremendous power alone will we submit.

— *Harry S. Truman*

The best part of our knowledge is that which teaches us where knowledge leaves off and ignorance begins.

— *Oliver Wendell Holmes*

A PRIMER OF AMERICAN SELF-GOVERNMENT

1. Understand, honor and preserve the Constitution of the United States.

2. Keep forever separate and distinct the legislative, executive and judicial functions of government.

3. Remember that government belongs to the people, is inherently inefficient, and that its activities should be limited to those which government alone can perform.

4. Be vigilant for freedom of speech, freedom of worship, and freedom of action.

5. Cherish the system of Free Enterprise which made America great.

6. Respect thrift and economy, and beware of debt.

7. Above all, let us be scrupulous in keeping our word and in respecting the rights of others.   — *Philip D. Reed*

Education is the process by which the individual relates himself to the universe, gives himself citizenship in the changing world, shares the race's mind and enfranchises his own soul.   — *Dr. John H. Finley*

It is true that we have not deliberately or wholly abandoned the Christian element in our tradition, but does that element count with us as it once did?   Is the moral tone of the nation — its politics, its business life, its literature, its theatre, its movies, its radio networks, its television stations — Christian?   — *Robert J. McCracken, D.D.*

Some morning it is likely that the headlines of the world will scream forth the news that New York has been bombed. As tragic as this will be, it will nevertheless accomplish the deep unity that Christians should have.   It is a sad commentary that our brotherhood, which exists by Christian love, is only truly cemented by Christian suffering.

— *James P. De Wolfe, D.D.*

Our problem is within ourselves. We have found the means to blow the world physically apart. Spiritually, we have yet to find the means to put together the world's broken pieces. — *Thomas E. Dewey*

The mind is found most acute and most uneasy in the morning. Uneasiness is, indeed, a species of sagacity — a passive sagacity. Fools are never uneasy. — *Goethe*

He hath riches sufficient, who hath enough to be charitable. — *Sir T. Browne*

Let a man try faithfully, manfully to be right, he will daily grow more and more right. It is at the bottom of the condition on which all men have to cultivate themselves. — *Carlyle*

It's amazing what ordinary people can do if they set out without preconceived notions. — *Charles F. Kettering*

New discoveries in science . . . will continue to create a thousand new frontiers for those who would still adventure. — *Herbert Hoover*

Mistakes are costly and somebody must pay. The time to correct a mistake is before it is made. The causes of mistakes are, first, " I didn't know "; second, " I didn't think "; third, " I didn't care." — *Henry H. Buckley*

A man who is at the top is a man who has the habit of getting to the bottom. — *Joseph E. Rogers*

Good habits, which bring our lower passions and appetites under automatic control, leave our natures free to explore the larger experiences of life. Too many of us divide and dissipate our energies in debating actions which should be taken for granted.   — *Ralph W. Sockman, D.D.*

Always there will be, along the sidelines of life, inferior souls who throw mud at those whose attainments they do not quite understand. The man who really accomplishes doesn't pay attention to such detractors. If he did, he'd be on their level. He keeps an eye singled on the higher goal — and the mud never touches him.   — *Jerome P. Fleishman*

Business is like a man rowing a boat upstream. He has no choice; he must go ahead or he will go back.
        — *Lewis E. Pierson*

We are on the threshold of an age that will raise the standards of living of all men everywhere.
        — *Samuel T. Dana*

To try too hard to make people good is one way to make them worse. The only way to make them good is to be good, remembering well the beam and the mote.
        — *George McDonald*

Perhaps the most important lesson the world has learned in the past fifty years is that it is not true that " human nature is unchangeable." Human nature, on the contrary, can be changed with the greatest ease and to the utmost possible extent. If in this lies huge potential danger, it also contains some of the brightest hopes that we have for the future of mankind.   — *Bruce Bliven*

I wonder if the human touch, which people have, is not one of the greatest assets that one can have. You meet some people, and immediately you feel their warmth of mind or heart. You read a book, sit before the performance of a fine actor, or read a poem — and there it is — something that streams into your consciousness. . . . Those who keep climbing higher, in their chosen work, all have this outstanding something. The nurse in the hospital, the man who delivers your mail, the clerk behind many a store counter, and the effective minister or public speaker. Without this human touch, hope has little on which to feed or thrive.   *— George Matthew Adams*

Give us the fortitude to endure the things which cannot be changed, and the courage to change the things which should be changed, and the wisdom to know one from the other.   *— Bishop Oliver J. Hart*

Men are so constituted that every one undertakes what he sees another successful in, whether he has aptitude for it or not.   *— Goethe*

Nothing can be more destructive to vigor of action than protracted, anxious fluctuation, through resolutions adopted, rejected, resumed, and suspended, and nothing causes a greater expense of feeling. A man without decision can never be said to belong to himself; he is as a wave of the sea, or a feather in the air which every breeze blows about as it listeth.   *— John Foster*

The development of desirable traits and characteristics — that intangible something which we style personality — is the chief work of the school.   *— Dr. Frank Cody*

Every noble acquisition is attended with its risks; he who
fears to encounter the one must not expect to obtain the
other.   — *Metastasio*

The question is not whether a doctrine is beautiful but
whether it is true. When we wish to go to a place, we do
not ask whether the road leads through a pretty country, but
whether it is the right road.   — *Hare*

We can't take a slipshod and easygoing attitude toward
education in this country. And by " we " I don't mean
" somebody else," but I mean me and I mean you. It is the
future of our country — yours and mine — which is at
stake.   — *Henry Ford II*

Conversation should be pleasant without scurrility, witty
without affectation, free without indecency, learned without
conceitedness, novel without falsehood.   — *Shakespeare*

It will generally be found that those who sneer habitually
at human nature, and affect to despise it, are among its
worst and least pleasant samples.   — *Dickens*

To me — old age is 15 years older than I am.
                                        — *Bernard M. Baruch*

We must make automatic and habitual, as early as
possible, as many useful actions as we can. . . . The more
of the details of our daily life we can hand over to the
effortless custody of automatism, the more our higher
powers of mind will be set free for their own proper work.
                                         — *William James*

I thoroughly believe in a university education for both men and women, but I believe a knowledge of the Bible without a college course is more valuable than a college course without the Bible. — *William Lyon Phelps*

🌿

Indecision is debilitating; it feeds upon itself; it is, one might almost say, habit-forming. Not only that, but it is contagious; it transmits itself to others. . . . Business is dependent upon action. It cannot go forward by hesitation. Those in executive positions must fortify themselves with facts and accept responsibility for decisions based upon them. Often greater risk is involved in postponement than in making a wrong decision. — *H. A. Hopf*

🌿

The whole art of teaching is only the art of awakening the natural curiosity of young minds for the purpose of satisfying it afterwards. — *Anatole France*

🌿

If you would not have affliction visit you twice, listen at once to what it teaches. — *James Burgh*

🌿

Life is a mirror and will reflect back to the thinker what he thinks into it. — *Ernest Holmes*

🌿

One who is too wise an observer of the business of others, like one who is too curious in observing the labor of bees, will often be stung for his curiosity. — *Pope*

🌿

Progress in every age results only from the fact that there are some men and women who refuse to believe that what they knew to be right cannot be done.
— *Russell W. Davenport*

The essential element in personal magnetism is a consuming sincerity — an overwhelming faith in the importance of the work one has to do.   — *Bruce Barton*

Capitalism and communism stand at opposite poles. Their essential difference is this: The communist, seeing the rich man and his fine home, says: " No man should have so much." The capitalist, seeing the same thing, says: " All men should have as much."   — *Phelps Adams*

It is a socialist idea that making profits is a vice. I consider the real vice is making losses.   — *Winston Churchill*

If there be anything that can be called genius, it consists chiefly in ability to give that attention to a subject which keeps it steadily in the mind, till we have surveyed it accurately on all sides.   — *Reid*

Avarice, in old age, is foolish; for what can be more absurd than to increase our provisions for the road the nearer we approach to our journey's end?   — *Cicero*

The practical effect of a belief is the real test of its soundness.   — *Froude*

In this world it is not what we take up, but what we give up, that makes us rich.   — *Henry Ward Beecher*

No art can conquer the people alone — the people are conquered by an ideal of life upheld by authority.
          — *William Butler Yeats*

A man cannot utter two or three sentences without disclosing to intelligent ears precisely where he stands in life and thought, whether in the kingdom of the senses and the understanding, or in that of ideas and imagination, or in the realm of intuitions and duty. — *Emerson*

The Sermon on the Mount does not provide humanity with a complete guide to personal, social and economic problems. It sets forth spiritual attitudes, moral principles of universal validity, such as " Love your enemies," " Whatsoever ye would that men should do to you, do ye even so to them," and it leaves to Christians the task — the admittedly difficult task — of applying them in any given situation. — *Robert James McCracken, D.D.*

It is well for people who think to change their minds occasionally in order to keep them clean. For those who do not think, it is best at least to rearrange their prejudices once in a while. — *Luther Burbank*

The pursuit of truth shall set you free — even if you never catch up with it. — *Clarence Darrow*

Nothing is a waste of time if you use the experience wisely. — *Rodin*

Righteousness, or *justice*, is, undoubtedly of all the virtues, the surest foundation on which to create and establish a new state. But there are two nobler virtues, *industry* and *frugality*, which tend more to increase the wealth, power and grandeur of the community, than all the others without them. — *Benjamin Franklin*

America has believed that in differentiation, not in uniformity, lies the path of progress. It acted on this belief; it has advanced human happiness, and it has prospered.

— *Louis D. Brandeis*

Fool me once, shame on you; fool me twice, shame on me.

— *Chinese Proverb*

Five great enemies to peace inhabit with us: viz., avarice, ambition, envy, anger and pride. If those enemies were to be banished, we should infallibly enjoy perpetual peace.

— *Petrarch*

Aim at perfection in everything, though in most things it is unattainable. However, they who aim at it, and persevere, will come much nearer to it than those whose laziness and despondency make them give it up as unattainable.

— *Lord Chesterfield*

There is no royal road to anything. One thing at a time, and all things in succession. That which grows slowly endures.   — *J. G. Holland*

The difficulties, hardships and trials of life, the obstacles one encounters on the road to fortune are positive blessings. They knit the muscles more firmly, and teach self-reliance. Peril is the element in which power is developed.

— *W. Mathews*

Agriculture, manufactures, commerce and navigation, the four pillars of our prosperity, are most thriving when left most free to individual enterprise.   — *Thomas Jefferson*

The social fabric of a well-established nation is tough stuff. It can be pulled around and stretched a considerable distance before it breaks. But when the final rupture comes, the damage done is beyond repair.

— *H. W. Prentis, Jr.*

Those who love deeply never grow old; they may die of old age, but they die young. — *Arthur Wing Pinero*

Sympathy is never wasted except when you give it to yourself. — *John W. Raper*

One man can completely change the character of a country, and the industry of its people, by dropping a single seed in fertile soil. — *John C. Gifford*

Discreetly keep most of your radical opinions to yourself. When with people be a listener a large part of the time. Be considerate in every word and act, and resist the tendency to say clever things. The best evidence of your culture is the tone and temper of your conversation.

— *Grenville Kleiser*

What you have outside you counts less than what you have inside you. — *B. C. Forbes*

If all the gold in the world were melted down into a solid cube it would be about the size of an eight-room house. If a man got possession of all that gold — billions of dollars worth, he could not buy a friend, character, peace of mind, clear conscience, or a sense of eternity.

— *Charles F. Banning*

Dividing industry into " big " and " little " is artificial. Industry is *both* — *that* makes it Industry. Ninety-eight per cent of American industries employ less than 500 men each. Today's big industries were small within our lifetime, many of today's small industries will become big before our lifetime ends. Large industries make small industries necessary, and small industries make large ones possible. Wipe out large industries and you wipe out three-fourths of the small ones; wipe out the small ones and the large ones cannot go on. They work together. Each has a part in the nation's job.   — *W. J. Cameron*

No matter how much work a man can do, no matter how engaging his personality may be, he will not advance far in business if he cannot work through others.
                                              — *John Craig*

I do not understand what the man who is happy wants in order to be happier.   — *Cicero*

All brave men love; for he only is brave who has affections to fight for, whether in the daily battle of life, or in physical contests.   — *Hawthorne*

Some things have not changed since the dawn of history, and bid fair to last out time itself. One of these things is the capacity for greatness in man — his capacity for being often the master of the event — and sometimes even more — the changer of the course of history itself. This capacity for greatness is a very precious gift, and we are under a danger in our day of stifling it.
                                  — *Dr. William Clyde de Vane*

We demand that big business give people a square deal; in return we must insist that when anyone engaged in big business honestly endeavors to do right, he shall himself be given a square deal. — *Theodore Roosevelt*

Experience seems to be the only thing of any value that's widely distributed. — *William Feather*

The gem cannot be polished without friction, nor man perfected without trials. — *Chinese Proverb*

It was necessary for us to discover greater powers of destruction than our enemies. We did. But after every war we have followed through with a new rise in our standard of living by the application of war-taught knowledge for the benefit of the world. It will be the same with the atomic bomb principles. — *Thomas J. Watson*

Contrary to the commonly accepted belief, it is the risk element in our capitalistic system which produces an economy of security. Risk brings out the ingenuity and resourcefulness which insure the success of enough ventures to keep the economy growing and secure.
— *Robert Rawls*

Here in our land, and in other lands, many have been drifting toward a religion which says much about rights but little about duties; a religion which thinks only about humanity and little about God; which lays great stress on service but little stress on faith; which puts all the emphasis on man and his power and very little on God and His power.
— *William T. Manning, D.D.*

The strong man meets his crisis with the most practical
tools at hand. They may not be the best tools but they are
available, which is all-important. He would rather use
them, such as they are, than do nothing.

— *Raymond Clapper*

Worry is evidence of an ill-controlled brain; it is merely
a stupid waste of time in unpleasantness. If men and
women practiced mental calisthenics as they do physical
calisthenics, they would purge their brains of this foolish-
ness.   — *Arnold Bennett*

The consideration that human happiness and moral duty
are inseparably connected will always continue to prompt
me to promote the former by inculcating the practice of the
latter.   — *George Washington*

Get the facts, or the facts will get you. And when you
get 'em, get 'em right, or they will get you wrong.

— *Fuller*

A great many people think they are thinking when they
are really rearranging their prejudices.

— *Edward R. Murrow*

I may safely predict that the education of the future will
be inventive-minded. It will believe so profoundly in the
high value of the inventive or creative spirit that it will set
itself to develop that spirit by all means within its power.

— *Harry A. Overstreet*

The man that dares traduce, because he can with safety
to himself, is not a man.   — *Cowper*

As for the differences of opinion upon speculative questions, if we wait till they are reconciled, the action of human affairs must be suspended forever. But neither are we to look for perfection in any one man, nor for agreement among many. — *Junius*

The weakest among us has a gift, however seemingly trivial, which is peculiar to him and which worthily used will be a gift also to his race. — *Ruskin*

Big business can't prosper without small business to supply its needs and buy its products. Labor can't prosper so long as capital lies idle. Capital can't prosper while labor is unemployed. — *DeWitt M. Emery*

The great and glorious masterpiece of men is to live to the point. All other things — to reign, to hoard, to build — are, at most, but inconsiderable props and appendages. — *Montaigne*

Nothing is ever lost by courtesy. It is the cheapest of the pleasures; costs nothing and conveys much. It pleases him who gives and him who receives, and thus, like mercy, is twice blessed. — *Erastus Wiman*

There is a healthful hardiness about real dignity that never dreads contact and communion with others, however humble. — *Washington Irving*

If we would guide by the light of reason we must let our minds be bold. — *Louis D. Brandeis*

In the business of life, Man is the *only* product. And
there is only *one* direction in which man can possibly develop
if he is to make a better living or yield a bigger dividend to
himself, to his race, to nature or to God. He must *grow* in
knowledge, wisdom, kindliness and understanding.

— V. C. Kitchen

When you look at the world in a narrow way, how narrow
it seems! When you look at it in a mean way, how mean it
is! When you look at it selfishly, how selfish it is! But
when you look at it in a broad, generous, friendly spirit,
what wonderful people you find in it.

— Horace Rutledge

You can't see clearly if you insist on smoking up your
glasses.   *— Amos Parrish*

Delusions, errors and lies are like huge, gaudy vessels,
the rafters of which are rotten and worm-eaten, and those
who embark in them are fated to be shipwrecked.

— Buddha

The world is full of cactus, but we don't have to sit on it.
— Will Foley

The gates of wisdom and truth are forever closed to those
who are wise in their own conceits; they have always opened
before the expectancy of the humble and the teachable.
The great need of the religious soul is the capacity to be
receptive. It is a matter of record that no generation of
religious people throughout history has ever been lacking
in the fellowship and leadership of men and women of rare
intellectual power.   *— Theodore C. Speers, D.D.*

We have no more right to consume happiness without producing it, than to consume wealth without producing it.
— *George Bernard Shaw*

If this world afford true happiness, it is to be found in a home where love and confidence increase with the years, where the necessities of life come without severe strain, where luxuries enter only after their cost has been carefully considered.
— *A. Edward Newton*

If a man be endowed with a generous mind, this is the best kind of nobility.
— *Plato*

Absence diminishes little passions and increases great ones, as wind extinguishes candles and fans a fire.
— *La Rochefoucauld*

The man who is worthy of being " a leader of men " will never complain about the stupidity of his helpers, the ingratitude of mankind nor the inappreciation of the public. These are all a part of the great game of life. To meet them and overcome them and not to go down before them in disgust, discouragement or defeat — that is the final proof of power.
— *Wm. J. H. Boetcker*

It is with life as with a play — it matters not how long the action is spun out, but how good the acting is.
— *Seneca*

No enterprise can exist for itself alone. It ministers to some great need, it performs some great service, not for itself, but for others; or failing therein, it ceases to be profitable and ceases to exist.
— *Calvin Coolidge*

Too many young people itch for what they want without scratching for it.   — *Tom D. Taylor*

If we want to possess poise and to be capable of clear thinking, it is essential, first of all, to rise above the confusion of conflicting rumors and diverse opinions and listen to the eternal verities which God has given to men for their guidance and preservation.
                         — *Leon Merle Flanders, D.D.*

Shall any of us repine that it is our lot to live in perilous and sacrificial days?   Rather I say we are glad that we live in this time of mortal struggle and are doing our share to put to flight the powers of darkness.   Our children and grandchildren will be proud that this country saved freedom for itself by helping to preserve it for the world.
                         — *Thomas W. Lamont*

We cannot employ the mind to advantage when we are filled with excessive food and drink.   — *Cicero*

Those who do the most for the world's advancement are the ones who demand the least.   — *Henry L. Doherty*

The antithesis of democracy is class dictatorship, whether by groups of bankers, investors, managers, politicians, lawyers or union members.   Over a considerable part of the world the unspeakable doctrine is being preached that the ideal of a democratic State is a snare and a delusion. A politician if he denies the existence of the essentials of democracy and denies it in such a way as to create class feeling, is not working in the interest of democracy even though he protests to the high heavens that that is his objective.   — *Raymond E. Moley*

Habit is a cable; we weave a thread of it each day, and at last we cannot break it.   — *Horace Mann*

Someone has well said, " Success is a journey, not a destination." Happiness is to be found along the way, not at the end of the road, for then the journey is over and it is too late. Today, this hour, this minute is the day, the hour, the minute for each of us to sense the fact that life is good, with all of its trials and troubles, and perhaps more interesting because of them.   — *Robert R. Updegraff*

Fear not that thy life shall come to an end, but rather fear that it shall never have a beginning.
                          — *Cardinal Newman*

The parent can train the natures of children to remain fast while their habits change through the years. We must have a citizenry which will by long inner training be able to feel secure in a storm. No parent can raise that kind of child till he is himself that kind of *person*.
                          — *H. Clay Mitchell, D.D.*

It is a poor and disgraceful thing not to be able to reply, with some degree of certainty, to the simple questions, " What will you be? What will you do? "
                          — *John Foster*

All the good things of the world are no further good to us than as they are of use; and of all we may heap up we enjoy only as much as we can use, and no more.
                          — *DeFoe*

Three men were laying brick.
The first was asked: " What are you doing? "
He answered: " Laying some brick."
The second man was asked: " What are you working
for? "
He answered: " Five dollars a day."
The third man was asked: " What are you doing? "
He answered: " I am helping to build a great cathedral."
Which man are you?   — *Charles M. Schwab*

Prepare yourself for the world, as athletes used to do for
their exercises; oil your mind and your manners, to give
them the necessary suppleness and flexibility; strength
alone will not do.   — *Lord Chesterfield*

Knowledge and human power are synonymous, since the
ignorance of the cause frustrates the effect.   — *Bacon*

Knowledge alone does not stop men from evil. The poor
and the ignorant are not the greatest sinners. Man's
mind may unfold, his intellect grow more keen, his understanding more profound, yet side by side with this may
be a moral degeneration such as existed in pagan Greece
and Rome.   — *William A. Scully, D.D.*

The thing that impresses me most about this country is
its hopefulness. It is this which distinguishes it from
Europe, where there is hopeless depression and fear.
                                        — *Aldous Huxley*

He who freely praises what he means to purchase, and he
who enumerates the faults of what he means to sell, may
set up a partnership with honesty.   — *Lavater*

Character is the foundation stone upon which one must build to win respect. Just as no worthy building can be erected on a weak foundation, so no lasting reputation worthy of respect can be built on a weak character. Without character, all effort to attain dignity is superficial, and results are sure to be disappointing. — *R. C. Samsel*

A good name, like good will, is got by many actions and lost by one. — *Lord Jeffrey*

Conceit is to nature what paint is to beauty; it is not only needless, but it impairs what it would improve. — *Pope*

As the mind must govern the hands, so in every society the man of intelligence must direct the man of labor. — *Johnson*

From its very inaction, idleness ultimately becomes the most active cause of evil; as a palsy is more to be dreaded than a fever. The Turks have a proverb which says that the devil tempts all other men, but that idle men tempt the devil. — *Colton*

I wonder if there is anyone in the world who can really direct the affairs of the world, or of his country, with any assurance of the result his actions would have. — *Montagu C. Norman*

We have employments assigned to us for every circumstance in life. When we are alone, we have our thoughts to watch; in the family, our tempers; and in company, our tongues. — *H. More*

People generally quarrel because they cannot argue.
　　　　　　　　　　　　— *Gilbert K. Chesterton*

No wild enthusiast ever yet could rest, till half mankind
were, like himself, possest.　　　　　　　— *Cowper*

He is the happiest, be he king or peasant, who finds peace
in his home.　　　　　　　　　　　　— *Goethe*

Thinking well is wise; planning well, wiser; doing well
wisest and best of all.　　　　　　— *Persian Proverb*

Rapidity does not always mean progress, and hurry is
akin to waste. The old fable of the hare and the tortoise
is just as good now, and just as true, as when it was first
written.　　　　　　　　　　　　— *C. A. Stoddard*

When confronted with two courses of action I jot down
on a piece of paper all the arguments in favor of each one —
then on the opposite side I write the arguments against
each one. Then by weighing the arguments pro and con and
canceling them out, one against the other, I take the course
indicated by what remains.　　　　— *Benjamin Franklin*

Quiet minds cannot be perplexed or frightened but go on
in fortune or misfortune at their own private pace, like a
clock during a thunderstorm.　　— *Robert Louis Stevenson*

Manners are the happy ways of doing things; each one a
stroke of genius or of love, now repeated and hardened into
usage.　　　　　　　　　　　　— *Emerson*

He who reigns within himself, and rules passions, desires, and fears, is more than a king. — *Milton*

If you will help run our government in the American way, then there will never be any danger of our government running America in the wrong way.
— *Gen. Omar N. Bradley*

It is not half as important to burn the midnight oil as it is to be awake in the daytime. — *E. W. Elmore*

Just how we fit into the plans of the Great Architect and how much He has assigned us to do, we do not know, but if we fail in our assignment it is pretty certain that part of the job will be left undone. But fit in we certainly do somehow, else we would not have a sense of our own responsibility. A purely materialistic philosophy is to me the height of unintelligence. — *Robert A. Millikan*

A splendid storehouse of integrity and freedom has been bequeathed to us by our forefathers. In this day of confusion, of peril to liberty, our high duty is to see that this storehouse is not robbed of its contents.
— *Herbert Hoover*

We should place confidence in our employee. Confidence is the foundation of friendship. If we give it, we will receive it. Any person in a managerial position, from supervisor to president, who feels that his employee is basically not as good as he is and who suspects his employee is always trying to put something over on him, lacks the necessary qualities for human leadership — to say nothing of human friendship. — *Harry E. Humphreys, Jr.*

Remember, every time you open your mouth to talk,
your mind walks out and parades up and down the words.
— *Edwin H. Stuart*

You need not choose evil; but have only to fail to choose
good, and you drift fast enough toward evil. You do not
need to say, " I will be bad," you have only to say, " I
will not choose God's choice," and the choice of evil is
already settled. — *W. J. Dawson*

Make money your God, and it will plague you like the
devil. — *Henry Fielding*

Certain thoughts are prayers. There are certain moments
when, whatever be the attitude of the body, the soul is on
its knees. — *Victor Hugo*

You take all the experience and judgment of men over
50 out of the world and there wouldn't be enough left to
run it. — *Henry Ford*

The reason American cities are prosperous is that there is
no place for people to sit down. — *Alfred J. Talley*

Truth is tough. It will not break, like a bubble, at a
touch; nay, you may kick it about all day, like a football,
and it will be round and full at evening.
— *Oliver Wendell Holmes*

We cannot hold a torch to light another's path without
brightening our own. — *Ben Sweetland*

All ambitions are lawful except those which climb upward on the miseries or credulities of mankind.

— Joseph Conrad

Liberty is the only thing you cannot have unless you are willing to give it to others. *— William Allen White*

What the church should be telling the worker is that the first demand religion makes on him is that he should be a good workman. If he is a carpenter he should be a competent carpenter. Church by all means on Sundays — but what is the use of church if at the very center of life a man defrauds his neighbor and insults God by poor craftsmanship. *— Dwight D. Eisenhower*

Business is a combination of war and sport.

— André Maurois

Never give a man up until he has failed at something he likes. *— Lewis E. Lawes*

Good resolutions are a pleasant crop to sow. The seed springs up so readily, and the blossoms open so soon with such a brave show, especially at first. But when the time of flowers has passed, what as to the fruit? *— L. Malet*

If the masses of men were one-half as faithful to God — and obedient to His commands — as a dog is faithful to his master — and obedient to his commands — we would have a far better world to live in than we yet have found.

— R. B. Harris

The private and personal blessings we enjoy, the blessings
of immunity, safeguard, liberty and integrity, deserve the
thanksgiving of a whole life.   — *Jeremy Taylor*

Man never fastened one end of a chain around the neck
of his brother, that God did not fasten the other end around
the neck of the oppressor.   — *Lamartine*

Plenty and indigence depend upon the opinion every one
has of them; and riches, like glory or health, have no more
beauty or pleasure than their possessor is pleased to lend
them.   — *Montaigne*

Simplicity of character is the natural result of profound
thought.   — *Hazlitt*

There is no right without a parallel duty, no liberty
without the supremacy of the law, no high destiny without
earnest perseverance, no greatness without self-denial.
          — *Lieber*

Never rise to speak till you have something to say; and
when you have said it, cease.   — *Witherspoon*

If one should give me a dish of sand, and tell me there
were particles of iron in it, I might look for them with my
eyes, and seaich for them with my clumsy fingers, and
be unable to detect them; but let me take a magnet and
sweep through it, and how would it draw to itself the almost
invisible particles by the mere power of attraction! The
unthinkful heart, like my finger in the sand, discovers no
mercies; but let the thankful heart sweep through the day,
and as the magnet finds the iron, so it will find, in every
hour, some heavenly blessings.   — *Henry Ward Beecher*

Nobody grows old by merely living a number of years; people grow old only by deserting their ideals.

— *Samuel Ullman*

Nothing can stop the man with the right mental attitude from achieving his goal; nothing on earth can help the man with the wrong mental attitude. — *W. W. Ziege*

Let us keep our mouths shut and our pens dry until we know the facts. — *Dr. A. J. Carlson*

No theory of the universe can be satisfactory which does not adequately account for the phenomena of life, especially in that richest form which finds expression in human personality. — *B. H. Streeter*

Men cannot for long live hopefully unless they are embarked upon some great unifying enterprise — one for which they may pledge their lives, their fortunes and their honor.

— *C. A. Dykstra*

It is a good rule to face difficulties at the time they arise and not allow them to increase unacknowledged.

— *Edward W. Ziegler*

The goal of life is imminent in each moment, each thought, word, act, and does not have to be sought apart from these. It consists in no specific achievement, but the state of mind in which everything is done, the quality infused into existence. The function of man is not to attain an object, but to fulfill a purpose; not to accomplish but to be accomplished. — *S. E. Stanton*

We must be truthful and fair in the ordinary affairs of
life before we can be truthful and fair in patriotism and
religion.   — *Ed. Howe*

A man has to live with himself, and he should see to it
that he always has good company.
                              — *Charles Evans Hughes*

We are always much better pleased to see those whom
we have obliged than those who have obliged us.
                                    — *La Rochefoucauld*

He will always be a slave who does not know how to live
upon a little.   — *Horace*

Egotism is the anesthetic which nature gives us to deaden
the pain of being a fool.   — *Dr. Herbert Shofield*

A fresh mind keeps the body fresh. Take in the ideas of
the day, drain off those of yesterday. As to the morrow,
time enough to consider it when it becomes today.
                                              — *Bulwer*

Each citizen contributes to the revenues of the State a
portion of his property in order that his tenure of the rest
may be secure.   — *Montesquieu*

A gentleman is one who never hurts anyone's feelings
unintentionally.   — *Oliver Herford*

The multitude which does not reduce itself to unity is confusion. — *Pascal*

Small opportunities are often the beginning of great enterprises. — *Demosthenes*

Religious faith may very well be considered a science, for it responds invariably to certain formulae. Perform the technique of faith according to the laws which have been proved workable in human experience and you will always get a result of power.
— *Norman Vincent Peale, D.D.*

The young man of native ability, the will to work and good personality will, in the long run, get the equivalent of a college education in the tasks he will set for himself. If he has ability and determination, he will find ways to learn and to get ahead. — *Edward G. Seubert*

Suffering becomes beautiful when anyone bears great calamities with cheerfulness, not through insensibility but through greatness of mind. — *Aristotle*

Progress in industry depends very largely on the enterprise of deep-thinking men, who are ahead of the times in their ideas. — *Sir William Ellis*

The world will never have lasting peace so long as men reserve for war the finest human qualities. Peace, no less than war, requires idealism and self-sacrifice and a righteous and dynamic faith. — *John Foster Dulles*

No man is so great as mankind. — *Theodore E. Parker*

We cannot always oblige, but we can always speak
obligingly.   — *Voltaire*

We have forgotten in America that a democracy is the
most difficult kind of government to maintain. It is the
hardest kind of government under which to live. It is
hardest to maintain because of the widespread political
corruption to which it so easily lends itself. Our drift today
toward complete totalitarian bureaucracy is one that
threatens immediately the very freedoms for which our
own boys are dying.   — *Ernest R. Palen, D.D.*

Time mends all, ends all things earthly.
                                         — *B. C. Forbes*

The proper means of increasing the love we bear to our
native country is to reside some time in a foreign one.
                                         — *Shenstone*

In the long run, digging for truth has always proved not
only more interesting but more profitable than digging
for gold.   — *George R. Harrison*

Self-reliance can turn a salesman into a merchant; a
politician into a statesman; an attorney into a jurist; an
unknown youth into a great leader. All are to be tomorrow's big leaders — those who in solitude sit above the clang
and dust of time, with the world's secret trembling on their
lips.   — *Hillis*

Have patience and the mulberry leaf will become satin.
                                         — *Spanish Proverb*

There can be no profit in the making or selling of things to be destroyed in war. Men may think that they have such profit, but in the end the profit will turn out to be a loss. — *Alexander Hamilton*

In the long run I firmly believe only one answer can emerge. Always before, in world history, the frailty and weakness which the dictator has postulated in the masses of mankind has finally been uncovered in himself by the inexorable march of events, and the world as a whole has somehow managed to achieve, over the years, continually higher and nobler modes of thinking and of living.
— *Dr. Harvey N. Davis*

We are living in a period which all too readily scraps the old for the new. . . . As a nation, we are in danger of forgetting that the new is not true because it is novel, and that the old is not false because it is ancient.
— *Joseph Kennedy*

I am not afraid of tomorrow, for I have seen yesterday and I love today. — *William Allen White,*
on his 70th birthday.

Men in general are too material and do not make enough human contacts. If we search for the fundamentals which actually motivate us we will find that they come under four headings: love, money, adventure and religion. It is to some of them that we always owe that big urge which pushes us onward. Men who crush these impulses and settle down to everyday routine are bound to sink into mediocrity. No man is a complete unit of himself; he needs the contact, the stimulus and the driving power which is generated by his contact with other men, their ideas, and constantly changing scenes. — *Edward S. Jordan*

The simple virtues of willingness, readiness, alertness and courtesy will carry a man farther than mere smartness.

— *Davidson*

The cynic makes fun of all earnestness; he makes fun of everything and everyone who feels that something can be done. . . . But in his heart of hearts he knows that he is a defeated man and that his cynicism is merely an expression of the fact that he has lost courage and is beaten.

— *George E. Vincent*

No man is self-made who unmakes others.

— *Stephen Voris*

The priceless treasure of boyhood is his endless enthusiasm, his high store of idealism, his affections and his hopes. When we preserve these, we have made men. We have made citizens and we have made Americans.

— *Herbert Hoover*

So when the crisis is upon you, remember that God, like a trainer of wrestlers, has matched you with a tough and stalwart antagonist — that you may prove a victor at the Great Games. Yet without toil or sweat this may not be.

— *Epictetus*

The men who succeed best in public life are those who take the risk of standing by their own convictions.

— *James A. Garfield*

There are two kinds of failures: The man who will do nothing he is told, and the man who will do nothing else.

— *Dr. Perle Thompson*

Have confidence that if you have done a *little* thing well, you can do a *bigger* thing well, too. — *Storey*

Men of great parts are often unfortunate in the management of public business because they are apt to go out of the common road by the quickness of their imagination. — *Swift*

Mark this well, ye proud men of action! Ye are, after all, nothing but unconscious instruments of the men of thought. — *Heine*

Adversity has ever been considered the state in which a man most easily becomes acquainted with himself, then, especially, being free from flatterers. — *Johnson*

A comfortable old age is the reward of a well-spent youth. Instead of its bringing sad and melancholy prospects of decay, it should give us hopes of eternal youth in a better world. — *R. Palmer*

There is no doubt that the real destroyer of the liberties of any people is he who spreads among them bounties, donations and largess. — *Plutarch*

If a man harbors any sort of fear, it percolates through all his thinking, damages his personality, makes him landlord to a ghost. — *Lloyd C. Douglas*

If I have done the public any service, it is due to patient thought. — *Sir Isaac Newton*

Private opinion creates public opinion. Public opinion
overflows eventually into national behavior as things are
arranged at present, can make or mar the world. That is
why private opinion, and private behavior, and private
conversation are so terrifyingly important.

— Jan Struther

Humility is the part of wisdom, and is most becoming in
men. But let no one discourage self-reliance; it is, of all
the rest, the greatest quality of true manliness.

— Louis Kossuth

Every man should make up his mind that if he expects to
succeed, he must give an honest return for the other man's
dollar.   *— Edward H. Harriman*

Great men suffer hours of depression through introspec-
tion and self-doubt. That is why they are great. That is
why you will find modesty and humility the characteristics
of such men.   *— Bruce Barton*

The real gentleman is one who is gentle in everything, at
least in everything that depends on himself — in carriage,
temper, constructions, aims, desires. He is mild, calm, quiet,
even temperate — not hasty in judgment, not exorbitant
in ambition, not overbearing, not proud, not rapacious, not
oppressive.   *— Hare*

The man who builds a factory builds a temple; the man
who works there worships there; and to each is due not
scorn and blame but reverence and praise.

— Calvin Coolidge

If we can implant in our people the Christian virtues which we sum up in the word character, and, at the same time, give them a knowledge of the line which should be drawn between voluntary action and governmental compulsion in a democracy, and of what can be accomplished within the stern laws of economics, we will enable them to retain their freedom, and at the same time, make them worthy to be free.   — *Winthrop W. Aldrich*

It makes little difference what the trade, business, or branch of learning, in mechanical labor, or intellectual effort, the educated man is always superior to the common laborer. One who is in the habit of applying his powers in the right way will carry system into any occupation, and it will help him as much to handle a rope as to write a poem.   — *F. M. Crawford*

If we understand that the Lord has given us a doctrine of wholehearted, aggressive goodwill, even toward unfriendly people, we can save our world, even at a time when it was never more difficult to believe in ourselves and our fellowmen.   — *Lee Vaughn Barker, D.D.*

Any fool can criticize, condemn, and complain — and most fools do.   — *Dale Carnegie*

Big shots are only little shots who keep shooting.
                                    — *Christopher Morley*

The mind is like the stomach. It is not how much you put into it that counts, but how much it digests.
                                    — *A. J. Nock*

Some of us have turned our freedom into exploitation, our land into a dust bowl. We can't make a nation strong when it is held together by the rotten rope of self-interest. Too often we think of democracy only in terms of getting our rights.   — *Joseph R. Sizoo, D.D.*

Adequate distribution of goods makes, unmakes — or remakes — all capital values!   — *Kenneth Goode*

Most business men generally are so busy coping with immediate and piecemeal matters that there is a lamentable tendency to let the " long run " or future take care of itself. We often are so busy " putting out fires," so to speak, that we find it difficult to do the planning that would prevent those fires from occurring in the first place. As a prominent educator has expressed it, Americans generally " spend so much time on things that are *urgent* that we have none left to spend on those that are *important*."

— *Gustav Metzman*

If we could make a great bonfire of the thousands of laws we have in this country, and start all over again with only the Golden Rule and the Ten Commandments, I am sure we would get along much better.   — *Coleman Cox*

We sometimes speak of winning reputation as though that were the final goal. The truth is contrary to this. Reputation is a reward, to be sure, but it is really the beginning, not the end of endeavor. It should not be the signal for a let-down, but rather, a reminder that the standards which won recognition can never again be lowered. From him who gives much — much is forever after expected.

— *Alvan Macauley*

I have wandered all my life, and I have also traveled; the difference between the two being this, that we wander for distraction, but we travel for fulfillment.

— *Hilaire Belloc*

Those who never retract their opinions love themselves more than they love the truth. — *Venning*

I will govern my life and thoughts as if the whole world were to see the one and to read the other, for what does it signify to make anything a secret to my neighbor, when to God, who is the searcher of our hearts, all our privacies are open? — *Seneca*

Humanity may endure the loss of everything; all its possessions may be turned away without infringing its true dignity — all but the possibility of improvement.

— *Fichte*

Many politicians lay it down as a self-evident proposition that no people ought to be free till they are fit to use their freedom. The maxim is worthy of the fool in the old story, who resolved not to go into the water till he had learned to swim. — *Macaulay*

Fate is not the ruler, but the servant of Providence.

— *Bulwer*

So great has been the endurance, so incredible the achievement, that, as long as the sun keeps a set course in heaven, it would be foolish to despair of the human race.

— *Ernest L. Woodward*

The first great gift we can bestow on others is a good example. — *Morell*

Goodwill to others is constructive thought. It helps build you up. It is good for your body. It makes your blood purer, your muscles stronger, and your whole form more symmetrical in shape. It is the real elixir of life. The more such thought you attract to you, the more life you will have. — *Prentice Mulford*

If things are not going well with you, begin your effort at correcting the situation by carefully examining the service you are rendering, and especially the spirit in which you are rendering it. — *Roger Babson*

He who wishes to fulfill his mission in the world must be a man of one idea, that is, of one great overmastering purpose, overshadowing all his aims, and guiding and controlling his entire life. — *Bate*

Many have been ruined by their fortune, and many have escaped ruin by the want of fortune. To obtain it the great have become little, and the little great. — *Zimmermann*

More than ever before, in our country, this is the age of the individual. Endowed with the accumulated knowledge of centuries, armed with all the instruments of modern science, he is still assured personal freedom and wide avenues of expression so that he may win for himself, his family and his country greater material comfort, ease and happiness; greater spiritual satisfaction and contentment. — *Dwight D. Eisenhower*

As soon as government management begins it upsets the
natural equilibrium of industrial relations, and each interference only requires further bureaucratic control until
the end is the tyranny of the totalitarian state.

— Adam Smith (1776)

Young men are fitter to invent than to judge; fitter for
execution than for counsel; and fitter for new projects
than for settled business. *— Bacon*

He who is virtuous is wise; and he who is wise is good;
and he who is good is happy. *— Boethius*

Everyone knows that weeds eat out the life of the garden
and of the productive fields. The gardener and farmer
alike each has to keep the weeding process alive.
It's like that in the building and developing of character.
No one knows our own faults and tendencies better than
we do ourselves, so that it is up to each one of us to keep
the weeds out, and to keep all growth vigorous and fruitful.

— George Matthew Adams

Most of life is routine — dull and grubby, but routine is
the momentum that keeps a man going. If you wait for
inspiration you'll be standing on the corner after the
parade is a mile down the street. *— Ben Nicholas*

The important point is to be on the spot at the moment
most favorable for gaining the desired advantage; and it
will be found that of men who get what they want in this
world, both those who seem to hasten and those who seem
to lounge are always at the right place at the right time.

— David Graham Phillips

Business is never so healthy as when, like a chicken, it must do a certain amount of scratching for what it gets.

— *Henry Ford*

The cares of today are seldom those of tomorrow; and when we lie down at night we may safely say to most of our troubles, " Ye have done your worst, and we shall see you no more."   — *Cowper*

There is no such thing as chance or accident; the words merely signify our ignorance of some real and immediate cause.   — *Adam Clarke*

Character is a diamond that scratches every other stone.

— *Bartol*

Cheerfulness is as natural to the heart of a man in strong health as color to his cheek; and wherever there is habitual gloom there must be either bad air, unwholesome food, improperly severe labor, or erring habits of life.

— *Ruskin*

Circumstances are the rulers of the weak; they are but the instruments of the wise.   — *Samuel Lover*

The whole object of education is, or should be, to develop mind. The mind should be a thing that works. It should be able to pass judgment on events as they arise, make decisions.   — *Sherwood Anderson*

Solitude is as needful to the imagination as society is wholesome for the character.   — *James Russell Lowell*

Temper your enjoyments with prudence, lest there be
written on your heart that fearful word " satiety."

— *Quarles*

To do anything in this world worth doing, we must not
stand back shivering and thinking of the cold and danger,
but jump in, and scramble through as well as we can.

— *Sydney Smith*

The men who start out with the notion that the world
owes them a living generally find that the world pays its
debt in the penitentiary or the poorhouse.

— *W. G. Sumner*

A good man doubles the length of his existence; to have
lived so as to look back with pleasure on our past life is to
live twice.   — *Martial*

A government for the people must depend for its success
on the intelligence, the morality, the justice, and the interest
of the people themselves.   — *Grover Cleveland*

If any man seeks for greatness, let him forget greatness
and ask for truth, and he will find both.

— *Horace Mann*

Though we seem grieved at the shortness of life in general,
we are wishing every period of it at an end. The minor
longs to be at age, then to be a man of business, then to
make up an estate, then to arrive at honors, then to retire.

— *Addison*

A man there was, and they called him mad; the more he gave, the more he had. — *Bunyan*

America's future will be determined by the home and the school. The child becomes largely what it is taught, hence we must watch what we teach it, how we live before it.
— *Jane Addams*

They who give have all things; they who withhold have nothing. — *Hindu Proverb*

A little experience often upsets a lot of theory.
— *Cadman*

Culture is not just an ornament; it is the expression of a nation's character, and at the same time it is a powerful instrument to mould character. The end of culture is right living. — *W. Somerset Maugham*

Merely having an open mind is nothing. The object of opening the mind, as of opening the mouth, is to shut it again on something solid. — *Gilbert K. Chesterton*

In theory it is easy to convince an ignorant person; in actual life, men not only object to offer themselves to be convinced, but hate the man who has convinced them.
— *Epictetus*

I have brought myself by long meditation to the conviction that a human being with a settled purpose must accomplish it, and that nothing can resist a will which will stake even existence upon its fulfillment. — *Disraeli*

Regret is an appalling waste of energy. You can't build on it; it's only good for wallowing in.

— *Katherine Mansfield*

Poverty is uncomfortable; but nine times out of ten the best thing that can happen to a young man is to be tossed overboard and compelled to sink or swim.

— *James A. Garfield*

Time and happenings and the grace of God are the best solvers of puzzles. One must leave much to these, if he is not to worry himself into premature senility.

— *Alex Dow*

FUNDAMENTAL FACTS OF RELIGION

Man is condemned on account of his sins alone.
Salvation is the gift of God through grace alone.
Redemption is through the crucified Christ alone.
God's means of grace are effected through the Holy Spirit alone.
Justification before God by faith alone.
Authority through religion in the word of God alone.
The priesthood of believers exists through the risen Christ alone.
The brotherhood of believers is through the church alone.
The Christian life lives by love alone.
Liberty of conscience by truth alone.

— *Walton H. Greever, D.D.*

Taxing is an easy business. Any projector can contrive new impositions; any bungler can add to the old; but is it altogether wise to have no other bounds to your impositions than the patience of those who are to bear them?

— *Burke*

The man who will neither play nor do business unless everything is just to his liking and notions, retards rather than contributes to progress.   — *Henry L. Doherty*

A dangerous fallacy is to repudiate freedom in favor of an unknown future. What else but our own sturdy reliance on freedom can explain the unexampled record this country has made? In a period scarcely twice my own lifetime, it has risen from nothingness to become the world's greatest power. It has become the ark of the covenant of freedom.   — *Bernard M. Baruch*

The great business of man is to improve his mind, and govern his manners; all other projects and pursuits, whether in our power to compass or not, are only amusements.   — *Pliny*

Luck generally comes to those who look after it; and my notion is that it taps, once in a lifetime, at everybody's door, but if industry does not open it luck goes away.   — *Spurgeon*

Three things too much, and three too little are pernicious to man; to speak much, and know little; to spend much, and have little; to presume much, and be worth little.   — *Cervantes*

Real merit of any kind cannot long be concealed; it will be discovered, and nothing can depreciate it but a man exhibiting it himself. It may not always be rewarded as it ought; but it will always be known.   — *Lord Chesterfield*

Almost all men are intelligent. It is method that they
lack. —*F. W. Nichol*

If you pursue good with labor, the labor passes away but
the good remains; if you pursue evil with pleasure, the
pleasure passes away and the evil remains. —*Cicero*

So long as you live and in whatever circumstances the
kaleidoscope of life may place you, think for yourself and
act in accordance with the conclusions of that thinking;
avoid so far as possible drifting with the current of the mob
or being too easily influenced by the outward manifestation
of things. Take your own look beneath the surface and
don't trust others to look for you. If you will follow this
rule consistently, I am sure you will keep out of much
trouble, will make the most out of your life and, what is
more, will contribute most of value to the community life.
— *Dr. Frank B. Jewett*

Books come at my call and return when I desire them;
they are never out of humor and they answer all my questions with readiness. Some present in review before me
the events of past ages; others reveal to me the secrets of
Nature. These teach me how to live, and those how to die;
these dispel my melancholy by their mirth, and amuse me by
their sallies of wit. Some there are who prepare my soul
to suffer everything, to desire nothing, and to become
thoroughly acquainted with itself. In a word, they open
the door to all the arts and sciences. — *Petrarch*

Your market has a free choice, and only by supplying
what the market wants, and not by your efforts to impose
your merchandise, will you get your maximum share of the
market's potential. — *Walter H. Lowy*

The average man takes life as a trouble. He is in a chronic state of irritation at the whole performance. He does not learn to differentiate between troubles and difficulties, usually, until some real trouble bowls him over. He fusses about pin-pricks until a mule kicks him. Then he learns the difference.   — *Herbert N. Casson*

The world abhors closeness, and all but admires extravagance; yet a slack hand shows weakness, and a tight hand strength.   — *Sir Thomas Buxton*

The aim of education should be to convert the mind into a living fountain, and not a reservoir. That which is filled by merely pumping in, will be emptied by pumping out.
— *John M. Mason*

A man can be as truly a saint in a factory as in a monastery, and there is as much need of him in the one as in the other.   — *Robert J. McCracken, D.D.*

Human life may be regarded as a succession of frontispieces. The way to be satisfied is never to look back.
— *Hazlitt*

Be not afraid of life. Believe that life *is* worth living, and your belief will help create the fact.
—*William James*

How happy the station which every moment furnishes opportunities of doing good to thousands! How dangerous that which every moment exposes to the injuring of millions!   — *Bruyère*

The greater the obstacle the more glory in overcoming it.
— *Molière*

Consider how much more you often suffer from your anger and grief, than from those very things for which you are angry and grieved.
— *Marcus Antonius*

As long as we can keep our international relations in the realm of conference rather than open conflict, we are giving truth more time to vindicate itself. And what we ourselves need is more faith in the power of truth.
— *Ralph W. Sockman, D.D.*

Not failure, but low aim, is a crime.
— *Ernest Holmes*

A liberal is a man who is willing to spend somebody else's money.
— *Carter Glass*

When you make a mistake, don't look back at it long. Take the reason of the thing into your mind, and then look forward. Mistakes are lessons of wisdom. The past cannot be changed. The future is yet in your power.
— *Hugh White*

Only actions give life strength; only moderation gives it charm.
— *Richter*

He whose first emotion, on the view of an excellent work, is to undervalue or depreciate it, will never have one of his own to show.
— *Aikin*

The philosophy which affects to teach us a contempt of
money does not run very deep.   — *Henry Taylor*

Borrow trouble for yourself, if that's your nature, but
don't lend it to your neighbors.   — *Rudyard Kipling*

In all differences consider that both you and your op-
ponent or enemy are mortal, and that ere long your very
memories will be extinguished.   — *Aurel*

Fear not for the future, weep not for the past.
— *Shelley*

The making of friends who are real friends, is the best
token we have of a man's success in life.
— *Edward E. Hale*

Success in business implies optimism, mutual confidence,
and fair play. A business man must hold a high opinion of
the worth of what he has to sell and he must feel that he
is a useful public servant.   — *R. H. Cabell*

Home is the one place in all this world where hearts are
sure of each other. It is the place of confidence. It is the
spot where expressions of tenderness gush out without any
dread of ridicule.   — *Frederick W. Robertson*

No matter what the form of the government, the liberty
of a people consists in being governed by laws which they
have themselves made.   — *Abraham Cowley*

If war should sweep our commerce from the seas, another generation will restore it. If war exhausts our treasury, future industry will replenish it. If war desiccate and lay waste our fields, under new cultivation they will grow green again and ripen to future harvest. If the walls of yonder Capitol should fall and its decorations be covered by the dust of battle, all these can be rebuilt. But who shall reconstruct the fabric of a demolished government; who shall dwell in the well-proportioned columns of constitutional liberty; who shall frame together the skillful architecture which unites sovereignty with state's rights, individual security with prosperity? — *Daniel Webster*

Forty is the old age of youth; fifty is the youth of old age. — *Victor Hugo*

In my opinion, he only may be truly said to live and enjoy his being who is engaged in some laudable pursuit, and acquires a name by some illustrious action, or useful art. — *Sallust*

Make no man your friend before inquiring how he has used his former friends; for you must expect him to treat you as he has treated them. Be slow to give your friendship, but when you have given it, strive to make it lasting; for it is as reprehensible to make many changes in one's associates as to have no friends at all. Neither test your friends to your own injury nor be willing to forego a test of your companions. — *Isocrates*

The world is divided into people who do things and people who get the credit. Try, if you can, to belong to the first class. There's far less competition. — *Dwight Morrow*

What the world has to eradicate is fear and ignorance.

— *Jan Masaryk*

Those who give too much attention to trifling things become generally incapable of great ones.

— *La Rochefoucauld*

If you believe in the Lord, He will do half the work — but the last half. He helps those who help themselves.

— *Cyrus H. K. Curtis*

In all science error precedes the truth, and it is better it should go first than last.   — *Walpole*

Happiness quite unshared can scarcely be called happiness; it has no taste.   — *Brontë*

Empires built on force will always be destroyed. Those built on trust in Christ will remain.

— *Joseph R. Sizoo, D.D.*

Perfect freedom is as necessary to the health and vigor of commerce as it is to the health and vigor of citizenship.

— *Patrick Henry*

Common sense is the knack of seeing things as they are, and doing things as they ought to be done.   — *Stowe*

The reward of doing one duty is the power to do another.

— *Rabbi Ben Azai*

There is no easy method of learning difficult things.
The method is to close the door, give out that you are not
at home, and work. — *Joseph de Maistre*

Four things come not back — the spoken word, the
sped arrow, the past life, and the neglected opportunity.
— *Arabian Proverb*

Let us show, not merely in great crises, but in every day
affairs of life, qualities of practical intelligence, of hardi-
hood and endurance, and above all, the power of devotion to
a lofty ideal. — *Theodore Roosevelt*

I mistrust the judgment of every man in a case in which
his own wishes are concerned. — *Wellington*

A good book is the precious lifeblood of a master spirit,
embalmed and treasured up on purpose to life beyond life.
— *Milton*

Many ideas grow better when transplanted into another
mind than in the one where they sprang up.
— *Oliver Wendell Holmes*

We are lonely even in the milling crowds of a city, where
we may only be recognized as customers for goods and
services. Our personalities are weakened and starved by
the impersonal life in a city. That is why there is so much
wreckage in a city. Our families answer this need to some
degree, but not completely. And so, in the last analysis it
is only God who can give us the comfort of utter understanding. — *Lyman V. Cady, D.D.*

We're worn into grooves by Time — by our habits. In
the end, these grooves are going to show whether we've been
second rate or champions, each in his way in dispatching
the affairs of every day. By choosing our habits, we determine the grooves into which Time will wear us; and these
are grooves that enrich our lives and make for ease of
mind, peace, happiness — achievement.

— *Frank B. Gilberth*

Good intentions are very mortal and perishable things.
Like very mellow and choice fruit, they are difficult to keep.

— *G. Simmons*

Public sentiment is everything. With public sentiment,
nothing can fail. Without it, nothing can succeed.

— *Abraham Lincoln*

All problems become smaller if you don't dodge them, but
confront them. Touch a thistle timidly, and it pricks
you; grasp it boldly, and its spines crumble.

— *William S. Halsey*

Perfectionism is a dangerous state of mind in an imperfect world. The best way is to forget doubts and set about
the task in hand. . . . If you are doing your best, you
will not have time to worry about failure.

— *Robert Hillyer*

Personal magnetism is a mixture of rugged Honesty,
pulsating Energy, and self-organized Intelligence. I believe, absolutely, that truth is the strongest and most powerful weapon a man can use, whether he is fighting for a
reform or fighting for a sale.   — *Arthur Dunn*

It isn't the common man at all who is important; it's the uncommon man.   — *Lady Nancy Astor*

In a society safe and worthy to be free, teaching which produces a willingness to lead, as well as a willingness to follow, must be given to all.   — *William F. Russell*

The big things of life are never done by a fussy man.
Poise is one of the earmarks of mental strength.
                                    — *Preston Nolan*

I do not have to make over the universe; I have only to do my job, great or small, and to look often at the trees and the hills and the sky, and be friendly with all men.
                                    — *David Grayson*

Ideas must work through the brains and the arms of good and brave men, or they are no better than dreams.
                                    — *Emerson*

Small kindnesses, small courtesies, small considerations, habitually practiced in our social intercourse, give a greater charm to the character than the display of great talent and accomplishments.   — *Kelty*

We have got to begin a vast reclamation project to revitalize religion for those to whom it means little or nothing. This can be done not by trying to persuade those outside the church to believe what we believe but by pointing out to them the presence of the unrecognized religion that already exists in their lives.
                                — *Theodore C. Speers, D.D.*

The man who insists upon seeing with perfect clearness
before he decides, never decides. Accept life, and you
cannot accept regret. — *Amiel*

Opposition inflames the enthusiast, never converts him.
— *Schiller*

Faith gives the courage to live and do. Scientists, with
their disciplined thinking, like others, need a basis for the
good life, for aspiration, for courage to do great deeds.
They need a faith to live by. The hope of the world lies
in those who have such faith and who use the methods of
science to make their visions become real. Visions and hope
and faith are not part of science. They are beyond the
nature that science knows. Of such is the religion that
gives meaning to life. — *Arthur H. Compton*

Read not books alone, but men, and amongst them chiefly
thyself. If thou find anything questionable there, use the
commentary of a severe friend, rather than the gloss of a
sweet-lipped flatterer; there is more profit in a distasteful
truth than in deceitful sweetness. — *Quarles*

The parent's job year in and year out, here a little and
there a little, is to build up a disposition of good sportsmanship, of taking one's medicine, of facing the music, of
being reviled and reviling not. This sense of not always
being right, of recognition that perhaps we've made a mistake, seems left out of some grown-up children.
— *Samuel Smith Drury*

The man who follows the crowd will never be followed
by a crowd. — *Donnell*

The human spirit is stronger than anything that can
happen to it. — *C. C. Scott*

We want no dictatorship of physicists, as physicists. If
our democracy is to realize its full promise, we want no
dictatorship at all — of any species. What we want and
need is the enlightened and active interest of all men of
intelligence and goodwill in their government, and their par-
ticipation in its functions. — *Jerome Frank*

We cannot live only for ourselves. A thousand fibers
connect us with our fellow-men; and along those fibers, as
sympathetic threads, our actions run as causes, and they
come back to us as effects. — *Melville*

Leisure for men of business, and business for men of
leisure, would cure many complaints. — *Thrale*

Ideas go booming through the world louder than cannon.
Thoughts are mightier than armies. Principles have
achieved more victories than horsemen or chariots.
— *W. M. Paxton*

An idle brain is the devil's workshop.
— *English Proverb*

It is going to be a long, hard haul; it will require patience,
courage, faith that hangs on when hope fails, if we are to
tame the rude barbarity of man, so that the atomic age
becomes a blessing, not a curse. There never was such a day
for the Christian gospel. God help us all in these years
ahead to make that gospel live in men and nations!
— *Harry Emerson Fosdick, D.D.*

In some small field each child should attain, within the limited range of its experience and observation, the power to draw a justly limited inference from observed facts.
— *Charles W. Eliot*

The mere apprehension of a coming evil has put many into a situation of the utmost danger.   — *Lucan*

I love the man that can smile in trouble, that can gather strength from distress, and grow brave by reflection. 'Tis the business of little minds to shrink, but he whose heart is firm, and whose conscience approves his conduct, will pursue his principles unto death.   — *Thomas Paine*

An acre of performance is worth a whole world of promise.   —*W. D. Howells*

We all have to learn, in one way or another, that neither men nor boys get second chances in this world. We all get new chances to the end of our lives, but not second chances in the same set of circumstances; and the great difference between one person and another is how he takes hold and uses his first chance, and how he takes his fall if it is scored against him.   — *Thomas Hughes*

It is never safe to look into the future with eyes of fear.
— *E. H. Harriman*

We cannot possibly reconcile the principle of democracy, *which means co-operation*, with the principle of governmental omniscience under which everyone waits for an order before doing anything. That way lies loss of freedom, and dictatorship.   — *Lewis H. Brown*

If you divorce capital from labor, capital is hoarded, and labor starves.

— *Daniel Webster*

The habit of reading is the only one I know in which there is no alloy. It lasts when all other pleasures fade. It will be there to support you when all other resources are gone. It will be present to you when the energies of your body have fallen away from you. It will make your hours pleasant to you as long as you live.

— *Anthony Trollope*

It took thrift and savings, together with tremendous character and vision, to make our nation what it is today. And it will take thrift and savings, together with constant ingenuity and stamina, to conserve our remaining resources to enable us to continue to be a great nation.

— *John W. Snyder*

Wisdom thoroughly learned, will never be forgotten.

— *Pythagoras*

Anybody can become angry — that is easy; but to be angry with the right person, and to the right degree, and at the right time, and for the right purpose, and in the right way — that is not within everybody's power and is not easy.

— *Aristotle*

A tool is but the extension of a man's hand and a machine is but a complex tool; and he that invents a machine augments the power of man and the well-being of mankind.

— *Henry Ward Beecher*

A quiet conscience makes one so serene.

— *Byron*

Laziness grows on people; it begins in cobwebs and ends in iron chains. The more one has to do the more he is able to accomplish. — *Sir Thomas Buxton*

American business men must learn human nature to the point of accepting as necessary the Rabble Rouser of the Right. . . . To get fast action somebody must stir millions to genuine anger over conditions which are adversely affecting their lives. —*Walter B. Pitkin*

Public education is a great instrument of social change. Through it, if we so desire, we can make our country more nearly a democracy without classes. To do so will require the efforts of us all — teachers, administrators, taxpayers and statesmen. Education is a social process, perhaps the most important process in determining the future of our country; it should command a far larger portion of our national income than it does today.
— *Dr. James B. Conant*

There is hardly any place or any company where you may not gain knowledge, if you please; almost everybody knows some one thing, and is glad to talk about that one thing. — *Lord Chesterfield*

Lost, somewhere between sunrise and sunset, sixty golden minutes. Each set with sixty diamond seconds. No reward is offered, for they are gone forever.
— *Horace Mann*

We don't need democratization of privilege. What we need is the self-discipline of democracy.
— *Thomas I. Parkinson*

Fortunate is the person who has developed the self-control to steer a straight course toward his objective in life, without being swayed from his purpose by either commendation or condemnation.   — *Napoleon Hill*

The great truths of human life do not spring new born to each new generation. They derive from long experience. They are the gathered wisdom of the race. They are renewed in time of conflict and danger. If the times in which we are now living do not bring a fuller understanding of the great traditions of the Western European peoples and an almost Messianic desire to affirm them, we are not worthy of that heritage.   — *Frederick Osborn*

Two things, well considered, would prevent many quarrels: first, to have it well ascertained whether we are not disputing about terms rather than things and, second, to examine whether that on which we differ is worth contending about.   — *Colton*

The rung of a ladder was never meant to rest upon, but only to hold a man's foot long enough to enable him to put the other somewhat higher.   — *Thomas Huxley*

Science is teaching man to know and reverence truth, and to believe that only as far as he knows and loves it can he live worthily on earth, and vindicate the dignity of his spirit.   — *Moses Harvey*

I am inclined to put the zenith of success — the time of most consideration and public labor — as somewhere in the sixties, say from sixty-five to seventy.
                                          — *W. Robertson Nicoll*

Goodness is always an asset. A man who is straight, friendly and useful may never be famous, but he is respected and liked by all who know him. He has laid a sound foundation for success and he will have a worthwhile life.
— Herbert N. Casson

Toil, feel, think, hope; you will be sure to dream enough before you die, without arranging for it.
— J. Sterling

The life of every man is a diary in which he means to write one story, and writes another, and his humblest hour is when he compares the volume as it is with what he vowed to make it. *—J. M. Barrie*

Money may be the husk of many things, but not the kernel. It brings you food, but not appetite; medicine, but not health; acquaintances, but not friends; servants, but not faithfulness; days of joy, but not peace or happiness.
— Henrik Ibsen

No one can ask honestly or hopefully to be delivered from temptation unless he has himself honestly and firmly determined to do the best he can to keep out of it.
— Ruskin

No man lives without jostling and being jostled; in all ways he has to elbow himself through the world, giving and receiving offense. *— Carlyle*

If you wish your merit to be known, acknowledge that of other people. *— Oriental Proverb*

What a curious phenomenon it is that you can get men to die for the liberty of the world who will not make the little sacrifice that is needed to free themselves from their own individual bondage.
— Bruce Barton

No man has come to true greatness who has not felt in some degree that his life belongs to his race, and that what God gives him He gives him for mankind.
— Phillips Brooks

Luxury makes a man so soft that it is hard to please him, and easy to trcuble him; so that his pleasures at last become his burden. Luxury is a nice master, hard to be pleased.
— Mackenzie

Though a good motive cannot sanction a bad action, a bad motive will always vitiate a good action. In common and trivial matters we may act without motive, but in momentous ones the most careful deliberation is wisdom.
—W. Jay

Every good act is charity. Your smiling in your brother's face, is charity; an exhortation of your fellowman to virtuous deeds, is equal to alms-giving; your putting a wanderer in the right road, is charity; your assisting the blind, is charity; your removing stones, and thorns, and other obstructions from the road, is charity; your giving water to the thirsty, is charity. A man's true wealth hereafter, is the good he does in this world to his fellow-man. When he dies, people will say, " What property has he left behind him? " But the angels will ask, " What good deeds has he sent before him? "
— Mahomet

The clean tongue, the clear head, and the bright eye are
birthrights of each day.   *— Dr. William Osler*

You can't escape the responsibility of tomorrow by
evading it today.   *— Abraham Lincoln*

PEOPLE

They range from animals to gods. They pray for you
and they prey on you. They are bears for punishment
and brutes for revenge. They want to be Everyone, Everywhere, Everything. Their restlessness fills them with
wonderings and spurs them into wanderings. They are
creatures of moods and modes. They try to look different,
but deep down underneath they are all alike. They are
hero-worshippers and idol-destroyers. They are quick to
take sides and quick to swing from side to side. They
like individuals who can appraise and praise them. People
must be taken as they are and still they want to be taken
as they aren't. They have their ways and want to get
away with them. They cry for the moon and wail for a
place in the sun. They are happiest in the hurly-burly,
giving and taking, making and losing, to the tune of a hurdy-
gurdy. They try everything once and seldom stop to think
twice. But they are blessed with nine lives and often
strike twelve at eleventh hours. With people all things are
possible; without them, all things are impossible. They
must forever be felt and dealt with. To lose contact with
them is to lose contact with life.   *— P. K. Thomajan*

Mankind needs the American type of leadership. Let
it be not discredited by those who are out of sympathy
with it, who don't understand it or are incompetent to
administer it. In America, the demand for power to compel is a confession of incompetence to lead.
                        — Eugene E. Wilson

No man can, for any considerable time, wear one face to himself, and another to the multitude, without finally getting bewildered as to which is the true one.

— Hawthorne

It is foolish to try to live on past experience. It is very dangerous, if not a fatal habit, to judge ourselves to be safe because of something that we felt or did twenty years ago.

— Spurgeon

Neither great poverty nor great riches will hear reason.

— Henry Fielding

There is only one real failure in life that is possible, and that is, not to be true to the best one knows.   *— Farrar*

Science has sometimes been said to be opposed to faith, and inconsistent with it. But all science, in fact, rests on a basis of faith, for it assumes the permanence and uniformity of natural laws — a thing which can never be demonstrated.

— Tryon Edwards

A lie has always a certain amount of weight with those who wish to believe it.   *— E. W. Rice*

Five minutes, just before going to sleep, given to a bit of directed imagination regarding achievement possibilities of the morrow, will steadily and increasingly bear fruit, particularly if all ideas of difficulty, worry or fear are resolutely ruled out and replaced by those of accomplishment and smiling courage.   *— Frederick Pierce*

Ideas are the mightiest influence on earth. One great
thought breathed into a man may regenerate him.

— *Channing*

Inflexible in faith, invincible in arms.

— *James Beattie*

Courage in danger is half the battle.   — *Plautus*

We work day after day, not to finish things; but to make
the future better . . . because we will spend the rest of
our lives there.   — *Charles F. Kettering*

The New Dealers, labor politicians and Socialists have
tried to take advantage of the natural American instinct
for charity to forward their plans to socialize the furnishing
of the necessities of life to all. If the Government gives
free medical care to everybody, why not free food, clothing
and housing?   — *Robert A. Taft*

The legitimate aim of criticism is to direct attention to the
excellent. The bad will dig its own grave, and the imperfect may safely be left to that final neglect from which
no amount of present undeserved popularity can rescue it.

— *Bovée*

Obstinacy in opinions holds the dogmatist in the chains of
error, without hope of emancipation.

— *John C. Granville*

Thrift is that habit of character that prompts one to
work for what he gets, to earn what is paid him; to invest
a part of his earnings; to spend wisely and well; to save,
but not hoard.   — *Arthur Chamberlain*

Getters generally don't get happiness; givers get it. You simply give to others a bit of yourself — a thoughtful act, a helpful idea, a word of appreciation, a lift over a rough spot, a sense of understanding, a timely suggestion. You take something out of your mind, garnished in kindness out of your heart, and put it into the other fellow's mind and heart. *— Charles H. Burr*

Nature has written a letter of credit upon some men's faces that is honored wherever presented. You cannot help trusting such men. Their very presence gives confidence. There is " promise to pay " in their faces which gives confidence and you prefer it to another man's endorsement. Character is credit. *— Thackeray*

Pay as little attention to discouragement as possible. Plough ahead as a steamer does, rough or smooth — rain or shine. To carry your cargo and make your port is the point. *— Maltbie Babcock*

If we could only make our hands move as actively as our tongues, what wonders we could accomplish! Almost everyone loves to hear his own voice. It is so easy, too! Yet if we could say less and do more for each other's good, not alone would every home be happier, but communities would be enriched thereby. Instead of criticism by speech, to show someone a better way to do a thing would be of much greater value. *— John Wanamaker*

People are afraid to think, or they don't know how. They fail to realize that, while emotions can't be suppressed, the mind can be strengthened. All over the world people are seeking peace of mind, but there can be no peace of mind without strength of mind. *— Eric B. Gutkind*

When we have practiced good actions awhile, they become easy; when they are easy, we take pleasure in them; when they please us, we do them frequently; and then, by frequency of act, they grow into a habit.   — *Tillotson*

A really great man is known by three signs — generosity in the design, humanity in the execution, moderation in success.   — *Bismarck*

If we survive danger it steels our courage more than anything else.   — *Niebuhr*

Safe popular freedom consists of four things: The diffusion of liberty, of intelligence, of property, and of conscientiousness, and cannot be compounded of any three out of the four.   — *Joseph Cook*

My suggestion to ambitious young men would be to conserve and develop their physical and mental strength, cram their heads with all the useful knowledge they can, and work, work, work — not simply for their own advancement but to get worthwhile things done.
          — *Edward G. Seubert*

I am glad I am an optimist.   The pessimist is half-licked before he starts.   The optimist has won half the battle, the most important half that applies to himself, when he begins his approach to a subject with the proper mental attitude. The optimist may not understand, or if he understands he may not agree with, prevailing ideas; but he believes, yes, knows, that in the long run and in due course there will prevail whatever is right and best.
          — *Thomas A. Buckner*

We often rebel against the strenuousness and chaos of
our time. But historically it has always been in such time
that man won his great inner victories.

— *E. M. McKee, D.D.*

Courtesy is really nothing more than a form of friendliness. It is amazing what a warming influence it can have
on an otherwise dreary world. It has been said that a rise
of one degree Fahrenheit in the mean annual temperature
of the globe would free both polar regions from their ice.
It is thrilling to contemplate what frigidity might be dis-
pelled in the world of human relations if people made just
a little better effort to be friendly.   — *M. Bartos*

Action may not always bring happiness; but there is no
happiness without action.   — *Disraeli*

Three ideas stand out above all others in the influence
they have exerted and are destined to exert upon the development of the human race: The idea of the Golden Rule; the
idea of natural law; the idea of age-long growth or evolution.

— *Robert A. Millikan*

If a man is worth knowing at all, he is worth knowing
well.   — *Alexander Smith*

Don't be a fault-finding grouch; when you feel like finding
fault with somebody or something stop for a moment and
think; there is very apt to be something wrong within yourself. Don't permit yourself to show temper, and always
remember that when you are in the right you can afford to
keep your temper, and when you are in the wrong you
cannot afford to lose it.   — *J. J. Reynolds*

Better to be a strong man with a weak point, than to be a weak man without a strong point. A diamond with a flaw is more valuable than a brick without a flaw.

—Wm. J. H. Boetcker

There are three things which make a nation great and prosperous — a fertile soil, busy workshops, and easy conveyance for men and commodities.   *— Bacon*

No life can be barren which hears the whisper of the wind in the branches, or the voice of the sea as it breaks upon the shore; and no soul can lack happiness looking up to the midnight stars.   *— William Winter*

There is just as much honey in the flowers this year as there ever was. The soil will produce abundantly when fertilized well with elbow grease and good sense.

— Jacob Kindleberger

This country has achieved its commercial and financial supremacy under a regime of private ownership. It conquered the wilderness, built our railroads, our factories, our public utilities, gave us the telegraph, the telephone, the electric light, the automobile, the airplane, the radio and a higher standard of living for all the people than obtains anywhere else in the world. No great invention ever came from a government-owned industry.

— George B. Cortelyou

No man ever sank under the burden of the day. It is when to-morrow's burden is added to the burden of to-day that the weight is more than a man can bear.

— George MacDonald

Once you have sold a customer, make sure he is satisfied with your goods. Stay with him until the goods are used up or worn out. Your product may be of such long life that you will never sell him again, but he will sell you and your product to his friends. *— William Feather*

The question " Who ought to be boss? " is like asking " Who ought to be the tenor in the quartet? " Obviously, the man who can sing tenor. *— Henry Ford*

Each person has an ideal, a hope, a dream of some sort which represents his soul. In the long light of eternity this seed of the future is all that matters! We must find this seed no matter how small it is; we must give to it the warmth of love, the light of understanding and the water of encouragement. We must learn to deal with people as they are — not as we wish them to be. We must study the moral values which shape our thinking, arouse our emotions and guide our conduct. We must get acquainted with our inner stream and find out what's going on in our heads and hearts. We must put an end to blind, instinctive, sensory thought and feeling. We must take time to be human. *— Colby Dorr Dam*

Words are the voice of the heart. *— Confucius*

Genius is entitled to respect only when it promotes the peace and improves the happiness of mankind. *— Lord Essex*

He is wise who knows the sources of knowledge — who knows who has written and where it is to be found. *— A. A. Hodge*

Pleasures, riches, honor and joy are sure to have care,
disgrace, adversity and affliction in their train. There is
no pleasure without pain, no joy without sorrow. O the
folly of expecting lasting felicity in a vale of tears, or a
paradise in a ruined world.   — *Gotthold*

You don't have to preach honesty to men with creative
purpose. Let a human being throw the engines of his soul
into the making of something, and the instinct of workmanship will take care of his honesty.   — *Walter Lippmann*

There can be no freedom of the individual, no democracy,
without the capital system, the profit system, the private
enterprise system. These are, in the end, inseparable.
Those who would destroy freedom have only first to destroy
the hope of gain, the profit of enterprise and risk-taking,
the hope of accumulating capital, the hope to save something
for one's old age and for one's children. For a community
of men without property, and without the hope of getting
it by honest effort, is a community of slaves of a despotic
State.   — *Russell C. Leffingwell*

He who can wait for what he desires takes the course
not to be exceedingly grieved if he fails of it; he, on the
contrary, who labors after a thing too impatiently thinks the
success when it comes is not a recompense equal to all the
pains he has been at about it.   — *Bruyère*

Set about doing good to somebody. Put on your hat,
and go and visit the sick and poor of your neighborhood;
inquire into their circumstances, and minister to their wants.
Seek out the desolate, and afflicted, and oppressed, and tell
them of the consolations of religion. I have often tried
this method, and have always found it the best medicine for
a heavy heart.   — *Howard*

A duty dodged is like a debt unpaid; it is only deferred, and we must come back and settle the account at last.

— *Joseph Fort Newton*

Aim at the sun, and you may not reach it; but your arrow will fly far higher than if aimed at an object on a level with yourself.

— *J. Hawes*

Whatever difference there may appear to be in men's fortunes, there is still a certain compensation of good and ill in all, that makes them equal.

— *Charron*

A thought is often original, though you have uttered it a hundred times. It has come to you over a new route, by a new and express train of association.

— *Oliver Wendell Holmes*

Perfection does not exist; to understand it is the triumph of human intelligence; to expect to possess it is the most dangerous kind of madness.

— *Alfred de Musset*

Because a fellow has failed once or twice, or a dozen times, you don't want to set him down as a failure till he's dead or loses his courage — and that's the same thing.

— *George Horace Lorimer*

Despotism may govern without faith, but Liberty cannot.

— *De Tocqueville*

Every man has a right to his opinion, but no man has a right to be wrong in his facts.

— *Bernard M. Baruch*

It is not the number of books you read, nor the variety of sermons you hear, nor the amount of religious conversation in which you mix, but it is the frequency and earnestness with which you meditate on these things till the truth in them becomes your own and part of your being, that ensures your growth.   — *Frederick W. Robertson*

Don't let yourself say or even think " I am busy," " I haven't time," " I am tired." That makes you feel busier or more rushed or more tired than you actually are.

— *Wm. B. Given, Jr.*

Most of us have a pretty clear idea of the world we want. What we lack is an understanding of how to go about getting it.   — *Hugh Gibson*

Life is work, rest, and recreation, and depending on that " recreation " is the story of one's success or failure.

— *F. D. Van Amburgh*

He who floats with the current, who does not guide himself according to higher principles, who has no ideal, no convictions — such a man is a mere article of the world's furniture — a thing moved, instead of a living and moving being — an echo, not a voice.   — *Amiel*

No political dreamer was ever wild enough to think of breaking down the lines which separate the States and compounding the American people into one common mass.

— *John Marshall*

Second thoughts are ever wiser.   – *Euripides*

Work is the true elixir of life. The busiest man is the happiest man. Excellence in any art or profession is attained only by hard and persistent work. Never believe that you are perfect. When a man imagines, even after years of striving, that he has attained perfection, his decline begins. — *Sir Theodore Martin* (*92*)

We should lay up in our minds a store of goodly thoughts which will be a living treasure of knowledge always with us, and from which, at various times, and amidst all the shiftings of circumstances, we might be sure of drawing some comfort, guidance and sympathy.
— *Sir Arthur Helps*

Democracy is something we must always be working at. It is a process never finished, never ending. And each new height gained opens broader vistas for the future. Thus it has been as one looks back over the sweep of history; thus it must continue to be if democracy is to continue as a working tool in the hands of free men.
— *Edmund deS. Brunner*

It is an anomaly of modern life that many find giving to be a burden. Such persons have omitted a preliminary giving. If one first gives himself to the Lord, all other giving is easy. — *John S. Bonnell, D.D.*

He who considers too much will perform little.
— *Schiller*

I don't like to talk much with people who always agree with me. It is amusing to coquette with an echo for a little while, but one soon tires of it. — *Carlyle*

The men who build the future are those who know that greater things are yet to come, and that they themselves will help bring them about. Their minds are illumined by the blazing sun of hope. They never stop to doubt. They haven't time.   — *Melvin J. Evans*

If by saying that all men are born free and equal, you mean that they are all equally born, it is true, but true in no other sense; birth, talent, labor, virtue, and providence, are forever making differences.   — *Eugene Edwards*

The man who makes everything that leads to happiness depend upon himself, and not upon other men, has adopted the very best plan for living happily. This is the man of moderation, the man of manly character and of wisdom.   — *Plato*

Courage that grows from constitution often forsakes a man when he has occasion for it; courage which arises from a sense of duty acts in a uniform manner.   — *Addison*

Give vocational training to the manually minded, and the children's courts of the future will have less to do.   — *Lewis E. Lawes*

Education is the cheap defense of nations.   — *Burke*

Be not too presumptuously sure in any business; for things of this world depend on such a train of unseen chances that if it were in man's hands to set the tables, still he would not be certain to win the game.   — *Herbert*

True enjoyment comes from activity of the mind and exercise of the body; the two are ever united.

— *Humboldt*

Markets as well as mobs respond to human emotions; markets as well as mobs can be inflamed to their own destruction. — *Owen D. Young*

You find yourself refreshed by the presence of cheerful people. Why not make earnest effort to confer that pleasure on others? Half the battle is gained if you never allow yourself to say anything gloomy. — *L. M. Child*

To cultivate a garden is to walk with God. — *Bovée*

Nothing is so great an instance of ill-manners as flattery. If you flatter all the company, you please none; if you flatter only one or two, you affront the rest. — *Swift*

We are raising a generation that has a woefully small stock of ideas and interests and emotions. It must be amused at all costs but it has little skill in amusing itself. It pays some of its members to do what the majority can no longer do for themselves. It is this inner poverty that makes for the worst kind of boredom.

— *Robert J. McCracken, D.D.*

Man must work. That is certain as the sun. But he may work grudgingly or he may work gratefully; he may work as a man, or he may work as a machine. There is no work so rude, that he may not exalt it; no work so impassive, that he may not breathe a soul into it; no work so dull that he may not enliven it. — *Henry Giles*

The advertising man is a liaison between the products of business and the mind of the nation. He must know both before he can serve either.   — *Glenn Frank*

A. T. Stewart started life with a dollar and fifty cents. This merchant prince began by calling at the doors of houses in order to sell needles, thread and buttons. He soon found the people did not want them, and his small stock was thrown back on his hands. Then he said wisely, " I'll not buy any more of these goods, but I'll go and ask people what they do want." Thereafter he studied the needs and desires of people, found out just what they most wanted, endeavored to meet those wants, and became the greatest business man of his time.   — *Grenville Kleiser*

Industry need not wish, and he that lives upon hopes will die fasting. There are no gains without pains. He that hath a trade hath an estate, and he that hath a calling hath an office of profit and honor; but then the trade must be worked at, and the calling followed, or neither the estate nor the office will enable us to pay our taxes. If we are industrious, we shall never starve; for at the workingman's house hunger looks in, but dares not enter. Nor will the bailiff or the constable enter, for industry pays debts, while idleness and neglect increase them.

— *Benjamin Franklin*

People seldom want to walk over you until you lie down.
— *Elmer Wheeler*

Whatever mitigates the woes, or increases the happiness of others, is a just criterion of goodness; and whatever injures society at large, or any individual in it, is a criterion of iniquity.   — *Goldsmith*

The value of compassion cannot be over-emphasized. Anyone can criticize. It takes a true believer to be compassionate. No greater burden can be born by an individual than to know no one cares or understands.

— *Arthur H. Stainback, D.D.*

You cannot do away with the competitive system so long as trademarks remain to distinguish one product from another. You cannot cut out large-scale manufacture so long as there are established brands which breed consumer confidence and thus make mass production not only possible and profitable, but also economical. — *Philip Salisbury*

The Constitution of America only guarantees pursuit of happiness — you have to catch up with it yourself. Fortunately, happiness is something that depends not on position but on disposition, and life is what you make it.

— *Gill Robb Wilson*

There are two great classes of men: the people and the scholars, the men of science. For the former, nothing exists but that which directly leads to action. It is for the latter to see beyond. They are the free artists who create the future and its history, the conscious architects of the world.

— *Fichte*

The future of nations cannot be frozen . . . cannot be foreseen. If we are going to accomplish anything in our time we must approach our problem in the knowledge that there is nothing rigid or immutable in human affairs. History is a story of growth, decay and change. If no provision, no allowance is made for change by peaceful means, it will come anyway — and with violence. — *Herbert Hoover*

The glory of a people, and of an age, is always the work of a small number of great men, and disappears with them.

— *Grimm*

We [the Government] are here not as masters but as servants, we are not here to glory in power, but to attest our loyalty to the commands and restrictions laid down by our sovereign, the people of the United States, in whose name and by whose will we exercise our brief authority.

— *Charles Evans Hughes*

Success is good management in action.

— *William E. Holler*

The percentage of mistakes in quick decisions is no greater than in long-drawn-out vacillations, and the effect of decisiveness itself " makes things go " and creates confidence.   — *Anne O'Hare McCormick*

A man is relieved and gay when he has put his heart into his work and done his best.   — *Emerson*

Some have an idea that the reason we in this country discard things so readily is because we have so much. The facts are exactly opposite — the reason we have so much is simply because we discard things so readily. We replace the old in return for something that will serve us better.

— *Alfred P. Sloan, Jr.*

A man who lives right, and is right, has more power in his silence than another has by his words.

— *Phillips Brooks*

Cleverness is serviceable for everything, sufficient for nothing. — *Amiel*

It becomes no man to nurse despair, but, in the teeth of clenched antagonisms, to follow up the worthiest till he die.
— *Tennyson*

Life is like a game of cards. Reliability is the ace, industry the king, politeness the queen, thrift the jack. Commonsense is playing to best advantage the cards you draw. And every day, as the game proceeds, you will find the ace, king, queen, jack in your hand and opportunity to use them. — *Ed. Howe*

It is to law alone that men owe justice and liberty. It is this salutary organ of the will of all which establishes in civil rights the natural equality between men. It is this celestial voice which dictates to each citizen the precepts of public reason, and teaches him to act according to the rules of his own judgment and not to behave inconsistently with himself. It is with this voice alone that political leaders should speak when they command.
— *Jean Jacques Rousseau*

Tact is the unsaid part of what you think; its opposite, the unthought part which you say. — *Henry Van Dyke*

The great composer does not set to work because he is inspired, but becomes inspired because he is working. Beethoven, Wagner, Bach and Mozart settled down day after day to the job in hand with as much regularity as an accountant settles down each day to his figures. They didn't waste time waiting for inspiration. — *Ernest Newman*

There is no business, no avocation, whatever, which will not permit a man, who has the inclination, to give a little time, every day, to study.   — *Daniel Wyttenbach*

There have been a few moments when I have known complete satisfaction, but only a few. I have rarely been free from the disturbing realization that my playing might have been better.   — *Jan Ignace Paderewski*

We grow great by dreams. All big men are dreamers. They see things in the soft haze of a spring day or in the red fire of a long winter's evening. Some of us let these great dreams die, but others nourish and protect them, nurse them through bad days till they bring them to the sunshine and light which come always to those who sincerely hope that their dreams will come true.

— *Woodrow Wilson*

There is a point, of course, where a man must take the isolated peak and break with all his associates for clear principle; but until that time comes he must work, if he would be of use, with men as they are. As long as the good in them overbalances the evil, let him work with them for the best that can be obtained.   — *Theodore Roosevelt*

A man that seeks truth and loves it must be reckoned precious to any human society.   — *Frederick the Great*

There is far more danger in public than in private monopoly, for when Government goes into business it can always shift its losses to the taxpayers. Government never makes ends meet — and that is the first requisite of business.

— *Thomas A. Edison*

Progress in America has resulted from the freedom of the individual to venture for himself and to assure the gains and take all the losses as they come. — *Robert R. Wason*

Next in importance to freedom and justice is popular education, without which neither freedom nor justice can be permanently maintained. — *James A. Garfield*

May we never let the things we can't have, or don't have, or shouldn't have, spoil our enjoyment of the things we do have and can have. As we value our happiness let us not forget it, for one of the greatest lessons in life is learning to be happy without the things we cannot or should not have. — *Richard L. Evans*

The most successful business man is the man who holds onto the old just as long as it is good and grabs the new just as soon as it is better. — *Robert P. Vanderpoel*

There will be selfishness and greed and corruption and narrowness and intolerance in the world tomorrow and tomorrow's tomorrow. But pray God we may have the courage and the wisdom and the vision to raise a definite standard that will appeal to the best that is in man, and then strive mightily toward that goal. — *Harold E. Stassen*

Live your life each day as you would climb a mountain. An occasional glance toward the summit keeps the goal in mind, but many beautiful scenes are to be observed from each new vantage point. Climb slowly, steadily, enjoying each passing moment; and the view from the summit will serve as a fitting climax for the journey. — *Harold V. Melchert*

Be noble, and the nobleness that lies in other men, sleeping but never dead, will rise in majesty to meet thine own.

— James Russell Lowell

Never shrink from doing anything which your business calls you to do. The man who is above his business may one day find his business above him.   *— Drew*

There are but two powers in the world, the sword and the mind. In the long run the sword is always beaten by the mind.   *— Napoleon*

The man without religion is as a ship without a rudder.

— B. C. Forbes

Life is made up, not of great sacrifices or duties, but of little things, in which smiles and kindnesses, and small obligations, given habitually, are what win and preserve the heart and secure comfort.   *— Sir Humphry Davy*

There is a point at which even justice does injury.

— Sophocles

A man who neglects his duty as a citizen is not entitled to his rights as a citizen.   *— Tiorio*

Any man can work when every stroke of his hand brings down the fruit rattling from the tree to the ground; but to labor in season and out of season, under every discouragement, by the power of truth . . . that requires a heroism which is transcendent.   *— Henry Ward Beecher*

The superstition that all our hours of work are a minus quantity in the happiness of life, and all the hours of idleness are plus ones, is a most ludicrous and pernicious doctrine, and its greatest support comes from our not taking sufficient trouble, not making a real effort, to make work as near pleasure as it can be. — *Lord Balfour*

When a man has equipped himself by thought and study for a bigger job, it usually happens that promotion comes along even before it is expected. — *P. G. Winnett*

We have heard enough about being practical and efficient and prudent. We heard it preached through several decades that these things would save the world. I think that, with the salty taste of blood and sweat on our lips, we are learning that we had best talk once again about doing what is right. — *Ellis Arnall*

If I had my life to live over again, I would have made a rule to read some poetry and listen to some music at least once a week; for perhaps the parts of my brain now atrophied would have thus been kept active through use. The loss of these tastes is a loss of happiness, and may possibly be injurious to the intellect, and more probably to the moral character, by enfeebling the emotional part of our nature. — *Darwin*

What is the recipe for successful achievement? To my mind there are just four essential ingredients: Choose a career you love . . . Give it the best there is in you . . . Seize your opportunities . . . And be a member of the team. In no country but America, I believe, is it possible to fulfill all four of these requirements.
— *Benjamin F. Fairless*

God did not intend the human family to be wafted to
heaven on flowery beds of ease.   — *Frank Knox*

Principle — particularly moral principle — can never be
a weathervane, spinning around this way and that with
the shifting winds of expediency. Moral principle is a
compass forever fixed and forever true — and that is as
important in business as it is in the classroom.
          — *Edward R. Lyman*

Politeness is good nature regulated by good sense.
          — *Sydney Smith*

To be what we are, and to become what we are capable
of becoming, is the only end of life.   — *Spinoza*

The heart of all problems, whether economic, political or
social, is a human heart. The man comes first, then the plan.
          — *L. M. Charles-Edwards, D.D.*

Democracy, as I understand it, requires me to sacrifice
myself *for* the masses, not *to* them. Who knows not that
if you would save the people, you must often oppose them?
          — *John C. Calhoun*

A great factory with the machinery all working and
revolving with absolute and rhythmic regularity and with
the men all driven by one impulse, and moving in unison as
though a constituent part of the mighty machine, is one
of the most inspiring examples of directed force that the
world knows. I have rarely seen the face of a mechanic in
the action of creation which was not fine, never one which
was not earnest and impressive.   — *Thomas Nelson Page*

When you find a man who knows his job and is willing to take responsibility, keep out of his way and don't bother him with unnecessary supervision. What you may think is co-operation is nothing but interference.

— Thomas Dreier

You will never stub your toe standing still. The faster you go, the more chance there is of stubbing your toe, but the more chance you have of getting somewhere.

— Charles F. Kettering

One big reason why men do not develop greater abilities, greater sales strength, greater resourcefulness is because they use neither their abilities nor their opportunities. We don't need more strength or more ability or greater opportunity. What we need is to use what we have. Men fail and their families suffer deprivations when all the time these men have in their possession the same assets other men are utilizing to accumulate a fortune. . . . Life doesn't cheat. It doesn't pay in counterfeit coin. It doesn't lock up shop and go home when pay-day comes. It pays every man exactly what he has earned. The age-old law that a man gets what he earns hasn't been suspended. When we take that truth home and believe it, we've turned a big corner on the high road that runs straight through to success. *— Basil S. Walsh*

This is the first nation that organized government on the basis of universal liberty with a free Church and a free State. This meant much at the time; it means much now and will continue to be the beacon of light and guidance for ourselves and of other nations. All that is good and practical and wise in the new developments can best be worked out under our form of government without destroying any of the basic principles upon which it rests.

— Oscar S. Straus

The doctrine of human equality reposes on this: that there is no man really clever who has not found that he is stupid. There is no big man who has not felt small. Some men never feel small; but these are the few men who are.   — *Gilbert K. Chesterton*

Every human mind is a great slumbering power until awakened by keen desire and by definite resolution to do.
                                     — *Edgar F. Roberts*

Social progress makes the well-being of all more and more the business of each.   — *Henry George*

To keep the Golden Rule we must put ourselves in other people's places, but to do that consists in and depends upon picturing ourselves in their places. If we had the imagination to do that there would be fewer families estranged by misunderstanding between the older and the younger generations, fewer bitter judgments would pass our lips, fewer racial, national and class prejudices would stain our lives.   — *Harry Emerson Fosdick, D.D.*

True greatness is the most ready to recognize and most willing to obey those simple outward laws which have been sanctioned by the experience of mankind.   — *Froude*

We do not yet trust the unknown powers of thought. Whence came all these tools, inventions, book laws, parties, kingdoms? Out of the invisible world, through a few brains. The arts and institutions of men are created out of thought. The powers that make the capitalist are metaphysical, the force of method and force of will makes trade, and builds towns.   — *Emerson*

There are six things that " keep us going ":

First, the instinct to live, which we apparently have no part in making or deciding about.

Second, group consciousness and the desire that we have to win the approbation of our fellows within the group.

Third, the various interests that we may find in life, such as religion or art or some such other branch of esthetics.

Fourth, in our climate the habit of work.

Fifth, the sheer joy of physical life that we find in hours of well-earned recreation after hard work — games, fishing, tramping the hills, a good book before an open fire.

Sixth, and most important, the general feeling that we have that there is some abstract goodness or rightness in the world with which we may co-operate in making the world a fine place for a splendid race of men, women and children to live in. *— Frank Parker Day*

One should take good care not to grow too wise for so great a pleasure of life as laughter. *— Addison*

A man who is contented with what he has done will never become famous for what he will do.

— Fred Estabrook

Nature will not forgive those who fail to fulfill the law of their being. The law of human beings is wisdom and goodness, not unlimited acquisition.

— Robert Maynard Hutchins

Americanism is not an accident of birth, but an achievement in terms of worth. Government does not create Americanism, but Americanism creates Government. Americanism is not a race, but a vision, a hope and an ideal.

— Dr. Louis I. Mann

In life it is possible merely to throw a heap of stones
together, but this pile is not beautiful. We pyramid to the
heights only when we lay stone on stone according to a
beautiful plan. If we have no faith in the principles with
which we build life, we are defeated.

—*W. N. Thomas, D.D.*

Seek those who find your road agreeable, your personality
and mind stimulating, your philosophy acceptable, and
your experience helpful. Let those who do not, seek their
own kind.

— *Henri Fabre*

Life is a place of service, and in that service one has to
suffer a great deal that is hard to bear, but more often to
experience a great deal of joy. But that joy can be real only
if people look upon their life as a service, and have a definite object in life outside themselves and their personal happiness.   — *Tolstoi*

Most of the critical things in life, which become the starting points of human destiny, are little things.

— *R. Smith*

What we see depends mainly on what we look for.

— *John Lubbock*

Unless a business can stay in the black over the long
term, averaging the bad years with good, it cannot sustain
itself. A manager may have laudable social intentions of
providing security for his employees, better products at
lower prices for his customers. But if he cannot keep the
business going in realizing these intentions he is defeated
before he begins.   — *Paul Garrett*

Do not attempt to do a thing unless you are sure of yourself; but do not relinquish it simply because someone else is not sure of you. *— Stewart E. White*

When a great man has some one object in view to be achieved in a given time, it may be absolutely necessary for him to walk out of all the common roads. *— Burke*

Iron rusts from disuse; water loses its purity from stagnation and in cold weather becomes frozen; even so does inaction sap the vigors of the mind. *— L. da Vinci*

The old thought that one cannot be rich except at the expense of his neighbor, must pass away. True prosperity adds to the richness of the whole world, such as that of the man who makes two trees grow where only one grew before. The parasitical belief in prosperity as coming by the sacrifices of others has no place in the mind that thinks true. " My benefit is your benefit, your success is my success," should be the basis of all our wealth. *— Anne Rix Miltz*

Wear a smile and have friends; wear a scowl and have wrinkles. What do we live for if not to make the world less difficult for each other? *— George Eliot*

The dead are living all around us, watching with eager anticipation how we will handle the opportunities they left in our hands when they died. *— Theodore C. Speers, D.D.*

The man who can put himself in the place of other men, who can understand the workings of their minds, need never worry about what the future has in store for him.
— Owen D. Young

Sooner or later a democracy which is to survive has to be able to rely upon that enlargement of vision and purpose of those individuals who compose it, which means that their craving for devotion and self-sacrifice is satisfied in a democratic society on a nobler level, and with a finer recognition of the value of individual personality than is true of a national purpose of a totalitarian state under a dictator.

— *Ordway Tead*

Your morning thoughts may determine your conduct for the day. Optimistic thoughts will make your day bright and productive, while pessimistic thinking will make it dull and wasteful. Face each day cheerfully, smilingly and courageously, and it will naturally follow that your work will be a real pleasure and progress will be a delightful accomplishment.   — *William M. Peck*

The only limitless thing I know of is human want. Civilization itself is nothing more than the creation of wants, followed by methods of satisfying those wants. At the moment we had better give consideration to the fact that we may not be creating enough stuff to satisfy the wants this education has inspired.

— *Dr. James Shelby Thomas*

A desire for bigness has hurt many folks. Putting oneself in the limelight at the expense of others is a wrong idea of greatness. The secret of greatness rather than bigness is to acclimate oneself to one's place of service and be true to one's own convictions. A life of this kind of service will forever remain the measure of one's true greatness.

— *Richard W. Shelly, Jr.*

Wasted time means wasted lives.   — *R. Shannon*

The history of mankind is one long record of giving revolution another trial — and then limping back at last to sanity, safety and hard work!   — *Ed. Howe*

Business demands faith, compels earnestness, requires courage, is honestly selfish, is penalized for mistakes, and is the essence of life.   — *William Feather*

It is not at all likely that anyone ever had a totally original idea.   He may put together old ideas into a new combination, but the elements which made up the new combination were mostly acquired from other people.   Without many borrowed ideas there would be no inventions, new movements or anything else that is classed as new.

                   — *Dr. George Grier*

If you will call your " troubles " " experiences," and remember that every experience develops some latent force within you, you will grow vigorous and happy, however adverse your circumstances may seem to be.

                   — *J. R. Miller*

Do not think it wasted time to submit yourself to any influence that will bring upon you any noble feeling.

                   — *Ruskin*

Call on a business man only at business times, and on business; transact your business, and go about your business, in order to give him time to finish his business.

                   — *Wellington*

The power of imagination makes us infinite.

                   — *John Muir*

An executive is a man who decides; sometimes he decides right, but always he decides.   *— John H. Patterson*

It takes a highly intellectual individual to enjoy leisure. . . . Most of us had better count on working. What a man really wants is creative challenge with sufficient skills to bring him within the reach of success so that he may have the expanding joy of achievement. . . . Few people overwork; plenty overeat, overworry, overdrink. . . . Few realize real joy and happiness of conquest. The basis of mental health for the average adult is more work, provided the work is not mere drudgery.   *— Dr. Fay B. Nash*

Facts are the most important thing in business. Study facts and do more than is expected of you.
          — Frederick H. Ecker

In the New Testament it is taught that willing and voluntary service to others is the highest duty and glory in human life. . . . The men of talent are constantly forced to serve the rest. They make the discoveries and inventions, order the battles, write the books, and produce the works of art. The benefit and enjoyment go to the whole. There are those who joyfully order their own lives so that they may serve the welfare of mankind.   *— W. G. Sumner*

If anyone wants to understand the course of man on earth, he must consider the fact of the long pause, three million years on the level of savagery, ten thousand years on the level of dependence on the fruits of hand labor, and a hundred or a hundred and fifty years of sudden sharp rise. One hundred or 150 years is the time included in what we call progress in man's history.   *— E. Parmalee Prentice*

Freedom is no heritage. Preservation of freedom is a fresh challenge and a fresh conquest for each generation. It is based on the religious concept of the dignity of man. The discovery that man is free is the greatest discovery of the ages. —*C. Donald Dallas*

While an open mind is priceless, it is priceless only when its owner has the courage to make a final decision which closes the mind for action after the process of viewing all sides of the question has been completed. Failure to make a decision after due consideration of all the facts will quickly brand a man as unfit for a position of responsibility. Not all of your decisions will be correct. None of us is perfect. But if you get into the habit of making decisions, experience will develop your judgment to a point where more and more of your decisions will be right. After all, it is better to be right 51% of the time and get something done, than it is to get nothing done because you fear to reach a decision. —*H. W. Andrews*

Unless the job means more than the pay it will never pay more. —*H. Bertram Lewis*

The trouble with most people is that they think with their hopes or fears or wishes rather than with their minds. —*Walter Duranty*

A man isn't poor if he can still laugh. —*Raymond Hitchcock*

Always vote for a principle, though you vote alone, and you may cherish the sweet reflection that your vote is never lost. —*John Quincy Adams*

Believe, if you will, that there may have been faults in our industrial system, yet the fact remains that the welfare of the average man has not so far advanced under any other form of government, and that whatever evil exists will not be corrected by delegating to government, with all its weaknesses, the authority to run and control all business and to control the daily lives and activities of laboring mankind. Nor will any existing waste and extravagance of government be eliminated or appreciably diminished until the average man realizes that the burden of paying its bills will, through direct or indirect taxation, ultimately fall upon him, his children or his children's children.

— J. B. Hill

If thou wouldst conquer thy weakness thou must not gratify it.   *— William Penn*

Every one of us, unconsciously, works out a personal philosophy of life, by which we are guided, inspired, and corrected, as time goes on. It is this philosophy by which we measure out our days, and by which we advertise to all about us the man, or woman, that we are. . . . It takes but a brief time to scent the life philosophy of anyone. It is defined in the conversation, in the look of the eye, and in the general mien of the person. It has no hiding place. It's like the perfume of the flower — unseen, but known almost instantly. It is the possession of the successful, and the happy. And it can be greatly embellished by the absorption of ideas and experiences of the useful of this earth.   *— George Matthew Adams*

Believe in yourself, your neighbors, your work, your ultimate attainment of more complete happiness. It is only the farmer who faithfully plants seeds in the Spring, who reaps a harvest in the Autumn.   *— B. C. Forbes*

There is deep intuitive wisdom in this American tolerance of economic variety and in our refusal to commit ourselves to any one social and economic system. It is recognition of the fact that life and truth are too varied and complex to be confined within the pattern of any single deliberately planned economic system. *— Dr. Arthur E. Morgan*

It is more difficult to organize peace than to win a war; but the fruits of victory will be lost if the peace is not well organized. *— Aristotle*

Great men are the commissioned guides of mankind, who rule their fellows because they are wiser.
— Carlyle

Time is precious but truth is more precious than time.
— Disraeli

City folk need not feel sorry for themselves or be pessimistic about the soil in which Christianity is planted to live and bear fruit. The Christian faith was made for contest, and its best fruits are always produced out of the harsh soil of difficulty and danger.
— Theodore C. Speers, D.D.

True wisdom lies in gathering the precious things out of each day as it goes by. *— E. S. Bouton*

No accidents are so unlucky but that the wise may draw some advantage from them; nor are there any so lucky but that the foolish may turn them to their own prejudice.
— La Rochefoucauld

The wisest have the most authority.   —*Plato*

You can be deprived of your money, your job and your home by someone else, but remember that no one can ever take away your honor.   —*William Lyon Phelps*

Happiness has many roots, but none more important than security.   —*E. R. Stettinius, Jr.*

Reprove not, in their wrath, excited men; good counsel comes all out of season then; but when their fury is appeased and past, they will perceive their faults, and mend at last. When he is cool and calm, then utter it.

—*Randolph*

Either I will find a way, or I will make one.

—*Sir P. Sidney*

The best executive is the one who has sense enough to pick good men to do what he wants done, and self-restraint enough to keep from meddling with them while they do it.

—*Theodore Roosevelt*

If America is to be run by the people, it is the people who must think. And we do not need to put on sackcloth and ashes to think. Nor should our minds work like a sundial which records only sunshine. Our thinking must square against some lessons of history, some principles of government and morals, if we would preserve the rights and dignity of men to which this nation is dedicated.

—*Herbert Hoover*

The man who has accomplished all that he thinks worth
while, has begun to die.   — E. T. Trigg

Great discoveries and improvements invariably involve
the co-operation of many minds. I may be given credit for
having blazed the trail but when I look at the subsequent
developments I feel the credit is due to others rather than
to myself.   — Alexander Graham Bell

The Golden Rule is of no use to you whatever unless you
realize that it is your move.   — Dr. Frank Crane

Worry affects the circulation, the heart, the glands, the
whole nervous system, and profoundly affects the health.
I have never known a man who died from overwork, but
many who died from doubt.   — Dr. Charles Mayo

It is our individual performances, no matter how humble
our place in life may be, that will in the long run determine
how well ordered the world may become.
                    — Paul C. Packer

Let no man imagine that he has no influence. Whoever
he may be, and wherever he may be placed, the man who
thinks becomes a light and a power.   — Henry George

Inscription in lobby of the S. F. Bowser & Co. office
building, Fort Wayne, Ind.:
I acknowledge God's great help in all things, of which this
splendid office is one. One which all our office employees
can enjoy. God help us to be grateful.   — S. F. Bowser

The moment a question comes to your mind, see yourself mentally taking hold of it and disposing of it. In that moment is your choice made. Thus you learn to take the path to the right. Thus you learn to become the decider and not the vacillator. Thus you build character.

— *H. Van Anderson*

You generally hear that what a man doesn't know doesn't hurt him, but in business what a man doesn't know does hurt. — *E. S. Lewis*

A vigorous temper is not altogether an evil. Men who are easy as an old shoe are generally of little worth.

— *Spurgeon*

Government means politics, and interference by government carries with it always the implication of coercion. We may accept the expanding power of bureaucrats so long as we bask in their friendly smile. But it is a dangerous temptation. Today politics may be our friend and tomorrow we may be its victims. — *Owen D. Young*

The most important single influence in the life of a person is another person. We may say to our children: Here is art, science, philosophy, mathematics, music, psychology, history, religion — and we may open innumerable doors along the corridors of living so that they will have a broad and even a minute acquaintance with the segments of life; but these introductions are not as important as knowing people whose characters and actions, personalities and words have grown after similar introductions and have become worthy of emulation. — *Paul D. Shafer*

You'll find as you grow older that you weren't born
such a very great while ago after all. The time shortens up.
— *W. D. Howells*

It is the penalty of fame that a man must ever keep
rising. " Get a reputation, and then go to bed," is the
absurdest of all maxims. " Keep up a reputation or go to
bed," would be nearer the truth. — *E. H. Chapin*

All good government must begin in the home. It is useless to make good laws for bad people. Public sentiment
is more than law. — *H. R. Hawes*

The youth of today and the youth of tomorrow will be
accorded an almost unequaled opportunity for great accomplishment and for human service.
— *Dr. Nicholas Murray Butler*

Good listeners generally make more sales than good
talkers. — *B. C. Holwick*

Some of our problems can no more be solved correctly
by majority opinion than can a problem in arithmetic and
there are few problems that cannot be solved according
to what is just and right without resort to popular opinion.
— *Henry L. Doherty*

Every human being is intended to have a character of
his own; to be what no other is, and to do what no other
can do. — *Channing*

He who thinks his place below him, will certainly be
below his place.   — *Saville*

A man who knows how to mix pleasures with business is
never entirely possessed by them; he either quits or re-
sumes them at his will; and in the use he makes of them
he rather finds a relaxation than a dangerous charm that
might corrupt him.   — *St. Evremond*

Think not those faithful who praise all thy words and
actions, but those who kindly reprove thy faults.
                                              — *Socrates*

Beware prejudices. They are like rats, and men's minds
are like traps; prejudices get in easily, but it is doubtful
if they ever get out.   — *Lord Jeffrey*

Many a man fails to become a thinker for the sole reason
that his memory is too good.   — *Nietzsche*

If the power to do hard work is not talent, it is the best
possible substitute for it.   — *James A. Garfield*

The easiest thing of all is to deceive one's self; for what a
man wishes he generally believes to be true.
                                          — *Demosthenes*

At sixty a man has passed most of the reefs and whirl-
pools. Excepting only death, he has no enemies left to
meet. . . .   That man has awakened to a new youth. . . .
Ergo, he is young.   — *George Luks*

There is enough for all. The earth is a generous mother; she will provide in plentiful abundance food for all her children if they will but cultivate her soil in justice and in peace. — *Bourke Cockran*

Every individual has a place to fill in the world, and is important in some respect, whether he chooses to be so or not. — *Nathaniel Hawthorne*

It is to the United States that all freemen look for the light and the hope of the world. Unless we dedicate ourselves completely to this struggle, unless we combat hunger with food, fear with trust, suspicion with faith, fraud with justice — and threats with power, nations will surrender to the futility, the hopelessness, the panic on which wars feed. — *Gen. Omar N. Bradley*

Faith is positive, enriching life in the here and now. Doubt is negative, robbing life of glow and meaning. So though I do not understand immortality, I choose to believe. — *Webb B. Garrison*

He who would distinguish the true from the false must have an adequate idea of what is true and false. — *Spinoza*

Success is never final and Failure never fatal. It's courage that counts. — *George F. Tilton*

Life's greatest achievement is the continual re-making of yourself so that at last you know how to live. — *Winfred Rhodes*

Knowledge cannot be stolen from us. It cannot be bought or sold. We may be poor, and the sheriff may come and sell our furniture, or drive away our cow, or take our pet lamb, and leave us homeless and penniless; but he cannot lay the law's hand upon the jewelry of our minds.

— Burritt

There's no ceiling on effort!   *— Harvey C. Fruehauf*

It is an experiment worth trying to be alone and to be quiet for a brief period every day. Under city conditions it may be difficult to carry out, but most of us could do it if we tried. At any rate, we should moderate the pace at which we are living. If we remain at high gear, at top pressure, we are bound to suffer from fatigue and strain.

— Robert J. McCracken, D.D.

Any act often repeated soon forms a habit; and habit allowed, steadily gains in strength. At first it may be but as the spider's web, easily broken through, but if not resisted it soon binds us with chains of steel.   *— Tryon Edwards*

Service to a just cause rewards the worker with more real happiness and satisfaction than any other venture of life.   *— Carrie Chapman Catt*

Sensitiveness is closely allied to egotism. Indeed, excessive sensitiveness is only another name for morbid self-consciousness. The cure for it is to make more of our objects, and less of ourselves.   *— Bovée*

Ambition is the germ from which all growth of nobleness proceeds.   *— T. D. English*

Life in the country teaches one that the really stimulating things are the quiet, natural things, and the really wearisome things are the noisy, unnatural things. It is more exciting to stand still than to dance. Silence is more eloquent than speech. Water is more stimulating than wine. Fresh air is more intoxicating than cigarette smoke. Sunlight is more subtle than electric light. The scent of grass is more luxurious than the most expensive perfume. The slow, simple observations of the peasant are more wise than the most sparkling epigrams of the latest wit.

— *Beverley Nichols*

By a divine paradox, wherever there is one slave there are two. So in the wonderful reciprocities of being, we can never reach the higher levels until all our fellows ascend with us. There is no true liberty for the individual except as he finds it in the liberty of all. There is no true security for the individual except as he finds it in the security of all.

— *Edwin Markham*

Wise men learn more from fools than fools from the wise.

— *Cato*

If to do were as easy as to know what were good to do, chapels had been churches, and poor men's cottages princes' palaces. It is a good divine that follows his own instructions; I can easier teach twenty what were good to be done, than be one of the twenty to follow mine own teaching.

— *Shakespeare*

Discourage litigation. Persuade your neighbor to compromise whenever you can. As a peacemaker the lawyer has a superior opportunity of being a good man. There will still be business enough.   — *Abraham Lincoln*

Curiosity is one of the most permanent and certain
characteristics of a vigorous intellect.　　　*— Johnson*

Want and wealth equally harden the human heart, as frost
and fire are both alien to the human flesh.　Famine and
gluttony alike drive away nature from the heart of man.
　　　　　　　　　　　　　　　— Theodore E. Parker

Many a man who pays rent all his life owns his own
home; and many a family has successfully saved for a home
only to find itself at last with nothing but a house.
　　　　　　　　　　　　　　　　— Bruce Barton

The more noise a man or a motor makes the less power
there is available.　　　　　　*— W. R. McGeary*

Public money ought to be touched with the most scrupulous conscientiousness of honor.　It is not the produce of
riches only, but of the hard earnings of labor and poverty.
It is drawn even from the bitterness of want and misery.
Not a beggar passes, or perishes in the streets, whose mite
is not in that mass.　　　　　　*— Thomas Paine*

The recipe for perpetual ignorance is: Be satisfied with
your opinions and content with your knowledge.
　　　　　　　　　　　　　　　— Elbert Hubbard

Mirth is God's medicine; everybody ought to bathe in it.
Grim care, moroseness, anxiety — all the rust of life —
ought to be scoured off by the oil of mirth.
　　　　　　　　　　　　　　　— Orison Swett Marden

It is not permitted to the most equitable of men to be a judge in his own cause.   — *Pascal*

Spurts don't count. The final score makes no mention of a splendid start if the finish proves that you were an " also ran."   — *Herbert Kaufman*

You should have education enough so that you won't have to look up to people; and then more education so that you will be wise enough not to look down on people.
                    — *M. L. Boren*

A man without mirth is like a wagon without springs, in which one is caused disagreeably to jolt by every pebble over which it turns.   — *Henry Ward Beecher*

Talking and eloquence are not the same: to speak, and to speak well are two things. A fool may talk, but a wise man speaks.   — *Ben Jonson*

The test of our religion is whether it fits us to meet emergencies. A man has no more character than he can command in a time of crisis.   — *Ralph W. Sockman, D.D.*

There is no fire like passion, there is no shark like hatred, there is no snare like folly, there is no torrent like greed.
                    — *Buddha*

Philosophy should be an energy; it should find its aim and its effect in the amelioration of mankind.
                    — *Victor Hugo*

The man who works need never be a problem to anyone. Opportunities multiply as they are seized; they die when neglected. Life is a long line of opportunities. Wealth is not in making money, but in making the man while he is making money. Production, not destruction, leads to success.

— *John Wicker*

A vision of the future has been one of the sustaining marks of the American experience. Without that vision and without the men who devote themselves to realizing that vision, there can be no true American way of life. We must beware of the thoughtless men who proclaim that a particular stage of our social development, or any special set of conditions, is the best that progress can offer. These men would immobilize us in the great stream of history. They would let its great challenges and chances pass us by, . . . forgetting that the American way of life is a way of acting, not a state of inactivity.   — *C. W. De Kiewiet*

When you rise in the morning, form a resolution to make the day a happy one to a fellow-creature.

— *Sydney Smith*

The formation of right habits is essential to your permanent security. They diminish your chance of falling when assailed, and they augment your chance of recovery when overthrown.   — *John Tyndall*

We cannot too often tell ourselves that the real wealth of a nation — the only enduring, worthwhile wealth — is in the spiritual, mental and physical health of the citizens, and that in a democracy we are all trustees.

—*Sir Herbert Gepp*

He that wrestles with us strengthens our nerves and
sharpens our skill. Our antagonist is our helper.

— *Burke*

Each excellent thing, once learned, serves for a measure
of all other knowledge. — *Sir P. Sidney*

My clearest recollection of a long-ago interview with
Thomas A. Edison is of a single sentence that was painted
or hung on a wall in his room. In effect, the sentence
was: " It is remarkable to what lengths people will go to
avoid thought." That is tragically true. Some of us think,
more of us think we think, and most of us don't even think
of thinking. The result is a somewhat cockeyed world.

— *Pollack*

A determined soul will do more with a rusty monkey
wrench than a loafer will accomplish with all the tools in
a machine shop. — *Rupert Hughes*

When you want a thing deeply, earnestly and intensely,
this feeling of desire reinforces your will and arouses in you
the determination to work for the desired object. When
you have a distinct purpose in view, your work becomes of
absorbing interest. You bend your best powers to it; you
give it concentrated attention; you think of little else than
the realization of this purpose; your will is stimulated
into unusual activity, and as a consequence you do your
work with an increasing sense of power.

— *Grenville Kleiser*

Happiness is only a by-product of successful living.
— *Dr. Austen Fox Riggs*

Be glad of life because it gives you the chance to love
and to work and to play and to look at the stars.

— *Henry Van Dyke*

The rise of statism in our time is the natural result of the
longing of godless, unchurched people for some kind of
protection. When we lose to God we turn to what looks
like the next most powerful thing, which is the state. How
bad a choice that is, let Germany and Russia in recent
years testify.   — *Samuel M. Shoemaker, D.D.*

The question for each man to settle is not what he would
do if he had means, time, influence and educational advantages, but what he will do with the things he has.

— *Hamilton Wright Mabie*

Never does a man know the force that is in him till some
mighty affection or grief has humanized the soul.

— *Frederick W. Robertson*

Labor is rest from the sorrows that greet us; from all the
petty vexations that meet us; from the sin-promptings that
assail us; from the world-sirens that lure us to ill.

— *F. S. Osgood*

Every human soul is of infinite value, eternal, free; no
human being, therefore, is so placed as not to have within
his reach, in himself and others, objects adequate to infinite
endeavor.   — *Lord Balfour*

If a rich man is proud of his wealth, he should not be
praised until it is known how he employs it.   — *Socrates*

Omit a few of the most abstruse sciences, and mankind's study of man occupies nearly the whole field of literature. The burden of history is what man has been; of law, what he does; of physiology, what he is; of ethics, what he ought to be; of revelation, what he shall be.

— *George Finlayson*

Proverbs are in the world of thought what gold coin is in the world of business — great value in small compass, and equally current among all people. Sometimes the proverb may be false, the coin counterfeit, but in both cases the false proves the value of the true.   — *D. March*

Real life is, to most men, a long second-best, a perpetual compromise between the ideal and the possible; but the world of pure reason knows no compromise, no practical limitations, no barrier to the creative activity.

— *Bertrand Russell*

It takes courage to live — courage and strength and hope and humor. And courage and strength and hope and humor have to be bought and paid for with pain and work and prayers and tears.   — *Jerome P. Fleishman*

Leisure may prove to be a curse rather than a blessing, unless education teaches a flippant world that leisure is not a synonym for entertainment.   — *William J. Bogan*

When you have lived longer in this world and outlived the enthusiastic and pleasing illusions of youth, you will find your love and pity for the race increase tenfold, your admiration and attachment to a particular party or opinion fall away altogether.   — *Joseph Henry Shorthouse*

Emphasis on educational and vocational rehabilitation
must not be allowed to overshadow the profound need that
will exist for spiritual reorientation. Inevitably there will
exist, to a considerable degree, psychological maladjust-
ments manifested in disillusionment, resentment toward
civilians, depression, and a sense of guilt. Spiritual therapy
available in the resources of the Christian faith can accomplish most in overcoming these problems.

—*John S. Bonnell, D.D.*

What we have done for ourselves alone dies with us.
What we have done for others and the world remains and
is immortal.   — *Albert Pine*

Not on one string are all life's jewels strung.

— *William Morris*

Three-fourths of the mistakes a man makes are made
because he does not really know the things he thinks he
knows.   — *James Bryce*

Most men believe that it would benefit them if they could
get a little from those who *have* more. How much more
would it benefit them if they would learn a little from
those who *know* more.   — *Wm. J. H. Boetcker*

The inlet of a man's mind is what he learns; the outlet
is what he accomplishes. If his mind is not fed by a continued supply of new ideas which he puts to work with
purpose, and if there is no outlet in action, his mind becomes stagnant. Such a mind is a danger to the individual
who owns it and is useless to the community.

—*Jeremiah W. Jenks*

When possible make the decisions now, even if action is in the future. A reviewed decision usually is better than one reached at the last moment. — *Wm. B. Given, Jr.*

The man who works for the gold in the job rather than for the money in the pay envelope, is the fellow who gets on. — *Joseph French Johnson*

It is only after an unknown number of unrecorded labors, after a host of noble hearts have succumbed in discouragement, convinced that their cause is lost; it is only then that the cause triumphs. — *Guizot*

Cynics build no bridges; they make no discoveries; no gaps are spanned by them. Cynics may pride themselves in being realistic in their approach, but progress and the onward march of Christian civilization demand an inspiration and motivation that cynicism never affords. If we want progress we must take the forward look. — *Paul L. McKay, D.D.*

No legitimate business man ever got started on the road to permanent success by any other means than that of hard, intelligent work, coupled with an earned credit, plus character. — *F. D. Van Amburgh*

It is wonderful how preposterously the affairs of the world are managed. We assemble parliaments and councils to have the benefit of collected wisdom, but we necessarily have, at the same time, the inconvenience of their collected passions, prejudices and private interests: for regulating commerce an assembly of great men is the greatest fool on earth. — *Benjamin Franklin*

Those who are surly and imperious to their inferiors are generally humble, flattering and cringing to their superiors.

— *Fuller*

The transcendent importance of love and goodwill in all human relations is shown by their mighty beneficent effect upon the individual and society.   — *George D. Birkhoff*

Invention, strictly speaking, is little more than a new combination of those images which have been previously gathered and deposited in the memory. Nothing can be made of nothing; he who has laid up no materials can produce no combinations.   — *Sir J. Reynolds*

There are five types of men who fail in life; the machine, the miser, the hermit, the snob and the brute.

— *Walter Wilber Gruber*

Faith without works is like a bird without wings; though she may hop about on earth, she will never fly to heaven. But when both are joined together, then doth the soul mount up to her eternal rest.   — *Beaumont*

It is a maxim received in life that, in general, we can determine more wisely for others than for ourselves. The reason of it is so clear in argument that it hardly wants the confirmation of experience.   — *Junius*

Pursue not a victory too far. He hath conquered well that hath made his enemy fly; thou mayest beat him to a desperate resistance, which may ruin thee.   — *Herbert*

The strongest bond of human sympathy, outside of the family relation, should be one uniting all working people, of all nations, and tongues, and kindreds. Nor should this lead us to a war upon property, or the owners of property. Property is the fruit of labor; property is desirable; is a positive good in the world. That some should be rich shows that others may become rich and, hence, is just encouragement to industry and enterprise. Let not him who is houseless pull down the house of another, but let him labor diligently and build one for himself, thus, by example, assuring that his own shall be safe from violence when built.

— *Abraham Lincoln*

Human affairs inspire in noble hearts only two feelings — admiration or pity.   — *Anatole France*

Laws should be like clothes. They should be made to fit the people they are meant to serve.

— *Clarence Darrow*

Our way of living together in America is a strong but delicate fabric. It is made up of many threads. It has been woven over many centuries by the patience and sacrifice of countless liberty-loving men and women. It serves as a cloak for the protection of poor and rich, of black and white, of Jew and Gentile, of foreign and native born. Let us not tear it asunder. For no man knows, once it is destroyed, where or when man will find its protective warmth again.

— *Wendell Willkie*

Thinking, not growth, makes manhood. Accustom yourself, therefore, to thinking. Set yourself to understand whatever you see or read. To join thinking with reading is one of the first maxims, and one of the easiest operations.

— *Isaac Taylor*

Through our great good fortune, in our youth our hearts were touched with fire. It was given us to learn at the outset that life is a profound and passionate thing. While we are permitted to scorn nothing but indifference, and do not pretend to undervalue the worldly rewards of ambition, we have seen with our own eyes, beyond and above the gold fields, the snowy heights of honor, and it is for us to bear the report to those who come after us.   — *Oliver Wendell Holmes*

Give us, O give us the man who sings at his work! Be his occupation what it may, he is equal to any of those who follow the same pursuit in silent sullenness. He will do more in the same time . . . he will do it better . . . he will persevere longer. One is scarcely sensible to fatigue while he marches to music. The very stars are said to make harmony as they revolve in their spheres.   — *Carlyle*

No man will ever be a big executive who feels that he must, either openly or under cover, follow up every order he gives and see that it is done — nor will he ever develop a capable assistant.   — *John Lee Mahin*

Liberty — is one of the choicest gifts that heaven hath bestowed upon man, and exceeds in volume all the treasures which the earth contains within its bosom or the sea covers. Liberty, as well as honor, man ought to preserve at the hazard of his life, for without it, life is insupportable.
                                        — *Cervantes*

He who reveals to me what is in me and helps me to externalize it in fuller terms of self-trust, is my real helper, for he assists me in the birth of those things which he knows are in me and in all men.   — *W. John Murray*

The long span of the bridge of your life is supported by countless cables called habits, attitudes, and desires. What you do in life depends upon what you are and what you want. What you get from life depends upon how much you want it — how much you are willing to work and plan and co-operate and use your resources. The long span of the bridge of your life is supported by countless cables that you are spinning now, and that is why today is such an important day. Make the cables strong! — *L. G. Elliott*

Well-timed silence hath more eloquence than speech.
— *M. T. Tupper*

Provision for others is a fundamental responsibility of human life. — *Woodrow Wilson*

A man's life may stagnate as literally as water may stagnate, and just as motion and direction are the remedy for one, so purpose and activity are the remedy for the other.
— *John Burroughs*

The entire object of true education is to make people not merely do the right thing, but enjoy the right things; not merely industrious, but to love industry; not merely learned, but to love knowledge; not merely pure, but to love purity; not merely just, but to hunger and thirst after justice.
— *Ruskin*

To make one's own estate concentric with the public estate is to realize the conception of the church, the conception of the university, the conception of an essential democracy, and the conception of a business system that will really work. — *Ferguson*

Ultimately there can be no freedom for self unless it is vouchsafed for others; there can be no security where there is fear, and a democratic society presupposes confidence and candor in the relations of men with one another and eager collaboration for the larger ends of life instead of the pursuit of petty, selfish or vainglorious aims.

— Felix Frankfurter

Of all the things you wear, your expression is the most important. *— Janet Lane*

Do little things now; so shall big things come to thee by and by asking to be done. *— Persian Proverb*

The sweetest path of life leads through the avenues of learning, and whoever can open up the way for another, ought, so far, to be esteemed a benefactor to mankind.

— David Hume

Truth as old as the hills is bound up in the Latin proverb, "Necessity is the mother of invention." It is surprising what a man can do when he has to, and how little most men will do when they don't have to. *— Walter Linn*

Be discreet in all things, and so render it unnecessary to be mysterious about any. *— Wellington*

Genuine good taste consists in saying much in few words, in choosing among our thoughts, in having order and arrangement in what we say, and in speaking with composure.

— Fenelon

I care not what subject is taught if only it be taught well.
— *Thomas Huxley*

Don't knock your competitors. By boosting others you will boost yourself. A little competition is a good thing and severe competition is a blessing. Thank God for competition.
— *Jacob Kindleberger*

Heat and animosity, contest and conflict may sharpen the wits, although they rarely do; they never strengthen the understanding, clear the perspicacity, guide the judgment, or improve the heart.
— *Landor*

A work of real merit finds favor at last.
— *A. B. Alcott*

Just definitions either prevent or put an end to disputes.
— *Emmons*

We ought not to judge of men's merits by their qualifications, but by the use they make of them.
— *Charron*

Were we to take as much pains to be what we ought, as we do to disguise what we are, we might appear like ourselves without being at the trouble of any disguise at all.
— *La Rochefoucauld*

In those vernal seasons of the year when the air is calm and pleasant, it were an injury and sullenness against nature not to go out and see her riches, and partake in her rejoicing with heaven and earth.
— *Milton*

Let no man be sorry he has done good because others have done evil. If a man has acted right, he has done well, though alone; if wrong, the sanction of all mankind will not justify him.   *— Henry Fielding*

Let us do our duty in our shop or our kitchen, in the market, the street, the office, the school, the home, just as faithfully as if we stood in the front rank of some great battle, and knew that victory for mankind depended on our bravery, strength, and skill. When we do that, the humblest of us will be serving in that great army which achieves the welfare of the world.   *— Theodore Parker*

There is little peace or comfort in life if we are always anxious as to future events. He that worries himself with the dread of possible contingences will never be at rest.   *— Johnson*

If we did but know how little some enjoy of the great things that they possess, there would not be much envy in the world.   *— Young*

An intelligent class can scarce ever be, as a class, vicious, and never, as a class, indolent. The excited mental activity operates as a counterpoise to the stimulus of sense and appetite.   *— Everett*

Nothing is cheap which is superfluous, for what one does not need, is dear at a penny.   *— Plutarch*

Man is not born to solve the problem of the universe, but to find out what he has to do; and to restrain himself within the limits of his comprehension.   *— Goethe*

Never tell a young person that something can not be done. God may have been waiting for centuries for somebody ignorant enough of the impossible to do that thing.

— *Dr. J. A. Holmes*

Art is a human activity consisting in this, that one man consciously, by means of certain external signs, hands on to others feelings he has lived through, and that other people are infected by these feelings, and also experience them.

— *Tolstoi*

Never esteem anything as of advantage to thee that shall make thee break thy word or lose thy self-respect.

— *Marcus Aurelius*

The greatest asset of a man, a business or a nation is faith.

The men who built this country and those who made it prosper during its darkest days were men whose faith in its future was unshakable.

Men of courage, they dared to go forward despite all hazards; men of vision, they always looked forward, never backward.

Christianity, the greatest institution humanity has ever known, was founded by twelve men, limited in education, limited in resources, but with an abundance of faith and divine leadership.

The vision essential to clear thinking; the common sense needed for wise decisions; the courage of convictions based on facts not fancies; and the constructive spirit of faith as opposed to the destructive forces of doubt will preserve our Christian ways of life. — *Thomas J. Watson*

Every man's ability may be strengthened or increased by culture. — *J. Abbott*

I like business because it is competitive, because it rewards deeds rather than words. I like business because it compels earnestness and does not permit me to neglect today's task while thinking about tomorrow. I like business because it undertakes to please, not reform; because it is honestly selfish, thereby avoiding hypocrisy and sentimentality. I like business because it promptly penalizes mistakes, shiftlessness and inefficiency, while rewarding well those who give it the best they have in them. Lastly, I like business because each day is a fresh adventure.

— R. H. Cabell

What a man believes may be ascertained, not from his creed, but from the assumptions on which he habitually acts.   *— George Bernard Shaw*

The sense of ultimate truth is the intellectual counterpart of the esthetic sense of perfect beauty, or the moral sense of perfect good.   *— Lord Halifax*

As individuals find crime to be a dead-end street, so communities and nations are subject to the same psychology. The moral side of public opinion is traditionally lazy, but there is an indefinable point at which it can be and is aroused.   *— Allen E. Claxton, D.D.*

Uncertainty and expectation are the joys of life. Security is an insipid thing, though the overtaking and possessing of a wish discovers the folly of the chase.   *— Congreve*

By doing good with his money, a man, as it were, stamps the image of God upon it, and makes it pass current for the merchandise of heaven.   *— J. Rutledge*

My intimate contact with those great producing organizations and the men in them has given me great confidence in the machinery and the spirit now available for the building of a proper world. I do not mean that our industrial system is as good as it should be, but if I am looking for intelligent and unselfish understanding of our problems, and a generous approach to their solution, I shall seek it among the makers and builders with far more confidence than among the talkers, the manipulators and the vote seekers.

— Walter Teague

Whenever I hear a man or women express hatred for any race, I wonder just what it is in themselves they hate so much. You can always be sure of this: You cannot express hatred for anything or anybody unless you make use of the supply of hatred within yourself. The only hatred you can express is your own personal possession. To hate is to be enslaved by evil. *— Thomas Dreier*

The good that we take with us at the last call is the good that we do while here. *— William M. Peck*

Sameness is the mother of disgust, variety the cure.

— Petrarch

The world has a way of giving what is demanded of it. If you are frightened and look for failure and poverty, you will get them, no matter how hard you may try to succeed. Lack of faith in yourself, in what life will do for you, cuts you off from the good things of the world. Expect victory and you make victory. Nowhere is this truer than in business life, where bravery and faith bring both material and spiritual rewards. *— Preston Bradley*

History shows that great economic and social forces flow like a tide over communities only half conscious of that which is befalling them. Wise statesmen foresee what time is thus bringing, and try to shape institutions and mold men's thoughts and purposes in accordance with the change that is silently coming on. The unwise are those who bring nothing constructive to the process, and who greatly imperil the future of mankind by leaving great questions to be fought out between ignorant change on one hand and ignorant opposition to change on the other.

— *John Stuart Mill*

They who give have all things; they who withhold have nothing.   — *Hindu Proverb*

All the wild ideas of unbalanced agitators the world over in their ignorant and pitiable quest for happiness through revolution, confiscation of property, and crime, cannot overthrow the eternal truth that the one route to happiness through property or government is over the broad and open highway of service. And service always means industry, thrift, respect for authority, and recognition of the rights of others.   — *W. G. Sibley*

The future always holds something for the man who keeps his faith in it.   — *H. L. Hollis*

I wonder why it is that we are not all kinder to each other than we are. How much the world needs it! How easily it is done!   — *Henry Drummond*

Why and *how* are words so important that they cannot be too often used.   — *Napoleon*

We live in the present, we dream of the future and we learn eternal truths from the past.

— *Mme. Chiang Kai-shek*

If you are content, you have enough to live comfortably.

— *Plautus*

The experience of the ages that are past, the hopes of the ages that are yet to come, unite their voices in an appeal to us; they implore us to think more of the character of our people than of its vast numbers; to look upon our vast natural resources, not as tempters to ostentation and pride, but as means to be converted, by the refining alchemy of education, into mental and spiritual treasures — and thus give to the world the example of a nation whose wisdom increases with its prosperity, and whose virtues are equal to its power. — *Horace Mann*

One of man's finest qualities is described by the simple word " guts " — the ability to take it. If you have the discipline to stand fast when your body wants to run, if you can control your temper and remain cheerful in the face of monotony or disappointment, you have " guts " in the soldiering sense. This ability to take it must be trained — the training is hard, mental as well as physical. But once ingrained, you can face and flail the enemy as a soldier, and enjoy the challenges of life as a civilian.

— *Col. John S. Roosma*

One of the hardest lessons we have to learn in this life, and one that many persons never learn, is to see the divine, the celestial, the pure, in the common, the near at hand — to see that heaven lies about us here in this world.

— *John Burroughs*

In every country where man is free to think and to speak, difference of opinion will arise from difference of perception, and the imperfection of reason; but these differences, when permitted, as in this happy country, to purify themselves by free discussion, are but as passing clouds overspreading our land transiently, and leaving our horizon more bright and serene.   — *Thomas Jefferson*

Who hath not known ill fortune, never knew himself, or his own virtue.   — *Mallett*

The smallest good deed is better than the grandest good intention.   — *Duguet*

More people should learn to tell their dollars where to go instead of asking them where they went.

— *Roger Babson*

Parties who want milk should not seat themselves on a stool in the middle of a field in hope that the cow will back up to them.   — *Elbert Hubbard*

If men can be made to understand that society, with its rigid codes and stratifications, is in its confused infancy rather than in the apex of its development; if they can be made to understand that the conflicts and contradictions of society can only be resolved by scientific long-range planning — then we will succeed in maintaining what civilization we have and drive onward to greater culture.

— *A. M. Meerloo*

The bigger a man's head gets, the easier it is to fill his shoes.   — *Henry A. Courtney*

No man really becomes a fool until he stops asking
questions.   — *Charles P. Steinmetz*

The record of the last century has been impressive. The
problem for the future is to keep our capitalism dynamic —
continue to raise living standards and yet to reduce, as
much as possible, the human costs as reflected in insecurity
and instability.   — *W. Walter Williams*

How to forgive is something we have to learn, not as a
duty or an obligation but as an experience akin to the experience of love; it must come into being spontaneously.
                        — *Theodore Cuyler Speers, D.D.*

All good things of this world are no further good than as
they are of use; and whatever we may heap up to give to
others, we enjoy only as much as we can make useful to ourselves and others, and no more.   — *Defoe*

True fortitude of understanding consists in not suffering
what we do know to be disturbed by what we do not know.
                                              — *Paley*

The interests of society often render it expedient not to
utter the whole truth, the interests of science never: for in
this field we have much more to fear from the deficiency
of truth than from its abundance.   — *Colton*

Experience shows that success is due less to ability than
to zeal. The winner is he who gives himself to his work,
body and soul.   — *Charles Buxton*

Will is character in action.   — *William McDougall*

The best rules to form a young man are: to talk a little, to hear much, to reflect alone upon what has passed in company, to distrust one's own opinions, and value others' that deserve it.   — *Sir W. Temple*

Although words exist for the most part for the transmission of ideas, there are some which produce such violent disturbance in our feelings that the role they play in the transmission of ideas is lost in the background.

— *Albert Einstein*

An obligation rests upon each one of us to analyze the intellectual problem of his time and to attempt to formulate his statement of its significance, for the impact of modern science affects the individual as well as society. Each one of us must answer to himself what place it will find in the mansions of his spirit.   — *Hayward Keniston*

Memory is a capricious and arbitrary creature. You never can tell what pebble she will pick up from the shore of life to keep among her treasures, or what inconspicuous flower of the field she will preserve as the symbol of " thoughts that do often lie too deep for tears." . . . And yet I do not doubt that the most important things are always the best remembered.   — *Henry Van Dyke*

Believe me when I tell you that thrift of time will repay you in after life, with a usury of profit beyond your most sanguine dreams; and that waste of it will make you dwindle, alike in intellectual and moral stature, beyond your darkest reckoning.   — *Gladstone*

What is opportunity to the man who can't use it?   An unfecundated egg, which the waves of time wash away into nonentity.   — *George Eliot*

Every great man exhibits the talent of organization or construction, whether it be in a poem, a philosophical system, a policy, or a strategy.   And without method there is no organization nor construction.   — *Bulwer*

Plenty of men can do good work for a spurt and with immediate promotion in mind, but for promotion you want a man in whom good work has become a habit.
                                        — *Henry L. Doherty*

Talk happiness.   The world is sad enough without your woe.   — *Orison Swett Marden*

If we want more brotherhood and goodwill, more intelligence, more clear thinking, more honesty and sincerity, more tolerance and human understanding we must concentrate upon cultivating these qualities within ourselves.   There is a natural progression in social advancement from the individual spirit to the family, to the community, to the nation and to the world at large.   The line of progress can move in no other direction.   There is no substitute for personal integrity.   — *Howard W. Hintz. D.D.*

Thou mayest as well expect to grow stronger by always eating, as wiser by always reading.   Too much overcharges Nature, and turns more into disease than nourishment.   'Tis thought and digestion which make books serviceable, and give health and vigor to the mind.
                                                    — *Fuller*

I have done what I could do in life, and if I could not do better, I did not deserve it. In vain have I tried to step beyond what bound me. Despite my years, I am still trying! — *Maurice Maeterlinck (84)*

We do not need more national development, we need more spiritual development. We do not need more intellectual power, we need more spiritual power. We do not need more knowledge, we need more character. We do not need more law, we need more religion. We do not need more of the things that are seen, we need more of the things that are unseen. — *Calvin Coolidge*

All good activities which encourage people to learn how to live with one another pleasantly and to develop a sense of humor improve living. — *Leonard Carmichael*

A laugh is worth a hundred groans in any market. — *Lamb*

The profoundest affinities are the most readily felt; they remain a background and standard for all happiness and if we trace them out we succeed. — *Santayana*

There is a kind of dictatorship that can come about through a creeping paralysis of thought, readiness to accept paternalistic measures by government, and along with those measures comes a surrender of our own responsibilities and therefore a surrender of our own thought over our own lives and our own right to exercise the vote. The free system gives the right to every citizen to do something for himself. Because he has the right, the opportunity is always there. — *Dwight D. Eisenhower*

To live with beauty is not only to give oneself a joy, it is o have the power of beauty at one's call. A man's life would be in a deep and manly way purified and sweetened if each day he could gain a little of the inspiration that poets fuse into their verse and have it share his visions for that day. The wise poet was right who advised us, daily to see a beautiful picture, daily to read a beautiful poem. He was right, he was practical. *— Martin W. Sampson*

The secret of being tiresome is to tell everything.
— Voltaire

Beaten paths are for beaten men. *— Eric Johnston*

On the clarity of your ideas depends the scope of your success in any endeavor. *— James Robertson*

Whenever you commend, add your reasons for doing so; it is this which distinguishes the approbation of a man of sense from the flattery of sycophants and admiration of fools.
— Steele

The difficult tasks to be performed are not the ones that mean physical and mental labor, but the ones that you dislike, or the ones that you do not love. There are unpleasant angles to nearly every important job to be done in this world, but there must be an over-all love for doing each, else precious time and effort are uselessly wasted. I shall never forget noting a sign above a construction job that read: " *Builder of Difficult Foundations.*" That man must have loved that calling, else he would not have made a point of advertising the fact! *— George Matthew Adams*

Poverty is not dishonorable in itself, but only when it comes from idleness, intemperance, extravagance, and folly.

— *Plutarch*

The best security against revolution is in constant correction of abuses and the introduction of needed improvements. It is the neglect of timely repair that makes rebuilding necessary.   — *Whately*

In handling men, there are three feelings that a man must not possess — fear, dislike and contempt. If he is afraid of men he cannot handle them. Neither can he influence them in his favor if he dislikes or scorns them. He must neither cringe nor sneer. He must have both self-respect and respect for others.   — *Herbert N. Casson*

Perhaps the most valuable result of all education is the ability to make yourself do the thing you have to do when it has to be done, whether you like it or not.   — *Huxley*

How things look on the outside of us depends on how things are on the inside of us. Stay close to the heart of nature and forget this troubled world. Remember, there is nothing wrong with nature; the trouble is in ourselves.

— *Parks Cousins*

No matter how much madder it may make you, get out of bed forcing a smile. You may not smile because you are cheerful; but if you will force yourself to smile, you'll end up laughing. You will be cheerful because you smile. Repeated experiments prove that when man assumes the facial expression of a given mental mood — any given mood — then that mental mood itself will follow.

— *Kenneth Goode*

The very essence of all power to influence lies in getting the other person to participate. The mind that can do that has a powerful leverage on his human world.

— *Harry A. Overstreet*

One thing everybody in the world wants and needs is friendliness. — *William E. Holler*

Have no fear of change as such and, on the other hand, no liking for it merely for its own sake.

— *Robert Moses*

Respectable men and women content with the good and easy living are missing some of the most important things in life. Unless you give yourself to some great cause you haven't even begun to live. — *William P. Merrill, D.D.*

Don't bother about genius. Don't worry about being clever. Trust to hard work, perseverance and determination. And the best motto for a long march is: " Don't grumble. Plug on! " — *Sir Frederick Treves*

What a person praises is perhaps a surer standard, even, than what he condemns, of his character, information and abilities. No wonder, then, that most people are so shy of praising anything. — *Hare*

You cannot afford to make the mistake of thinking you cannot be replaced. And your employer cannot afford to have a man around that he cannot afford to do without.

— *Frank Irving Fletcher*

Peace is a militant state, which is not secured by wishful thinking. . . . If we are to be sure of our liberty, we must be ready to fight for it.   — *Gen. Jonathan Wainwright*

Minds are like parachutes — they only function when open.   — *Lord Thomas Dewar*

A great leader never sets himself above his followers except in carrying responsibilities.   — *Jules Ormont*

Reprove thy friend privately; commend him publicly.
                                                      — *Solon*

No man who continues to add something to the material, intellectual and moral well-being of the place in which he lives is left long without proper reward.
                                        — *Booker T. Washington*

Moral stimulation is good but moral complacency is the most dangerous habit of mind we can develop, and that danger is serious and ever-present.   — *Joseph C. Grew*

Few men during their lifetime come anywhere near exhausting the resources dwelling within them. There are deep wells of strength that are never used.
                                          — *Richard E. Byrd*

You will find men who want to be carried on the shoulders of others, who think that the world owes them a living. They don't seem to see that we must all lift together and pull together.   — *Henry Ford*

Two things are as big as the man who possesses them —
neither bigger nor smaller. One is a minute, the other a
dollar.   *— Channing Pollock*

Justice and power must be brought together, so that whatever is just may be powerful, and whatever is powerful may
be just.   *— Pascal*

Is life so dear, or peace so sweet, as to be purchased at
the price of chains and slavery? Forbid it, Almighty God!
                                           — Patrick Henry

No matter whose the lips that would speak, they must be
free and ungagged. The community which dares not protect its humblest and most hated member in the free
utterance of his opinions, no matter how false or hateful, is
only a gang of slaves. If there is anything in the universe
that can't stand discussion, let it crack.
                                        — Wendell Phillips

No man can tell whether he is rich or poor by turning
to his ledger. It is the heart that makes a man rich. He
is rich according to what he is, not according to what he has.
                                       — Henry Ward Beecher

Immense power is acquired by assuring yourself in your
secret reveries that you were born to control affairs.
                                        — Andrew Carnegie

The test of tolerance comes when we are in a majority;
the test of courage comes when we are in a minority.
                                     — Ralph W. Sockman, D.D.

One of the greatest pleasures to be derived from wealth in any form is the delight inherent in choosing the proper vocational program for one's life. The child who has toys that will amuse him in all kinds of weather is enjoying the luxuries of life. The man who selects the proper vocation in life has all the luxuries that life can provide.

— Lloyd E. Bougham

If you love men and they are unfriendly, look into your love; if you rule men and they are unruly, look into your wisdom; if you are courteous to them and they do not respond, look into your courtesy. If what you do is vain, always seek within. *— Mencius*

The use of money is all the advantage there is in having money. *— Benjamin Franklin*

I keep the telephone of my mind open to peace, harmony, health, love and abundance. Then, whenever doubt, anxiety or fear try to call me, they keep getting a busy signal — and they'll soon forget my number. *— Edith Armstrong*

I don't know what your destiny will be, but one thing I know: the only ones among you who will be really happy are those who will have sought and found how to serve.

— Dr. Albert Schweitzer

The fruits of the earth do not more obviously require labor and cultivation to prepare them for our use and subsistence, than our faculties demand instruction and regulation in order to qualify us to become upright and valuable members of society, useful to others, or happy ourselves.

— Barrow

To acquire wealth is not easy, yet to keep it is even more difficult. . . . It is said that wealth is like a viper which is harmless if a man know how to take hold of it; but, if he does not, it will twine around his hand and bite him.

— *Frank K. Houston*

Fear is an acid which is pumped into one's atmosphere. It causes mental, moral and spiritual asphyxiation, and sometimes death; death to energy and all growth.

— *Horace Fletcher*

Oh, the comfort, the inexpressible comfort, of feeling safe with a person, having neither to weigh thoughts nor measure words, but pouring them all right out, just as they are, chaff and grain together; certain that a faithful hand will take and sift them, keep what is worth keeping, and with the breath of kindness blow the rest away.   — *Rex Cole*

Life has no smooth road for any of us; and in the bracing atmosphere of a high aim the very roughness stimulates the climber to steadier steps, till the legend, " over steep ways to the stars," fulfills itself.   — *W. C. Doane*

It is with narrow-souled people as with narrow-necked bottles; the less they have in it, the more noise they make in pouring it out.   — *Pope*

That discipline which corrects the eagerness of worldly passions, which fortifies the heart with virtuous principles, which enlightens the mind with useful knowledge, and furnishes to it matter of enjoyment from within itself, is of more consequence to real felicity than all the provisions which we can make of the goods of fortune.   — *Blair*

He who will not apply himself to business, eventually discovers that he means to get his bread by cheating, stealing, or begging, or else is wholly void of reason.

— *Ischomachus*

I do not regret having braved public opinion, when I knew it was wrong and was sure it would be merciless.

— *Horace Greeley*

If you do not wish to be prone to anger, do not feed the habit; give it nothing which may tend to its increase. At first, keep quiet and count the days when you were not angry: " I used to be angry every day, then every other day: next, every two, then every three days! " and if you succeed in passing thirty days, sacrifice to the gods in thanksgiving. — *Epictetus*

The only worthwhile achievements of man are those which are socially useful. — *Dr. Alfred Adler*

Some people think that all the world should share their misfortunes, though they do not share in the sufferings of any one else. — *A. Poincelot*

A prudent person profits from personal experience, a wise one from the experience of others. — *Dr. Joseph Collins*

The spiritual life is indeed a life of struggle; but it is also a life of well-grounded hope. Hope is grounded in freedom, and freedom is grounded in all the high purposes and powers of spirit, human and divine. The last word of spirit is Victory. — *Edgar Sheffield Brightman*

Those who devise better methods of utilizing manpower, tools, machinery, materials and facilities are making real contributions toward our national security. Today, these ideas are a form of insurance for our national security; tomorrow, this same progressive thinking is insurance for our individual security — it is, in effect, job insurance.

— *R. Shannon*

Capital is to the progress of society what gas is to a car.

— *James Truslow Adams*

Let your heart feel for the affliction and distress of every one. — *George Washington*

Never take counsel of your fears. — *Andrew Jackson*

I hope that my children, at least, if not I myself, will see the day when ignorance of the primary laws and facts of science will be looked upon as a defect only second to ignorance of the primary laws of religion and morality.

— *Charles Kingsley*

Calamity, war, famine, plague, death, adversity, disease, injury do not necessarily produce repentance. We may become better in a calamity but it does not necessarily make us repent. The essence of repentance is that we cannot be repentant until we confront our own self-righteousness with God's righteousness. — *Fulton J. Sheen, D.D.*

Every act of every man is a moral act, to be tested by moral, and not by economic, criteria.

— *Robert Maynard Hutchins*

I have not been able to find a single useful institution which has not been founded either by an intensely religious man or by the son of a praying father or a praying mother. I have made the statement before the chambers of commerce of all the largest cities of the country and have asked them to bring forward a case that is an exception to this rule. Thus far, I have not heard of a single one.

— *Roger W. Babson*

Consideration is not merely a matter of emotional good-will but of intellectual vigor and moral self-sacrifice. Wisdom must combine with sympathy. That is why consideration underlies the phrase " a scholar and a gentleman," which really sums up the ideal of the output of a college education. — *Charles Seymour*

The best teacher is the one who suggests rather than dogmatizes, and inspires his listener with the wish to teach himself. — *Bulwer*

If we are to survive the Atomic Age, we must have something to live by, to live on, and to live for. We must stand aside from the world's conspiracy of fear and hate and grasp once more the great monosyllables of life: faith, hope and love. Men must live by these if they live at all under the crushing weight of history.

— *O. P. Kretzmann, D.D.*

Man is not merely a combination of appetites, instincts, passions and curiosity. Something more is needed to explain great human deeds, virtues, sacrifices, martyrdom. There is an element in the great mystics, the saints, the prophets, whose influence has been felt for centuries, which escapes mere intelligence. — *Lecomte Du Nouy*

To add a library to a house is to give that house a soul.

— *Cicero*

When blocked or defeated in an enterprise I had much at heart, I always turned immediately to another field of work where progress looked possible, biding my time for a chance to resume the obstructed road. — *Charles W. Eliot*

I cannot too often repeat that Democracy is a word the real gist of which still sleeps, quite unawakened, notwithstanding the resonance and the many angry tempests out of which its syllables have come, from pen or tongue. It is a great word, whose history, I suppose, remains unwritten because that history has yet to be enacted.

— *Walt Whitman*

When you talk about your troubles, your ailments, your diseases, your hurts, you give longer life to what makes you unhappy. Talking about your grievances merely adds to those grievances. Give recognition only to what you desire. Think and talk only about the good things that add to your enjoyment of your work and life. If you don't talk about your grievances, you'll be delighted to find them disappearing quickly. — *Thomas Dreier*

Every great man is always being helped by everybody; for his gift is to get good out of all things and all persons.

— *Ruskin*

The glory of a workman, still more of a master-workman, that he does his work well, ought to be his most precious possession; like the honor of a soldier, dearer to him than life.

— *Carlyle*

I believe that for permanent survival, man must balance
science with other qualities of life, qualities of body and
spirit as well as those of mind — qualities he cannot develop
when he lets mechanics and luxury insulate him too greatly
from the earth to which he was born.

— Charles A. Lindbergh

The noblest of all studies is the study of what man is and
of what life he should live.   *— Plato*

The nobler sort of man emphasizes the good qualities in
others, and does not accentuate the bad. The inferior does
the reverse. . . . The nobler sort of man pays special
attention to nine points. He is anxious to see clearly, to
hear distinctly, to be kindly in his looks, respectful in his
demeanor, conscientious in his speech, earnest in his affairs.
When in doubt, he is careful to inquire; when in anger, he
thinks of the consequences; when offered an opportunity for
gain, he thinks only of his duty.   *— Confucius*

The test of good manners is to be able to put up pleasantly
with bad ones.   *— Wendell Willkie*

I know of no manner of speaking so offensive as that of
giving praise, and closing with an exception.   *— Steele*

Unless man in the midst of all his modernism finds a
middle ground upon which to adjust his differences, there
can be no mutual progress, human liberty is sacrificed and
talent and free-will suffer. Improvement of the standards
of living of the whole people is paramount, if civilization is
to escape world fanaticism.   *— Arnold W. Craft*

Take two workers in an organization. One limits his giving by wages he is paid. He insists on being paid instantly for what he does. That shows he is a man of limited imagination and intelligence. The other is a natural giver. His philosophy of life compels him to make himself useful. He knows that if he takes care of other people's problems they will be forced to take care of him to protect their own interests. The more a man gives of himself to his work, the more he will get out of it, both in wages and satisfaction.

— *J. T. Mackey*

Behind every argument is someone's ignorance.

— *Louis D. Brandeis*

Great ability without discretion comes almost invariably to a tragic end. — *Gambetta*

The thoughts that come often unsought, and, as it were, drop into the mind, are commonly the most valuable of any we have, and therefore should be secured, because they seldom return again. — *Locke*

The object of living is work, experience, happiness. There is joy in work. All that money can do is buy us some one else's work in exchange for our own. There is no happiness except in the realization that we have accomplished something. — *Henry Ford*

The last, best fruit which comes to late perfection, even in the kindliest soul, is tenderness toward the hard, forbearance toward the unforbearing, warmth of heart toward the cold, philanthropy toward the misanthropic. — *Richter*

There is a life that is worth living now as it was worth living in the former days, and that is the honest life, the useful life, the unselfish life, cleansed by devotion to an ideal. There is a battle worth fighting now as it was worth fighting then, and that is the battle for justice and equality: to make our city and our state free in fact as well as in name; to break the rings that strangle real liberty, and to keep them broken; to cleanse, so far as in our power lies, the fountains of our national life from political, commercial, and social corruption; to teach our sons and daughters, by precept and example, the honor of serving such a country as America. That is work worthy of the finest manhood and womanhood.   — *Henry Van Dyke*

He who would acquire fame must not show himself afraid of censure. The dread of censure is the death of genius.

       — *Simms*

Autocracies may survive for intermittent periods with populations of " yes men," but democracies need a perennially renewed supply of " know men."

       — *Dr. Robert Gordon Sproul*

A gentleman is one who is too brave to lie, too generous to cheat, and who takes his share of the world and lets other people have theirs.   — *Hoffman*

I have seen boys on my baseball team go into slumps and never come out of them, and I have seen others snap right out and come back better than ever. I guess more players lick themselves than are ever licked by an opposing team. The first thing any man has to know is how to handle himself. Training counts. You can't win any game unless you are ready to win.   — *Connie Mack*

Fires can't be made with dead embers, nor can enthusiasm be stirred by spiritless men. Enthusiasm in our daily work lightens effort and turns even labor into pleasant tasks. — *Baldwin*

" I can't do it " never yet accomplished anything; " I will try " has performed wonders.
— *George P. Burnham*

I am a great believer in Luck. The harder I work the more of it I seem to have. — *Coleman Cox*

The one who keeps the stars in their place can keep us in our place. There is no depression for good deeds, and that is all that business consists of, and that is our real business. — *Henry N. Kost*

He that respects himself is safe from others; he wears a coat of mail that none can pierce. — *Longfellow*

Any man who leads the regular and temperate life, not swerving from it in the least degree where his nourishment is concerned, can be but little affected by other disorders or incidental mishaps. Whereas, on the other hand, I truly conclude that disorderly habits of living are those which are fatal. — *Cornaro*

It is a sad thing to begin life with low conceptions of it. It may not be possible for a young man to measure life; but it is possible to say, I am resolved to put life to its noblest and best use. — *T. T. Munger*

Democracy has the only approach to human relationships that can make for a free flow of life forces.

— *Dr. Frank Kingdon*

Just as you are unconsciously influenced by outside advertisement, announcement, and appeal, so you can vitally influence your life from within by auto-suggestion. The first thing each morning, and the last thing each night, suggest to yourself specific ideas that you wish to embody in your character and personality. Address such suggestions to yourself, silently or aloud, until they are deeply impressed upon your mind.   *Grenville Kleiser*

Money spent on ourselves may be a millstone about the neck; spent on others it may give us wings like eagles.

— *Raymond Hitchcock*

Neither human applause nor human censure is to be taken as the best of truth; but either should set us upon testing ourselves.   — *Whately*

There is no sound basis upon which it may be assumed that all poor men are godly and all rich men are evil, no more than it could be assumed that all rich men are good and all poor men are bad.

— *Norman Vincent Peale, D.D.*

A man watches his pear tree day after day, impatient for the ripening of the fruit. Let him attempt to *force* the process, and he may spoil both fruit and tree. But let him patiently *wait*, and the ripe fruit at length falls into his lap.   — *Abraham Lincoln*

As diamond cuts diamond, and one hone smooths a second, all the parts of intellect are whetstones to each other; and genius, which is but the result of their mutual sharpening, is character too. — *Bartol*

Try to forget yourself in the service of others. For when we think too much of ourselves and our own interests, we easily become despondent. But when we work for others, our efforts return to bless us. — *Sidney Powell*

Excellence is an art won by training and habituation. We do not act rightly because we have virtue or excellence, but we rather have those because we have acted rightly. We are what we repeatedly do. Excellence, then, is not an act but a habit. — *Aristotle*

It is said that it is far more difficult to hold and maintain leadership (liberty) than it is to attain it. Success is a ruthless competitor for it flatters and nourishes our weaknesses and lulls us into complacency. We bask in the sunshine of accomplishment and lose the spirit of humility which helps us visualize all the factors which have contributed to our success. We are apt to forget that we are only one of a team, that in unity there is strength and that we are strong only as long as each unit in our organization functions with precision. — *Tilden*

Our delight in any particular study, art or science rises in proportion to the application which we bestow upon it. Thus, what was at first an exercise becomes at length an entertainment. — *Addison*

The art of living rightly is like all arts; it must be learned and practiced with incessant care. — *Goethe*

Anyone who studies the state of things which preceded
the French Revolution will see that the tremendous catas-
trophe came about from so excessive a regulation of men's
actions in all their details, and such an enormous drafting
away of the products of their actions to maintain the regulating organization, that life was fast becoming imprac-
ticable. And if we ask what then made, and now makes,
this error possible, we find it to be the political superstition
that governmental power is subject to no restraints.

— Herbert Spencer

Men of vision caught glimpses of truth and beauty
shining aloft like stars: and in these glimpses was a new
hope for the unification of mankind through enlightenment.

— Sir Robert Falconer

The political machine triumphs because it is a united
minority acting against a divided majority.

— Will Durant

Any one who has had a long life of experiences is worth
listening to, worth emulating, and worth tying to as a
friend. No one can have too much experience in any line
of endeavor. We readily welcome to our group of friends
that one who talks with the voice of experience and common sense. We know that we are safe in his hands. He is
not going to get us into trouble. Rather is he going to
point out the pitfalls and mistakes that experience has
taught him to avoid. There is no experience but what
carries its lasting good for us along with it. And you don't
have to discard experience. It's a coat for life! It never
wears out   *— George Matthew Adams*

Ideas are a capital that bears interest only in the hands of
talent.   *— Rivarol*

A thought may be very commendable *as* a thought, but
I value it chiefly as a window through which I can obtain
insight on the thinker. — *Alexander Smith*

Mark, young man, the line you succeed in will be of your
own finding. The Davids in life do not slay the Goliaths of
difficulty and temptation in another's armor, even though
it be the king's, but with their own self-made weapons,
though they be nothing more formidable than a sling and
a pebble. — *G. E. Bishop*

Any man will usually get from other men just what he
is expecting of them. If he is looking for friendship he
will likely receive it. If his attitude is that of indifference, it will beget indifference. And if a man is looking
for a fight he will in all likelihood be accommodated in
that. Men can be stimulated to show off their good qualities
to the leader who seems to think they have good qualities.
— *John Richelsen*

Our most valuable possessions are those which can be
shared without lessening — those which, when shared,
multiply. Our least valuable possessions, on the other
hand, are those which, when divided, are diminished.
— *William H. Danforth*

A man should never be ashamed to own he has been in
the wrong, which is but saying in other words, that he is
wiser today than he was yesterday. — *Pope*

The power of words is immense. A well-chosen word
has often sufficed to stop a flying army, to change defeat
into victory, and to save an empire.
— *Emile De Girardin*

Personality is a person among persons. There is no
personality of one man on a desert island.   — *Kilpatrick*

Every young man should aim at independence and should
prepare himself for a. vocation; above all, he should so
manage his life that the steps of his progress are taken
without improper aids; that he calls no one master, that
he does not win or deserve the reputation of being a tool
of others, and that if called to public service he may assume
its duties with the satisfaction of knowing that he is free
to rise to the height of his opportunity.

— *Charles Evans Hughes*

The character and qualifications of the leader are
reflected in the men he selects, develops and gathers around
him. Show me the leader and I will know his men. Show
me the men and I will know their leader. Therefore,
to have loyal, efficient employees — be a loyal and efficient
employer.   — *Arthur W. Newcomb*

A home is no home unless it contains food and fire for
the mind as well as for the body. For human beings are
not so constituted that they can live without expansion.
If they do not get it in one way, they must in another, or
perish.   — *Margaret Fuller*

It is the privilege and duty of the present generation to
pass on to its successors, unimpaired, the heritage of liberty
bequeathed to it by the founders of the Republic.

— *George B. Cortelyou*

Nothing splendid has ever been achieved except by those
who dared believe that something inside them was superior
to circumstance.   — *Bruce Barton*

No citizen of this nation is worthy of the name unless he bears unswerving loyalty to the system under which he lives, the system that gives him more benefits than any other system yet devised by man. Loyalty leaves room to change the system when need be, but only under the ground rules by which we Americans live.   —*John A. Hannah*

Race tensions thrive on the restricted educational opportunities for Southern Negroes. When earning power is limited or foreshortened by lack of education, whole populations suffer. A potential great producing force, as well as a large possible market for goods, is thus being ignored.   —*Dr. Rufus E. Clement*

Good and bad luck is a synonym in the great majority of instances, for good and bad judgment.
                                    —*John Chatfield*

The nations of the world look to the people of this country for leadership. They have seen our youth in action. They have seen their courage and their strength. Off the battlefield they have seen and admired the human kindness and the tolerance of the men who went overseas for us and for them. May we stand firm in our conviction that America has achieved a way of life that we can all cherish — and cherishing, strive ever to guard and improve.
                                    —*George A. Sloan*

When a business firm attempts to mold its whole policy to meet the prices of its competitor that business is entering a labyrinth, the center of which is the chamber of despair. Highest quality never can be given nor obtained at the lowest prices. If a price must be sacrificed, quality must be sacrificed. If quality is sacrificed society is not truly served.   —*H. T. Garvey*

When no new thoughts fill the mind — when no horizons beckon — when life is in the past, not in the future — you are on the way to uselessness.

— Dr. Frederick K. Stamm

Method is like packing things in a box; a good packer will get in half as much again as a bad one.   *— Cecil*

A man with a surplus can control circumstances, but a man without a surplus is controlled by them, and often he has no opportunity to exercise judgment.

— Harvey S. Firestone

We are making stupendous effort to extend the physical and economic life of the many. But of what high consequence is that extension unless the activity of the mind is also extended, unless we strive ever to live better, rather than simply to make a better living?

— Dr. John H. Finley

The man who wins may have been counted out several times, but he didn't hear the referee.   *— H. E. Jansen*

Personal deficiencies might be termed negative qualities and include unreliability, failure to co-operate, laziness, untidiness, trouble making, interference and dishonesty.

Positive qualities would include willingness, cheerfulness, courtesy, honesty, neatness, reliability and temperance.

Many fail in their work because they are unable to overcome one personal deficiency. Check up on yourself. Don't be afraid to put yourself under a microscope.

Eliminate your negative qualities. Develop your positive ones. You can't win with the check mark in the wrong place.   *— M. Winette*

Save time thinking you can do the other fellow's job
better than he can — put it in doing your job better!
— *Herbert A. Schoenfeld*

To remember that one is God's child, His own, that
no matter what one has done God loves, even to the end,
with a love that never lets go — that is the word men and
women need when wars, hot and cold, mass movements
and mass production, sweep over and swamp the individual.
All else but this assurance fails the man in dire need.
— *Albert Peel, D.D.*

You will never be a leader unless you first learn to follow
and be led. — *Tiorio*

Facts mean nothing unless they are rightly understood,
rightly related and rightly interpreted. — *R. L. Long*

The best hope of raising our own standards lies in the
progressive expansion of production both here and abroad
and making sure that the gains of increased productivity are,
in fact, applied to social advance. — *Carter Goodrich*

Watch your step when you immediately know the one
way to do anything. Nine times out of ten, there are
several better ways. — *Wm. B. Given, Jr.*

Our Christian civilization, as well as our political democracy, has developed through the inspiration of a high
faith in man, the common man. He is the sovereign of
the State, not because he is always wise, but because he
and his fellow-citizens are the State.
— *Franklin P. Cole, D.D.*

Sincerity is impossible unless it pervades the whole being, and the pretense of it saps the very foundation of character.   — *James Russell Lowell*

The ability to keep a cool head in an emergency, maintain poise in the midst of excitement, and to refuse to be stampeded are true marks of leadership.   — *R. Shannon*

The first recipe for happiness is: Avoid too lengthy meditations on the past.   — *André Maurois*

To prosper soundly in business, you must satisfy not only your customers, but you must lay yourself out to satisfy also the men who make your product and the men who sell it.   — *Harry Bassett*

Before you organize you ought to analyze and see what the elements of the business are.   — *Gerard Swope*

The man who lives only by hope will die with despair.   — *Italian Proverb*

The forty-four-hour week has no charm for me. I'm looking for a forty-hour day.   — *Dr. Nicholas Murray Butler*

Help thy brother's boat across, and lo! thine own has reached the shore.   — *Hindu Proverb*

Only fools and dead men don't change their minds. Fools won't. Dead men can't.   — *John H. Patterson*

God has a plan of justice, mercy, truth, co-operation and brotherhood which will bring peace upon this earth. As we worship God these qualities become part of our nature and we become fit inhabitants of the world God created. Human beings should worship God not alone to show their allegiance and dependence upon their Creator, but to absorb from Him the essential qualities of a permanent civilization. — *Allen E. Claxton, D.D.*

Faith is not trying to believe something regardless of the evidence: faith is daring to do something regardless of the consequences. — *Sherwood Eddy*

You seldom get what you go after unless you know in advance what you want. Indecision has often given an advantage to the other fellow because he did his thinking beforehand. — *Maurice Switzer*

Those who deny freedom to others deserve it not for themselves, and, under a just God, they cannot long retain it. — *Charles Sumner*

Keep your thoughts right — for as you think, so you are. Thoughts are things, therefore, think only the things that will make the world better and you unashamed. — *Henry H. Buckley*

Guard within yourself that treasure kindness. Know how to give without hesitation, how to lose without regret, how to acquire without meanness. — *George Sand*

I love a hand that meets my own with a grasp that causes some sensation. — *F. S. Osgood*

There are important cases in which the difference between
half a heart and a whole heart makes just the difference
between signal defeat and a splendid victory.

— *A. H. K. Boyd*

Nothing can be more unphilosophical than to be positive
or dogmatical on any subject. When men are the most
sure and arrogant, they are commonly the most mistaken
and have there given reins to passion without that proper
deliberation and suspense which alone can secure them
from the grossest absurdities.   — *David Hume*

When any of the four pillars of government — religion,
justice, counsel, and treasure — are mainly shaken or
weakened, men had need to pray for fair weather.

— *Bacon*

The culminating point of administration is to know well
how much power, great or small, we ought to use in all
circumstances.   — *Montesquieu*

One well-cultivated talent, deepened and enlarged, is
worth 100 shallow faculties. The first law of success in
this day, when so many things are clamoring for attention,
is concentration — to bend all the energies to one point, and
to go directly to that point, looking neither to the right
nor to the left.   — *William Matthews*

Many people have the ambition to succeed; they may
even have special aptitude for their job. And yet they do
not move ahead. Why? Perhaps they think that since
they can master the job, there is no need to master themselves.   — *John Stevenson*

Wealth is not only what you *have* but it is also what you are. — *Sterling W. Sill*

Occasionally worshippers of the past put obstructions in the way of progress by saying that we must be true to our fathers, but no church can long continue to live on its past. There is only one way that we can be true to our fathers and that is to carry on to completion the work they have so nobly begun. — *John S. Bonnell, D.D.*

Ethical living is the indispensable condition of all that is most worthwhile in the world. — *Ernest Caldecott*

Men are tattooed with their special beliefs like so many South Sea Islanders; but a real human heart with divine love in it beats with the same glow under all the patterns of all earth's thousand tribes. — *Oliver Wendell Holmes*

I have two basic convictions: First, more harm has been done by weak persons than by wicked persons; secondly, the problems of the world are caused by the weakness of goodness rather than by the strength of evil. It is evident that we have allowed technology to outstrip social controls. . . . Man must catch up with what he has created. — *Harry S. Kennedy, D.D.*

The sorrow of knowing that there is evil in the best is far out-balanced by the joy of discovering that there is good in the worst. — *Dr. Austen Fox Riggs*

A good laugh is sunshine in a house. — *Thackeray*

The most beautiful thing we can experience is the mysterious. It is the source of all true art and science. He to whom the emotion is a stranger, who can no longer pause to wonder and stand wrapped in awe, is as good as dead; his eyes are closed. The insight into the mystery of life, coupled though it be with fear, has also given rise to religion. To know what is impenetrable to us really exists, manifesting itself as the highest wisdom and the most radiant beauty, which our dull faculties can comprehend only in their most primitive forms — this knowledge, this feeling is at the center of true religiousness.

— Albert Einstein

Concentration is my motto — first honesty, then industry, then concentration.   *— Andrew Carnegie*

One man with courage makes a majority.

— Andrew Jackson

Before you try to convince anyone else be sure you are convinced, and if you cannot convince yourself, drop the subject.   *— John H. Patterson*

The shortest and surest way to live with honor in the world is to be in reality what we would appear to be; and if we observe, we shall find that all human virtues increase and strengthen themselves by the practice and experience of them.   *— Socrates*

Whenever you look at a piece of work and you think the fellow was crazy, then you want to pay some attention to that. One of you is likely to be, and you had better find out which one it is. It makes an awful lot of difference.

— Charles F. Kettering

Art is like a border of flowers along the course of civilization.
— *Lincoln Steffens*

Modern business requires that its salesmen be business men in the best sense of the word — men who know the ins and outs of the product or service they are selling . . . men who can make an intelligent and effective presentation . . . and most of all, men who have the modern concept of service to the customer.
— *Hugh W. Coburn*

Real freedom comes from the mastery, through knowledge, of historic conditions and race character, which makes possible a free and intelligent use of experience for the purpose of progress.
— *Hamilton Wright Mabie*

It goes far toward making a man faithful to let him understand that you think him so; and he that does but suspect I will deceive him, gives me a sort of right to do so.
— *Seneca*

Sometimes a noble failure serves the world as faithfully as a distinguished success.
— *Dowden*

Usually there are responsible jobs going begging because not enough men are willing to sweat enough to master the problems involved.
— *W. Alton Jones*

An inexhaustible good nature is one of the most precious gifts of heaven, spreading itself like oil over the troubled sea of thought, and keeping the mind smooth and equable in the roughest weather.
— *Washington Irving*

Only that day dawns to which we are awake.

— *Thoreau*

In some measure all that comes after you is going to be
influenced and determined by the kind of life you make in
your business of living. When viewed from such a height
of vision, even the seemingly least important life gathers
round it a glory which truly passes understanding.

— *Laurence I. Neale, D.D.*

Accuracy is the twin brother of honesty; inaccuracy is
a near kin to falsehood.   — *Tryon Edwards*

There is a time in every man's education when he arrives
at the conviction that envy is ignorance; that imitation is
suicide; that he must take himself for better, for worse,
as his portion; that though the wide universe is full of
good, no kernel of nourishing corn can come to him but
through his toil bestowed on that plot of ground which
is given to him to till.   — *Emerson*

There is a courageous wisdom; there is also a false reptile
prudence, the result, not of caution, but of fear.

— *Burke*

Much has been said about the relative value of happiness;
but write it on your heart that happiness is the cheapest
thing in the world — when we buy it for someone else.

— *Flemming*

Mine honor is my life; both grow in one; take honor from
me and my life is done.   — *Shakespeare*

Unless man has the wit and the grit to build his civilization on something better than material power, it is surely idle to talk of plans for a stable peace.

— Francis B. Sayre

We need not be afraid of the future, for the future will be in our own hands. We shall need courage, energy and determination, but above all, we shall need faith — faith in ourselves, in our communities and in our country.

— Thomas E. Dewey

However good you may be you have faults; however dull you may be you can find out what some of them are, and however slight they may be you had better make some — not too painful, but patient efforts to get rid of them.

— Ruskin

We will never have real safety and security for the wage earners unless we provide for safety and security for the wage payers and the wage savers, investors, and then, by all means, protection for both against reckless wasters and wage spenders. *— Wm. J. H. Boetcker*

Perfect happiness, I believe, was never intended by the Deity to be the lot of one of his creatures in this world; but that he has very much put in our power the nearness of our approaches to it is what I have steadfastly believed.

— Thomas Jefferson

Tact is one of the first mental virtues, the absence of which is often fatal to the best of talents; it supplies the place of many talents. *— Simms*

Wisdom is the right use of knowledge. To know is not
to be wise. Many men know a great deal, and are all the
greater fools for it. There is no fool so great a fool as a
knowing fool. But to know how to use knowledge is to
have wisdom.   — *Spurgeon*

Develop in youth the devotion to home interests and
home affairs, to community interests and community
affairs that led the founding fathers to establish a nation
of communities upon this continent, dedicated to a decent,
free life of equal opportunity under God, and consecrated to
the principle that the State exists as an instrument for
serving the individual, not for enslaving him. So instructed, American youth can be trusted.
                                    — *Joseph Kennedy*

The most difficult thing in life is to know yourself.
                                    — *Thales*

If we choose to be no more than clods of clay, then we
shall be used as clods of clay for braver feet to tread on.
                                    — *Marie Corelli*

A business man's judgment is no better than his information.   — *R. P. Lamont*

Life is too short to be unhappy in business. If business
were not a part of the joy of living, we might almost say
that we have no right to live, because it is a pretty poor man
who cannot get into the line for which he is fitted.
                                    — *George L. Brown*

The only way in which one human being can properly attempt to influence another is by encouraging him to think for himself, instead of endeavoring to instill ready-made opinions into his head. — *Leslie Stephen*

Any fool can waste, any fool can muddle, but it takes something of a man to save, and the more he saves the more of a man does it make of him. — *Kipling*

The mind's the standard of the man. — *Watts*

Many men absorbed in business show such a rare quality of culture that we are surprised at it. The reason invariably is partly because hard work and even the weariness it leaves carry a nobility with them, but also because there is no room in such lives for inferior mental occupation. — *Ernest Dimnet*

I believe that the time given to refutation in philosophy is usually time lost. Of the many attacks directed by many thinkers against each other, what now remains? Nothing, or assuredly very little. That which counts and endures is the modicum of positive truth which each contributes. The true statement is, of itself, able to displace the erroneous idea, and becomes, without our having taken the trouble of refuting anyone, the best of refutations. — *Henri Bergson*

A religion that serves today's needs and holds tomorrow's promise should not consist of dying forms and cold rituals, but of living hope and friendly righteousness. Justice, honor, and truth will be found where righteousness is found. If all people return to religion and find peace, the world will find peace. — *Wayland Zwayer, D.D.*

Praise, like gold and diamonds, owes its value to its
scarcity.   — *Johnson*

Nobody can think straight who does not work. Idleness
warps the mind. Thinking without constructive action
becomes a disease.   — *Henry Ford*

The discovery of what is true and the practice of that
which is good, are the two most important aims of philosophy.   — *Voltaire*

Quality is never an accident; it is always the result of
high intention, sincere effort, intelligent direction and skillful execution; it represents the wise choice of many alter-
natives, the cumulative experience of many masters of
craftsmanship. Quality also marks the search for an ideal
after necessity has been satisfied and mere usefulness
achieved.   — *Will A. Foster*

There is an easier, better and quicker way to do most
everything, and now as never before, we must seek those
easier, better, quicker ways and methods.
      — *Gustav Metzman*

Evils in the journey of life are like the hills which alarm
travelers on the road. Both appear great at a distance,
but when we approach them we find they are far less in-
surmountable than we had conceived.   — *Colton*

A good name is seldom regained. When character is
gone, all is gone, and one of the richest jewels of life is
lost forever.   — *J. Hawes*

When I was young I was sure of everything; in a few years, having been mistaken a thousand times, I was not half so sure of most things as I was before; at present, I am hardly sure of anything but what God has revealed to me.

— *John Wesley*

He is happy whose circumstances suit his temper; but he is more excellent who can suit his temper to any circumstances. — *David Hume*

There are joys which long to be ours. God sends ten thousand truths, which come about us like birds seeking inlet; but we are shut up to them, and so they bring us nothing, but sit and sing awhile upon the roof, and then fly away. — *Henry Ward Beecher*

The mere lapse of years is not life. To eat, to drink, and sleep; to be exposed to darkness and the light; to pace around in the mill of habit, and turn thought into an instrument of trade — this is not life. Knowledge, truth, love, beauty, goodness, faith, alone can give vitality to the mechanism of existence. — *James Martineau*

We gain nothing by being with such as ourselves; we encourage each other in mediocrity. I am always longing to be with men more excellent than myself. — *Lamb*

Fear is not in the habit of speaking truth; when perfect sincerity is expected, perfect freedom must be allowed; nor has anyone who is apt to be angry when he hears the truth any cause to wonder that he does not hear it.

— *Tacitus*

The miracle, or the power, that elevates the few is to be found in their industry, application, and perseverance under the promptings of a brave, determined spirit.

— *Mark Twain*

When a man's knowledge is not in order, the more of it he has the greater will be his confusion.

— *Herbert Spencer*

We have committed the Golden Rule to memory. Let us now commit it to life.   — *Edwin Markham*

A man should inure himself to voluntary labor, and not give up to indulgence and pleasure, as they beget no good constitution of body nor knowledge of mind.   — *Socrates*

Let all your views in life be directed to a solid, however moderate, independence; without it no man can be happy, nor even honest.   — *Junius*

The soldier who dies to save his brothers reaches the highest of all degrees of charity, and this is the virtue of a single act of charity: It cancels a whole lifetime of sin.

— *Cardinal Mercier*

To provide for the future is a part of one's responsibility in life; and the world has scant consideration for the man who neglects it.   — *Henry L. Doherty*

Take the course opposite to custom and you will almost always do well.   — *Jean Jacques Rousseau*

Example has more followers than reason. We unconsciously imitate what pleases us, and approximate to the characters we most admire. A generous habit of thought and action carries with it an incalculable influence.

— Bovée

You exist but as a part inherent in a greater whole. Do not live as though you had a thousand years before you. The common due impends; while you live, and while you may, be good. *— Marcus Aurelius*

The real secret of how to use time is to pack it as you would a portmanteau, filling up the small spaces with small things. *— Sir Henry Haddow*

Every one expects to go further than his father went; every one expects to be better than he was born and every generation has one big impulse in its heart — to exceed all the other generations of the past in all the things that make life worth living. *— William Allen White*

The journey of a thousand miles starts with a single step. *— Chinese Proverb*

Nothing worthwhile comes easily. Half effort does not produce half results. It produces no results. Work, continuous work and hard work, is the only way to accomplish results that last. *— Hamilton Holt*

There is no readier way for a man to bring his own worth into question than by endeavoring to detract from the worth of other men. *— Tillotson*

To be seeing the world made new every morning, as if it were the morning of the first day, and then to make the most of it for the individual soul, as if it were the last day — is the daily curriculum of the mind's desire.

— *Dr. John H. Finley*

Better to slip with the foot than with the tongue.

— *English Proverb*

A big corporation is more or less blamed for being big; it is only big because it gives service. If it doesn't give service, it gets small faster than it grew big.

— *William S. Knudsen*

If thou wouldst preserve a sound body, use fasting and walking; if a healthful soul, fasting and praying. Walking exercises the body; praying exercises the soul; fasting cleanses both.   — *Quarles*

The sole meaning of life is to serve humanity.

— *Tolstoi*

Kind words do not cost much. They never blister the tongue or lips. Mental trouble was never known to arise from such quarters. Though they do not cost much yet they accomplish much. They make other people good natured. They also produce their own image on men's souls, and a beautiful image it is.   — *Pascal*

Not a day passes over this earth, but men and women of no note do great deeds, speak great words and suffer noble sorrows.   — *Charles Reed*

The technical progress of industry has been a reflection of our ability to apply increasingly accurate methods of measurement to material things. The art of measuring psychological human dimensions is relatively undeveloped. To all of the complexities of management we must bring to bear infinite patience and persistence, consistency and complete sincerity.　　　　　— *Louis Ruthenburg*

The future of religion is connected with the possibility of developing a faith in the possibilities of human experience and human relationships that will create a vital sense of the solidarity of human interests and inspire action to make that sense a reality.　　　　　— *John Dewey*

There is a burden of care in getting riches; fear in keeping them; temptation in using them; guilt in abusing them; sorrow in losing them; and a burden of account at last to be given concerning them.　　　　　— *M. Henry*

When my external environment is clouded in doubt and despair . . . when the tempests of destruction are making my dreams of success tremble like the topmost spar of a helpless ship — when the skies seem to hold the closing ruin of all my fondest hopes, my mind, superior amid the outrages of this material world, rests upon the solid, immovable foundation of Faith. There is nothing in myself, but all is in my Master.　　　　　— *F. D. Van Amburgh*

He possesses dominion over himself, and is happy, who can every day say, " I have lived." Tomorrow the heavenly Father may either involve the world in dark clouds, or cheer it with clear sunshine; he will not, however, render ineffectual the things which have already taken place.　　　　　— *Horace*

Things are not always what they seem; the first appearance deceives many; the intelligence of few perceives what has been carefully hidden in the recesses of the mind.

— *Phaedrus*

Every person is responsible for all the good within the scope of his abilities, and for no more, and none can tell whose sphere is the largest.   — *Gail Hamilton*

When two men in a business always agree, one of them is unnecessary.   — *William Wrigley, Jr.*

The surplus wealth we have gained to some extent at least belongs to our fellow beings; we are only the temporary custodians of our fortunes, and let us be careful that no just complaint can be made against our stewardship.   — *Jacob H. Schiff*

Haste and rashness are storms and tempests, breaking and wrecking business; but nimbleness is a full, fair wind, blowing it with speed to the haven.   — *Fuller*

The two most precious things this side the grave are our reputation and our life. But it is to be lamented that the most contemptible whisper may deprive us of the one, and the weakest weapon of the other. A wise man, therefore, will be more anxious to deserve a fair name than to possess it, and this will teach him so to live as not to be afraid to die.   — *Cotton*

A man to carry on a successful business must have imagination. He must see things as in a vision, a dream of the whole thing.   — *Charles M. Schwab*

The worst bankrupt in the world is the man who has lost his enthusiasm. Let a man lose everything else in the world but his enthusiasm and he will come through again to success.
— *H. W. Arnold*

Beware of dissipating your powers; strive constantly to concentrate them. Genius thinks it can do whatever it sees others doing, but it is sure to repent of every ill-judged outlay.
— *Goethe*

We need justice. We need toleration, honesty and moral courage. These are modern virtues without which we cannot hope to control the forces science has let loose among us.
— *I. A. R. Wylie*

Life is like music, it must be composed by ear, feeling and instinct, not by rule. Nevertheless one had better know the rules, for they sometimes guide in doubtful cases, though not often.
— *Samuel Butler*

The principle of liberty and equality, if coupled with mere selfishness, will make men only devils, each trying to be independent that he may fight only for his own interest. And here is the need of religion and its power, to bring in the principle of benevolence and love to men.
— *Randolph*

Whatever you lend let it be your money, and not your name. Money you may get again, and, if not, you may contrive to do without it; name once lost you cannot get again, and, if you cannot contrive to do without it, you had better never have been born.
— *Bulwer*

The human mind cannot create anything. It produces
nothing until after having been fertilized by experience and
meditation; its acquisitions are the germs of its production.   *— Buffon*

Necessity may render a doubtful act innocent, but it
cannot make it praiseworthy.   *— Joubert*

Send the harmony of a Great Desire vibrating through
every fiber of your being. Pray for a task that will call
forth your faith, your courage, your perseverance, and your
spirit of sacrifice. Keep your hands and your soul clean,
and the conquering current will flow freely.
                                    — Thomas Dreier

Fear less, hope more; eat less, chew more; whine less,
breathe more; talk less, say more; hate less, love more; and
all good things are yours.   *— Swedish Proverb*

Many a man never fails because he never tries.
                                    — Norman MacEwan

It is very sad for a man to make himself servant to a
single thing; his manhood all taken out of him by the hy-
draulic pressure of excessive business.
                                    — Theodore Parker

Culture is what is left after everything we have learned
has been forgotten. It consists of a deepened understanding, a breadth of outlook, an unbiased approach and a heart
that has deep sympathy and strength of courage.
                                    — Dr. G. Bromley Oxnam

A man of meditation is happy, not for an hour or a day,
but quite round the circle of all his years.

— Isaac Taylor

We hear a good deal about business confidence, which
means confidence of business in itself, in its government,
and in its capacity for expansion. But confidence is only
another way of saying that people believe each other, keep
their promises, pay their debts, and regard their duty to
society. As long as business observes these rules, it will
have the confidence of the community and it will be safe
from all of the irresponsible attacks of its enemies.

— Will H. Hays

What the world craves today is a more spiritual and less
formal religion. To the man or woman facing death, great
conflict, the big problems of human life, the forms of religion are of minor concern, while the spirit of religion is
a desperately needed source of inspiration, comfort and
strength. *— John D. Rockefeller, Jr.*

On earth there is nothing great but man; in man there is
nothing great but mind. *— Sir William Hamilton*

To meet the great tasks that are before us, we require all
our intelligence, and we must be sound and wholesome in
mind. We must proceed in order. The price of anger is
failure. *— Elwood Hendricks*

Every man has three characters — that which he exhibits,
that which he has, and that which he thinks he has.

— Karr

There can be no economy where there is no efficiency.
— *Beaconsfield*

If I were to prescribe one process in the training of men which is fundamental to success in any direction, it would be thoroughgoing training in the habit of accurate observation. It is a habit which every one of us should be seeking ever more to perfect.   — *Eugene G. Grace*

Although words exist for the most part for the transmission of ideas, there are some which produce such violent disturbance in our feelings that the role they play in the transmission of ideas is lost in the background.
— *Albert Einstein*

One can advise comfortably from a safe port.
— *Schiller*

It is the peculiar quality of a fool to perceive the faults of others and to forget his own.   — *Cicero*

Man offers himself to God. He stands before Him like the canvas before the painter or the marble before the sculptor. At the same time he asks for His grace, expresses his needs and those of his brothers in suffering. Such a type of prayer demands complete renovation. The modest, the ignorant, and the poor are more capable of this self-denial than the rich and the intellectual.
— *Dr. Alexis Carrel*

It is surmounting difficulties that makes heroes.
— *Louis Kossuth*

When you have spoken the word, it reigns over you.
When it is unspoken you reign over it.

— Arabian Proverb

The great man is he who does not lose his child's heart.

— Mencius

The one and only formative power given to man is
thought. By his thinking he not only makes character,
but body and affairs, for " as he thinketh within himself, so
is he." *— Charles Fillmore*

Without freedom of thought, there can be no such thing
as wisdom; and no such thing as public liberty without
freedom of speech; which is the right of every man as far
as by it he does not hurt or control the right of another; and
this is the only check it ought to suffer and the only bounds
it ought to know. . . . Whoever would overthrow the
liberty of a nation must begin by subduing the freedom of
speech, a thing terrible to traitors.

— Benjamin Franklin

We as a people seem to be losing all sense of respect for
ourselves and our fellow men, with the result that in a
thoroughly intolerant attitude we hesitate not a minute to
secure an organized minority, or even a majority, to attempt by resolution or law to impose our will on a large
body of people in matters where no moral wrong is involved
and where liberty is curtailed. *— John J. Raskob*

Most men remember obligations, but not often to be
grateful; the proud are made sour by the remembrance
and the vain silent. *— Simms*

All great questions of politics and economics come down
in the last analysis to the decisions and actions of individual
men and women. They are questions of human relations,
and we ought always to think about them in terms of men
and women — the individual human beings who are involved in them. If we can get human relations on a proper
basis, the statistics, finance and all other complicated
technical aspects of these questions will be easier to solve.
— *Thomas J. Watson*

Prejudice is a mist, which in our journey through the
world often dims the brightest and obscures the best of all
the good and glorious objects that meet us on our way.
— *Shaftesbury*

Zeal for the public good is the characteristic of a man
of honor and a gentleman, and must take the place of
pleasures, profits and all other private gratifications.
— *Steele*

Education is the mother of leadership.
— *Wendell Willkie*

No totalitarians, no wars, no fears, famines or perils of
any kind can really break a man's spirit until he breaks it
himself by surrendering. Tyranny has many dread powers,
but not the power to rule the spirit.
— *Edgar Sheffield Brightman*

All finite things have their roots in the infinite, and if
you wish to understand life at all, you cannot tear out its
context. And that context, astounding even to bodily eyes,
is the heaven of stars and the incredible procession of the
great galaxies.   — *W. MacNeile Dixon*

Anything will give up its secrets if you love it enough.
— *Dr. George Washington Carver*

To be ignorant of the lives of the most celebrated men
of antiquity is to continue in a state of childhood all our
days. — *Plutarch*

He that gives good advice builds with one hand; he that
gives good counsel and example builds with both; but he
that gives good admonition and bad example builds with
one hand and pulls down with the other. — *Bacon*

Everyone has his superstitions. One of mine has always
been when I started to go anywhere, or to do anything,
never to turn back or to stop until the thing intended was
accomplished. — *Ulysses S. Grant*

Decision is a sharp knife that cuts clean and straight;
indecision, a dull one that hacks and tears and leaves
ragged edges behind it. — *Gordon Graham*

Many do with opportunities as children do at the sea-
shore; they fill their little hands with sand, and then let
the grains fall through, one by one, till all are gone.
— *T. Jones*

The effective impact upon us of men of honor, rectitude
and goodwill is to arouse kindred impulses within us. We
begin to detect in ourselves undeveloped capacities. The
touch of the heroic awakens in us the slumbering hero.
Fellowship with a true servant of mankind calls into action
our latent impulses to minister.
— *Charles Malcolm Douglas, D.D.*

Decision and determination are the engineer and fire-
man of our train to opportunity and success.

— *Burt Lawlor*

The wayside of business is full of brilliant men who
started out with a spurt, and lacked the stamina to finish.
Their places were taken by patient and unshowy plodders
who never knew when to quit.   — *J. R. Todd*

Language is the armory of the human mind, and at once
contains the trophies of its past and the weapons of its
future conquests.   — *Coleridge*

If we have no faith in ourselves and in the kind of future
we can create together, we are fit only to follow, not to
lead. Let us remember that the Bible contains two proverbs
we cannot afford to forget. The first is " Man does not
live by bread alone " and the second is " Where there is no
vision, the people perish."   — *Charles Luckman*

In the advance of civilization, it is new knowledge which
paves the way, and the pavement is eternal.

— *W. R. Whitney*

Unless the man who works in an office is able to " sell "
himself and his ideas, unless he has the power to convince
others of the soundness of his convictions, he can never
achieve his goal. He may have the best ideas in the
world, he may have plans which would revolutionize entire
industries. But unless he can persuade others that his
ideas are good, he will never get the chance to put them
into effect. Stripped of non-essentials, all business activity
is a sales battle. And everyone in business must be a
salesman.   — *Robert E. M. Cowie*

Whenever I may be tempted to slack up and let the business run for awhile on its own impetus, I picture my competitor sitting at a desk in his opposition house, thinking and thinking with the most devilish intensity and clearness, and I ask myself what I can do to be prepared for his next brilliant move.
— H. Gordon Selfridge

To brag little, to lose well,
To crow gently if in luck,
To pay up, to own up,
To shut up if beaten,
Are the virtues of a sportingman.
— Oliver Wendell Holmes

The superior man will watch over himself when he is alone. He examines his heart that there may be nothing wrong there, and that he may have no cause of dissatisfaction with himself.
— Confucius

Learn to depend upon yourself by doing things in accordance with your own way of thinking. Make your judgment trustworthy by trusting it. Cultivate regular periods of silence and meditation. The best time to build judgment is in solitude, when you can think out things for yourself without the probability of interruption.
— Grenville Kleiser

Two kinds of gratitude: The sudden kind we feel for what we take; the larger kind we feel for what we give.
— E. A. Robinson

It is easier to do a job right than to explain why you didn't.
— Martin Van Buren

The common people of America display a quality of
good common sense which is heartening to anyone who
believes in the democratic process.   — *George Gallup*

There is, and always has been, one tremendous ruler of
the human race — and that ruler is that combination of
the opinions of all, the leveling up of universal sense which
is called public sentiment.   That is the ever-present regu-
lator and police of humanity.   — *Thomas B. Reed*

Worry is a thin stream of fear trickling through the mind.
If encouraged, it cuts a channel into which all other
thoughts are drained.   — *Arthur Somers Roche*

It is by the goodness of God that in our country we have
those three unspeakably precious things: freedom of speech,
freedom of conscience, and the prudence never to practice
either.   — *Mark Twain*

Democracy is never a thing done.   Democracy is always
something that a nation must be doing.   What is necessary
now is one thing and one thing only . . . that democracy
become again democracy in action, not democracy accomplished and piled up in goods and gold.
                        — *Archibald MacLeish*

When you awaken some morning and hear that somebody or other has been discovered, you can put it down as
a fact that he discovered himself years ago — since which
time he has been working, toiling and striving to make himself worthy of general discovery.
                        — *James Whitcomb Riley*

Anyone who stops learning is old, whether this happens at twenty or eighty. Anyone who keeps on learning not only remains young, but becomes constantly more valuable regardless of physical capacity.   — *Harvey Ullman*

If you succeed in life, you must do it in spite of the efforts of others to pull you down. There is nothing in the idea that people are willing to help those who help themselves. People are willing to help a man who can't help himself, but as soon as a man is able to help himself, and does it, they join in making his life as uncomfortable as possible.   — *Ed. Howe*

We never enjoy perfect happiness; our most fortunate successes are mingled with sadness; some anxieties always perplex the reality of our satisfaction.   — *Corneille*

Psychologists have found that music does things to you whether you like it or not. Fast tempos invariably raise your pulse, respiration, and blood pressure; slow music lowers them.   — *Doron K. Antrim*

Acquire good physique and mental robustness which comes from fresh air, sound and plain food, constant and compelling attention to waste matter, proper and peaceful sleep, and concentration on true religion, ethics, art and literature.   — *Fisher*

Such as are thy habitual thoughts, such also will be the character of thy soul — for the soul is dyed by the thoughts. Dye it then, with a continuous series of such thoughts as these — that where a man can live, there if he will, he can also live well.   — *Marcus Antonius*

My share of the work of the world may be limited, but the fact that it is work makes it precious. Darwin could work only half an hour at a time; but in many diligent half-hours he laid anew the foundations of philosophy. Green, the historian, tells us that the world is moved not only by the mighty shoves of the heroes, but also by the aggregate of the tiny pushes of each honest worker. — *H. Kellogg*

Without free speech no search for truth is possible; without free speech progress is checked and the nations no longer march forward toward the nobler life which the future holds for man. Better a thousandfold abuse of free speech than denial of free speech. The abuse dies in a day, but the denial stays the life of the people, and entombs the hope of the race. — *Charles Bradlaugh*

The brave man carves out his fortune, and every man is the son of his own works. — *Cervantes*

There is no moment like the present. The man who will not execute his resolutions when they are fresh upon him can have no hope from them afterwards; they will be dissipated, lost, and perish in the hurry and scurry of the world, or sunk in the slough of indolence.
— *Marie Edgeworth*

The greatest difficulties lie where we are not looking for them. — *Goethe*

Any one entrusted with power will abuse it if not also animated with the love of truth and virtue, no matter whether he be a prince, or one of the people.
— *La Fontaine*

We should have a great many fewer disputes in the world if words were taken for what they are, the signs of our ideas only, and not for things themselves.   *— Locke*

Life is but one continual course of instruction. The hand of the parent writes on the heart of the child the first faint characters which time deepens into strength so that nothing can efface them.   *— R. Hill*

If you ask me which is the real hereditary sin of human nature, do you imagine I shall answer pride, or luxury, or ambition, or egotism? No; I shall say indolence. Who conquers indolence will conquer all the rest. Indeed all good principles must stagnate without mental activity.

— Zimmermann

When Rome's youth became debased and enervated, when regard was lost for men's honor and women's purity, when the sanctity of the home was violated, when her literature became cynical and debased, her dominion ended. The moral life of any people rises or falls with the vitality or decay of its religious life.   *— John S. Bonnell, D.D.*

What excites and interests the looker-on at life, what the romances and the statues celebrate, and the grim civic monuments remind us of, is the everlasting battle of the powers of light with those of darkness; with heroism reduced to its bare chance, yet ever and anon snatching victory from the jaws of death.   *— William James*

If all the people in this world, in which we live, were as selfish as a few of the people in this world, in which we live, there would be no world in which to live.

—W. L. Orme

You generally hear that what a man doesn't know doesn't hurt him, but in business what a man doesn't know does hurt.   — *E. St. Elmo Lewis*

Contentment is a pearl of great price, and whoever procures it at the expense of ten thousand desires makes a wise and a happy purchase.   — *Balguy*

Be sincere. Be simple in words, manners, and gestures. Amuse as well as instruct. If you can make a man laugh, you can make him think and make him like and believe you.   — *Alfred E. Smith*

Read every day something no one else is reading. Think every day something no one else is thinking. It is bad for the mind to be always a part of a unanimity.
                                    — *Christopher Morley*

Elected leaders who forget how they got there won't the next time.   — *Malcolm Forbes*

The manner in which the hours of freedom are spent determines, no less than labor and war, the moral worth of a nation.   — *Maurice Maeterlinck*

Confidence and enthusiasm are the greatest sales producers in any kind of economy. Have confidence in your products and the house backing them, have enthusiasm for your job, call on your trade regularly and consistently, treat your trade courteously, and you will find that your customers will not have to be sold — they will be glad to buy.   — *O. B. Smith*

Whenever nature leaves a hole in a person's mind, she
generally plasters it over with a thick coat of self-conceit.
— Longfellow

Things in which we do not take joy are either a burden
upon our minds to be got rid of at any cost; or they are
useful, and therefore in temporary and partial relation to us,
becoming burdensome when their utility is lost; or they are
like wandering vagabonds, loitering for a moment on the
outskirts of our recognition, and then passing on. A thing
is only completely our own when it is a thing of joy to us.
— Rabindranath Tagore

Certainly it is true that the constant striving for something better — the price of progress — adds to the total of
human happiness. It stimulates industry by creating new
wants. It multiplies opportunities for the employment of
brain and brawn. And it bridges the gaps between peaks
of prosperity and helps take up the slack during times of
reaction. *— John N. Willys*

Psychologically I should say that a person becomes an
adult at the point when he produces more than he consumes
or earns more than he spends. This may be at the age of
eighteen, twenty-five, or thirty-five. Some people remain
unproductive and dependent children forever and therefore
intellectually and emotionally immature.
— Henry C. Link

As one may bring himself to believe almost anything he
is inclined to believe, it makes all the difference whether we
begin or end with the inquiry, " What is truth? "
— Whately

There's a man in the world who is never turned down,
wherever he chances to stray; he gets the glad hand in the
populous town, or out where the farmers make hay; he's
greeted with pleasure on deserts of sand, and deep in the
aisles of the woods; wherever he goes there's a welcoming
hand — he's the man who delivers the goods.

— Walt Whitman

Violence ever defeats its own ends. Where you cannot
drive you can always persuade. A gentle word, a kind look,
a good-natured smile can work wonders and accomplish
miracles. There is a secret pride in every human heart
that revolts at tyranny. You may order and drive an individual, but you cannot make him respect you.

— Hazlitt

You can only govern men by serving them. The rule is
without exception.   *— Victor Cousin*

The machine can free man or enslave him; it can make
of this world something resembling a paradise or a purga-
tory. Men have it within their power to achieve a security
hitherto dreamed of only by the philosophers, or they may
go the way of the dinosaurs, actually disappearing from
the earth because they fail to develop the social and political intelligence to adjust to the world which their mechanical intelligence has created.   *— William G. Carleton*

The first lesson in civics is that efficient government
should begin at home.   *— Charles Evans Hughes*

Education makes a people easy to lead, but difficult to
drive; easy to govern, but impossible to enslave.

— Gen. Omar N. Bradley

We are coming to see that there should be no stifling of labor by capital, or of capital by labor; and also that there should be no stifling of labor by labor, or of capital by capital.　　　　　　　　　　　　*— John D. Rockefeller, Jr.*

Don't bother about genius. Don't worry about being clever. Trust to hard work, perseverance and determination. And the best motto for a long march is: " Don't grumble. Plug on! "　　　　　　*— Sir Frederick Treves*

The influences that really make and mar human happiness are beyond the reach of the law. The law can keep neighbors from trespassing, but it cannot put neighborly courtesy and goodwill into their relations.

— Walter Rauschenbusch

There are admirable potentialities in every human being. Believe in your strength and your youth. Learn to repeat endlessly to yourself: " It all depends on me."

— André Gide

It is better to give than to lend, and it costs about the same.　　　　　　　　　　　　*— Sir Philip Gibbs*

The four cornerstones of character on which the structure of this nation was built are: Initiative, Imagination, Individuality and Independence.

— Capt. Edward V. Rickenbacker

Analyzing what you haven't got as well as what you have is a necessary ingredient of a career.　　*— Grace Moore*

It is not the facts which guide the conduct of men, but
their opinions about facts; which may be entirely wrong.
We can only make them right by discussion.

— *Sir Norman Angell*

One is never done with knowing the greatest men or the
greatest works of art — they carry you on and on, and at
the last you feel that you are only beginning.

— *T. R. Glover*

For me, happiness came from prayer to a kindly God,
faith in a kindly God, love for my fellow man, and doing
the very best I could every day of my life. I had looked
for happiness in fast living, but it was not there. I tried
to find it in money, but it was not there, either. But when I
placed myself in tune with what I believe to be fundamental truths of life, when I began to develop my limited
ability, to rid my mind of all kinds of tangled thoughts,
and fill it with zeal and courage and love, when I gave myself a chance by treating myself decently and sensibly I
began to feel the stimulating, warm glow of happiness, and
life for me began to flow like a stream between smooth
banks.   — *Young*

The more sand has escaped from the hourglass of our life,
the clearer we should see through it.   — *Jean Paul*

He who by an exertion of mind or body, adds to the aggregate of enjoyable wealth, increases the sum of human
knowledge, or gives to human life higher elevation or
greater fullness — he is, in the larger meaning of the words,
a " producer," a " working man," a " laborer," and is
honestly earning honest wages.   — *Henry George*

The all-round liberally educated man, from Palaeolithic times to the time when the earth shall become a cold cinder, will always be the same, namely, the man who follows his standards of truth and beauty, who employs his learning and observation, his reason, his expression, for purposes of production, that is, to add something of his own to the stock of the world's ideas. — *H. F. Osborn*

By whatever basis human desires are classified, the promise of an abundant life covers virtually all. To the spiritual it suggests escape from futility; to the sensuous it calls up visions of luxury; to the defeated it is a dream of success. To the idle it pledges ease; to the weary, rest; to the frightened it means safety; to the anxious, security; and to the improvident it conjures inexhaustible resources. Persuade a man that you can give him the thing he most desires and you will be his hero; offer him justification for his failures and he will be your disciple; assure him a boundless supply of " loaves and fishes " and he will seek to make you king. — *Cadman*

Generosity during life is a very different thing from generosity in the hour of death; one proceeds from genuine liberality and benevolence, the other from pride or fear. — *Horace Mann*

If you treat with courtesy your equal, who is privileged to resent an impertinence, how much more cautious should you be to your dependents, from whom you demand a respectful demeanor. — *Chambers*

Get away from the crowd when you can. Keep yourself to yourself, if only for a few hours daily. — *Arthur Brisbane*

It is sometimes frightening to observe the success which comes even to the outlaw with a polished technique, and we find ourselves doubting the validity of the virtues we have been taught. But I believe we must reckon with character in the end, for it is as potent a force in world conflict as it is in our own domestic affairs. It strikes the last blow in any battle. — *Philip D. Reed*

It is no good making a fortune if you do not know how to enjoy it. Higher material standards are no good if you do not know how to use them for a better life. Economic ideals must include the ideal of beauty as well as the ideal of plenty. We want new capital, far more capital than is being created today, but we want it not only to advance material well-being but because we want a better and more beautiful life for the citizens. — *Sir Basil Blackett*

A vacant mind invites dangerous inmates, as a deserted mansion tempts wandering outcasts to enter and take up their abode in its desolate apartments. — *Hilliard*

Great merit, or great failings, will make you respected or despised; but trifles, little attentions, mere nothings, either done or neglected, will make you either liked or disliked in the general run of the world.

— *Lord Chesterfield*

A man's reach should exceed his grasp, or what's heaven for? — *Robert Browning*

Most people are about as happy as they make up their minds to be. — *Abraham Lincoln*

It is easy to dodge our responsibilities, but we cannot
dodge the consequences of dodging our responsibilities.
— *Sir Josiah Stamp*

If wrinkles must be written upon our brows, let them
not be written upon the heart. The spirit should not grow
old.   — *James A. Garfield*

He who is taught to live upon little owes more to his
father's wisdom than he who has a great deal left him does
to his father's care.   — *William Penn*

The way of a superior man is threefold: virtuous, he is
free from anxieties; wise, he is free from perplexities;
bold, he is free from fear.   — *Confucius*

The only time some people work like a horse is when
the boss rides them.   — *Gabriel Heatter*

Many persons wonder why they don't amount to more
than they do, have good stuff in them, energetic, persevering, and have ample opportunities. It is all a case of trim-
ming the useless branches and throwing the whole force
of power into the development of something that counts.
— *W. J. Johnston*

It is not enough to begin; continuance is necessary.
Mere enrollment will not make one a scholar; the pupil
must continue in the school through the long course, until
he masters every branch. Success depends upon staying
power. The reason for failure in most cases is lack of
perseverance.   — *J. R. Miller*

I do not believe you can do today's job with yesterday's methods and be in business tomorrow.

— *Nelson Jackson*

Public relations, in this country, is the art of adapting big business to a democracy so that the people have confidence that they are being well served and at the same time the business has freedom to serve them well.

— *Arthur W. Page*

Do not condemn the judgment of another because it differs from your own. You may both be wrong.

— *Dandemis*

Do not let yourself be tainted with a barren skepticism.

— *Louis Pasteur*

Each thought that is welcomed and recorded is a nest egg, by the side of which more will be laid.   — *Thoreau*

Life is given for wisdom, and yet we are not wise; for goodness, and we are not good; for overcoming evil, and evil remains; for patience and sympathy and love, and yet we are fretful and hard and weak and selfish. We are keyed not to attainment, but to the struggle toward it.

— *T. T. Munger*

There is no Fate that plans men's lives. Whatever comes to us, good or bad, is usually the result of our own action or lack of action.   — *Herbert N. Casson*

He who is false to the present duty breaks a thread in the loom, and you will see the effect when the weaving of a life-time is unraveled.   — *Channing*

Some men give up their designs when they have almost reached the goal; while others, on the contrary, obtain a victory by exerting, at the last moment, more vigorous efforts than before.

— *Polybius*

The more you learn what to do with yourself, and the more you do for others, the more you will learn to enjoy the abundant life.   — *Wm. J. H. Boetcker*

Those who believe that we have reached the limit of business progress and employment opportunity in this country are like the farmer who had two windmills and pulled one down because he was afraid there was not enough wind for both.   — *Morris S. Tremaine*

You will become as small as your controlling desire; as great as your dominant aspiration.   — *James Allen*

A man has generally the good or ill qualities which he attributes to mankind.   — *Shenstone*

Ignorance of all things is an evil neither terrible nor excessive, nor yet the greatest of all; but great cleverness and much learning, if they be accompanied by a bad training, are a much greater misfortune.   — *Plato*

The super-salesman neither permits his subconscious mind to " broadcast " negative thoughts nor give expression to them through words, for the reason that he understands that " like attracts like " and negative suggestions attract negative action and negative decisions from prospective buyers.

— *Napoleon Hill*

It is better to be old-fashioned and right than to be up-
to-date and wrong.   — *Tiorio*

I think that to have known one good, old man . . . one
man who, through the chances and mischances of a long life,
has carried his heart in his hand, like a palm branch waving
all discords into peace . . . helps our faith in God, in ourselves and in each other more than many sermons.
                                                — *Curtis*

I believe the recipe for happiness to be just enough money
to pay the monthly bills you acquire, a little surplus to give
you confidence, a little too much work each day, enthusiasm
for your work, a substantial share of good health, a couple
of real friends, and a wife and children to share life's
beauty with you.   — *J. Kenfield Morley*

To give real service you must add something which cannot be bought or measured with money, and that is sincerity
and integrity.   — *Donald A. Adams*

There are two ways of being happy: We must either
diminish our wants or augment our means — either may
do — the result is the same and it is for each man to decide for himself and to do that which happens to be easier.
                                        — *Benjamin Franklin*

Do not waste a minute — not a second — in trying to
demonstrate to others the merits of your performance. If
your work does not vindicate itself, you cannot vindicate it.
                                        — *Thomas W. Higginson*

The history of the past interests us only in so far as it
illuminates the history of the present.   — *Ernest Dimnet*

Human history is, in essence, a history of ideas.
— *H. G. Wells*

To live in the presence of great truths and eternal laws, to be led by permanent ideals — that is what keeps a man patient when the world ignores him, and calm and unspoiled when the world praises him. — *Balzac*

So much to do, so little done. — *Cecil Rhodes*

Commerce is the great civilizer. We exchange ideas when we exchange fabrics. — *Robert Ingersoll*

There are certain fundamental requisites for wise and resolute democratic leadership. It must build on hope, not on fear; on honesty, not on falsehood; on justice, not on injustice; on public tranquility, not on violence; on freedom, not on enslavement. It must weave a social fabric in which the most important strands are a devotion to truth and a commitment to righteousness. These are essential ingredients of the American way of life. They are the necessary conditions for the achievement of freedom and human progress the world over. — *Dr. Edmund Ezra Day*

It takes more than Capital to swing business. You've got to have the A. I. D. degree to get by — Advertising, Initiative and Dynamics. — *Ren Mulford, Jr.*

It is those moral and spiritual qualities which rise alone in free men, which will fulfill the meaning of the word American. And with them will come centuries of further greatness to our country. — *Herbert Hoover*

The people to fear are not those who disagree with you, but those who disagree with you and are too cowardly to let you know.
— *Napoleon*

That which is to be most desired in America is oneness and not sameness. Sameness is the worst thing that could happen to the people of this country. To make all people the same would lower their quality, but oneness would raise it.
— *Rabbi Stephen S. Wise*

History down through the centuries has proved again and again that there can be but one outcome to a struggle for selfish power against forces fighting to protect and advance human rights. Those genuinely serving humanity always ultimately emerge triumphant. It is under their standards that the [Western] allies choose to throw in their lot for humanity's defense.
— *Francis B. Sayre*

It may be that we should stop putting so much emphasis in our own minds on the monetary value of a college education and put more emphasis on the intangible social and cultural values to be derived from learning. The time may be coming when we will have to start accepting the idea that education is life, not merely a preparation for it.
— *Seymour E. Harris*

Fame is what you have taken, character is what you give. When to this truth you awaken, then you begin to live.
— *Bayard Taylor*

Necessity of action takes away the fear of the act, and makes bold resolution the favorite of fortune.
— *Quarles*

It is the law of our humanity that man must know good through evil. No great principle ever triumphed but through much evil. No man ever progressed to greatness and goodness but through great mistakes.

— *Frederick W. Robertson*

Talk is by far the most accessible of pleasures. It costs nothing in money, it is all profit, it completes our education, founds and fosters our friendships, and can be enjoyed at any age and in almost any state of health.

— *Robert Louis Stevenson*

There is no trifling with nature, it is always true, grave, and severe, it is always in the right, and the faults and errors fall to our share. It defies incompetency, but reveals its secrets to the competent, the truthful, and the pure.

— *Goethe*

It is well known to all great men, that by conferring an obligation they do not always procure a friend, but are certain of creating many enemies.   — *Henry Fielding*

To attain happiness in another world we need only to believe something, while to secure it in this world we must do something.   — *C. P. Gilman*

I know this world is ruled by Infinite Intelligence. It required Infinite Intelligence to create it and it requires Infinite Intelligence to keep it on its course. Everything that surrounds us — everything that exists — proves that there are Infinite Laws behind it. There can be no denying this fact. It is mathematical in its precision.

— *Thomas Alva Edison*

Great men sometimes lose the reins and lose their heads. This time, let us hope that they will retain them and that when victory is assured they will sit down and reckon what the future is going to be for their countries as well as for other lands.   — *David Lloyd George*

There isn't any luck that enters into anything, unless it's poker or shooting dice, maybe. There is no luck to merchandising. There is no luck in going out and working from early in the morning to long after dinner. That is not luck, it's work.   — *Fred W. Fitch*

Knowledge comes by eyes always open and working hands, and there is no knowledge that is not power.

— *Jeremy Taylor*

The lives and happiness of our children, as far ahead as the mind can reach, depend on us today. If we succeed, posterity looking back will record that this was indeed man's finest hour.   — *Carl A. Berendsen*

Man's life would be wretched and confined if it were to miss the candid intimacy developed by mutual trust and esteem.   — *Edwin Dummer*

When we pray " Our Father," I am praying for you, you are praying for me. In fact, if men everywhere would only learn to pray aright, " Our Father," there would be no differences to settle. It would not be long before Communist, imperialist, capitalist and what have you would stop their cold war and start to live at peace with one another.

— *Albert N. Neibacker, D.D.*

Deliver me from all evildoers that talk nothing but sickness and failure.

Grant me the companionship of men who think success and men who work for it.

Loan me associates who cheerfully face the problems of a day and try hard to overcome them.

Relieve me of all cynics and critics.

Give me good health and the strength to be of real service to the world, and I'll get all that's good for me, and will what's left to those who want it. — *William Feather*

Mere words are cheap and plenty enough, but ideas that rouse and set multitudes thinking come as gold from the mines. — *A. Owen Penny*

It's great to be great, but it's greater to be human.
— *Will Rogers*

The only way to compel men to speak good of us is to do it. — *Voltaire*

The measure of a man is not the number of his servants but in the number of people whom he serves.
— *Dr. Paul D. Moody*

All government is a trust. Every branch of government is a trust, and immemorially acknowledged to be so.
— *Jeremy Bentham*

Necessity is the plea for every infringement of human freedom. It is the argument of tyrants; it is the creed of slaves. — *William Pitt*

A man can do what he ought to do; and when he says he cannot, it is because he will not.   — *Froude*

Today the world is the victim of propaganda because people are not intellectually competent. More than anything the United States needs effective citizens competent to do their own thinking.   — *Dr. William Mather Lewis*

Man must realize his own unimportance before he can appreciate his importance.   — *R. M. Baumgardy*

Research teaches a man to admit he is wrong and to be proud of the fact that he does so, rather than try with all his energy to defend an unsound plan because he is afraid that admission of error is a confession of weakness when rather it is a sign of strength.   — *Prof. H. E. Stocher*

Life is a glass given to us to fill; a busy life is filling it with as much as it can hold; a hurried life has had more poured into it than it can contain.
      — *William Adams Brown*

Do not be duped by little duties. Do not be a chore man all your days.   — *Samuel Smith Drury*

Books are the open avenues down which, like kings coming to be crowned, great ideas and inspirations move to the abbey of man's soul. There are some people still left who understand perfectly what Fenelon meant when he said, " If the crowns of all the kingdoms of the empire were laid down at my feet in exchange for my books and my love of reading, I would spurn them all."
      — *Ernest Dressel North*

With all its alluring promise that some one else will guarantee for the rainy day, social security can never replace the program that man's future welfare is, after all, a matter of individual responsibility.

— Dr. Harold Stonier

Give, if thou canst, an alms; if not, afford, instead of that, a sweet and gentle word. *— Herrick*

Show me the leader and I will know his men. Show me the men and I will know their leader.

— Arthur W. Newcomb

Don't mistake pleasure for happiness. They are a different breed of dogs. *— Josh Billings*

We are living at a time when creeds and ideologies vary and clash. But the gospel of human sympathy is universal and eternal. *— Samuel Hopkins Adams*

Our country is still young and its potential is still enormous. We should remember, as we look toward the future, that the more fully we believe in and achieve freedom and equal opportunity — not simply for ourselves but for others — the greater our accomplishments as a nation will be.

— Henry Ford II

Industry is not only the instrument of improvement, but the foundation of pleasure. He who is a stranger to it may possess, but cannot enjoy, for it is labor only which gives relish to pleasure. It is the indispensable condition of possessing a sound mind in a sound body, and is the appointed vehicle of every good to man. *— Blair*

Of the whole sum of human life no small part is that
which consists of a man's relations to his country, and his
feelings concerning it.   — *Gladstone*

It takes vision and courage to create — it takes faith
and courage to prove.   — *Owen D. Young*

A man is never astonished that he doesn't know what another does, but he is surprised at the gross ignorance of the
other in not knowing what he does.   — *Haliburton*

From the little spark may burst a mighty flame.
     — *Dante*

The most distinctive mark of a cultured mind is the
ability to take another's point of view; to put one's self in
another's place, and see life and its problems from a point
of view different from one's own. To be willing to test a
new idea; to be able to live on the edge of difference in all
matters intellectually; to examine without heat the burn-
ing question of the day; to have imaginative sympathy, open-
ness and flexibility of mind, steadiness and poise of feeling,
cool calmness of judgment, is to have culture.
     — *A. H. R. Fairchild*

There are one-story intellects, two-story intellects, and
three-story intellects with skylights. All fact collectors,
who have no aim beyond their facts, are one-story men.
Two-story men compare, reason, generalize, using the labors
of fact collectors as well as their own. Three-story men
idealize, imagine, predict; their best illumination comes
from above, through the skylight.
     — *Oliver Wendell Holmes*

Get over the idea that only children should spend their time in study. Be a student so long as you still have something to learn, and this will mean all your life.

— *Henry L. Doherty*

The conception of perfect service is constantly expanding and must be handled by broad and liberal minded men who put equity and fairness above gain — who put a proper valuation upon a satisfied customer as an asset running into the thousands of dollars, and who love a job thoroughly well done and get a kick out of doing it.

— *Alvan Macauley*

True religion is the life we *live,* not the creed we profess, and some day will be recognized by quality and quantity, and not by brand.   — *J. F. Wright*

Even in the meanest sorts of labor, the whole soul of a man is composed into a kind of real harmony the instant he sets himself to work.   — *Carlyle*

Dishonesty, cowardice and duplicity are never impulsive.

— *George A. Knight*

Many men owe the grandeur of their lives to their tremendous difficulties.   — *Spurgeon*

Great steps in human progress are made by things that don't work the way philosophy thought they should. If things always worked the way they should, you could write the history of the world from now on. But they don't, and it is those deviations from the normal that make human progress.   — *Charles F. Kettering*

True scholarship consists in knowing not what things exist, but what they mean; it is not memory but judgment.

— James Russell Lowell

Nothing so needs reforming as other people's habits.

— Mark Twain

Remember, that *time* is money. . . . Remember, that *credit* is money. . . . Remember, that money is of the prolific, generating nature. . . . Remember, that six pounds a year is but a groat a day. . . . Remember this saying, *The good payer is lord of another man's purse.* He that is known to pay punctually and exactly to the time he promises, may at any time, and on any occasion, raise all the money his friends can spare. . . . In short, the way to wealth, if you desire it, is as plain as the way to market. It depends chiefly on two words, *industry* and *frugality;* that is, waste neither *time* nor *money,* but make the best use of both.   *— Benjamin Franklin*

What I am thinking and doing day by day is resistlessly shaping my future — a future in which there is no expiation except through my own better conduct. No one can save me. No one can live my life for me. If I am wise I shall begin today to build my own truer and better world from within.   *— H. W. Dresser*

The humanities of business in this age have become more important than the techniques of business. Each business and industry has to sweep the public misunderstandings and the false notions off its own tront walk. Thus will a pathway be cleared for popular appreciation of the important rôle of business in our freedom and in our way of life.   *— Harry A. Bullis*

There is no kind of bondage which life lays upon us that may not yield both sweetness and strength; and nothing reveals a man's character more fully than the spirit in which he bears his limitations. — *Hamilton W. Mabie*

If we are to have a stabilized market demand, selling pressure should be maintained . . . perhaps increased . . . at the first sign of a decline in business. I know of no single way business managers can do more to stabilize market demand than through greater stabilization of sales and advertising expenditures. — *Paul G. Hoffman*

Laws just or unjust may govern men's actions. Tyrannies may restrain or regulate their words. The machinery of propaganda may pack their minds with falsehood and deny them truth for many generations of time. But the soul of man thus held in trance or frozen in a long night can be awakened by a spark coming from God knows where and in a moment the whole structure of lies and oppression is on trial for its life. — *Winston Churchill*

Ninety per cent of the world's woe comes from people not knowing themselves, their abilities, their frailties, and even their real virtues. Most of us go almost all the way through life as complete strangers to ourselves — so how can we know anyone else? — *Sydney J. Harris*

The individual who cultivates grievances, and who is perpetually exacting explanations of his assumed wrongs, can only be ignored, and left to the education of time and of development. . . . One does not argue or contend with the foul miasma that settles over stagnant water; one leaves it and climbs to a higher region, where the air is pure and the sunshine fair. — *Lillian Whiting*

Only that traveling is good which reveals to me the
value of home and enables me to enjoy it better.

                                        — Thoreau

In a letter to a friend the thought is often unimportant,
and the feeling, if it be only a desire to entertain him, everything.   *— Sir Walter Raleigh*

No age or time of life, no position or circumstance, has a
monopoly on success. Any age is the right age to *start
doing!*   *— Gerard*

No cause is hopeless if it is just. Errors, no matter
how popular, carry the seeds of their own destruction.

                                        — John W. Scoville

Other relaxations are peculiar to certain times, places and
stages of life, but the study of letters is the nourishment of
our youth, and the joy of our old age. They throw an additional splendor on prosperity, and are the resource and consolation of adversity; they delight at home, and are no em-
barrassment abroad; in short, they are company to us at
night, our fellow travelers on a journey, and attendants in
our rural recesses.   *— Cicero*

In actual life every great enterprise begins with and takes
its first forward step in faith.   *— Schlegel*

We do not know, in most cases, how far social failure and
success are due to heredity, and how far to environment.
But environment is the easier of the two to improve.

                                        — J. B. S. Haldane

It is right to be contented with what we have, never with
what we are.   — *Mackintosh*

Intellect and industry are never incompatible. There is
more wisdom, and will be more benefit, in combining them
than scholars like to believe, or than the common world
imagine; life has time enough for both, and its happiness
will be increased by the union.   — *S. Turner*

Where we cannot invent, we may at least improve; we
may give somewhat of novelty to that which was old, con-
densation to that which was diffuse, perspicuity to that
which was obscure, and currency to that which was rec-
ondite.   — *Colton*

It is twice as hard to crush a half-truth as a whole lie.
                                              — *Austin O'Malley*

Good taste is the modesty of the mind; that is why it
cannot be either imitated or acquired.
                                            — *Emile De Girardin*

There are two lives to each of us, the life of our actions,
and the life of our minds and hearts. History reveals men's
deeds and their outward characters, but not themselves.
There is a secret self that has its own life, unpenetrated and
unguessed.   — *Bulwer*

Every civilization rests on a set of promises. . . . If the
promises are broken too often, the civilization dies, no
matter how rich it may be, or how mechanically clever.
Hope and faith depend on the promises; if hope and faith
go, everything goes.   — *Herbert Agar*

A pessimist is one who makes difficulties of his opportunities; an optimist is one who makes opportunities of his difficulties. — *Reginald B. Mansell*

Irresolution on the schemes of life which offer themselves to our choice, and inconstancy in pursuing them, are the greatest causes of all our unhappiness. — *Addison*

To complain that life has no joys while there is a single creature whom we can relieve by our bounty, assist by our counsels, or enliven by our presence, is to lament the loss of that which we possess, and is just as rational as to die of thirst with the cup in our hands. — *Fitzosborne*

A man's ideal, like his horizon, is constantly receding from him as he advances toward it. — *W. G. T. Shedd*

Many have no happier moments than those that they pass in solitude, abandoned to their own imagination, which sometimes puts sceptres in their hands or miters on their heads, shifts the scene of pleasure with endless variety, bids all the forms of beauty sparkle before them, and gluts them with every change of visionary luxury. — *Johnson*

It is not a merit to tolerate, but rather a crime to be intolerant. — *Shelley*

The acceptance of the truth that joy and sorrow, laughter and tears are not confined to any particular time, place or people, but are universally distributed, should make us more tolerant of and more interested in the lives of others. — *William M. Peck*

Knowledge of our duties is the most essential part of the philosophy of life. If you escape duty you avoid action. The world demands results. — *George W. Goethals*

There is often as much independence in not being led, as in not being driven. — *Tryon Edwards*

Fortunately or otherwise we live at a time when the average individual has to know several times as much in order to keep informed as he did only thirty or forty years ago. Being " educated " today requires not only more than a superficial knowledge of the arts and sciences, but a sense of inter-relationship such as is taught in few schools. Finally, being " educated " today, in terms of the larger needs, means preparation for world citizenship; in short, education for survival. — *Norman Cousins*

It is a thing of no great difficulty to raise objections against another man's oration — nay, it is a very easy matter; but to produce a better in its place is a work extremely troublesome. — *Plutarch*

Life is made up, not of great sacrifices or duties, but of little things, in which smiles and kindness, and small obligations given habitually, are what preserve the heart and secure comfort. — *William Davy*

Associate with men of faith. This tends to be reciprocal. Your faith will communicate itself to them, and their faith to you. Do your work in a " faith " atmosphere, and you will work at a maximum advantage. You impress others by your own faith, and they will have faith in you only in the degree that you have faith in yourself. — *Grenville Kleiser*

Every great example takes hold of us with the authority of a miracle, and says to us, " If ye had but faith, ye, also, could do the same things."   — Jacobi

Columbus found a world, and had no chart save one that Faith deciphered in the skies.   — G. Santayana

If these distracted times prove anything, they prove that the greatest illusion is reliance upon the security and permanence of material possessions. We must search for some other coin. And we will discover that the treasure-house of education has stood intact and unshaken in the storm. The man of cultivated life has founded his house upon a rock. You can never take away the magnificent mansion of his mind.   — John Cudahy

Steel can be tempered and hardened, and so can men. In this world of struggle, which was not designed for softies, a man must be harder than what hits him. Yes, he must be diamond-hard. Then he'll not be " fed up " with his little personal troubles.   — Herbert N. Casson

You can employ men and hire hands to work *for* you, but you must win their hearts to have them work *with* you.   — Tiorio

Our emotions are the driving powers of our lives. When we are aroused emotionally, unless we do something great and good, we are in danger of letting our emotions become perverted. William James used to tell the story of a Russian woman who sat weeping at the tragic fate of the hero in the opera while her coachman froze to death outside.   — Earl Riney

If we have need of a strong will in order to do good, it is still more necessary for us in order not to do evil.

— *Mole*

Each day of your life, as soon as you open your eyes in the morning, you can square away for a happy and successful day. It's the mood and the purpose at the inception of each day that are the important facts in charting your course for the day. We can always square away for a fresh start, no matter what the past has been. It's today that is the paramount problem always. Yesterday is but history.

— *George Matthew Adams*

By patience and determination, rather than by a harsh upsetting of tradition, we move toward our national aspirations. . . . This is the way we get things done in America. One man tells another, does what he can, till the sum of these efforts grows into a national aspiration — a precious goal. Then occurs our miracle of democracy: because the groundwork has been surely laid, the goal is already within our grasp.

— *Newton B. Drury*

The force of selfishness is as inevitable and as calculable as the force of gravitation.

— *Hilliard*

Associate with men of judgment, for judgment is found in conversation, and we make another man's judgment ours by frequenting his company.

— *Fuller*

Learning, like money, may be of so base a coin as to be utterly void of use; or, if sterling, may require good management to make it serve the purposes of sense or happiness.

— *Shenstone*

Music is the only language in which you cannot say a
mean or sarcastic thing. — *John Erskine*

Despite world unrest, the frontiers of the future lie in-
vitingly before us. They stretch to fabulous horizons of
scientific and technological discovery — all holding promise
of contribution to the national welfare. But these frontiers of tomorrow call for bold enterprise — for optimism,
for the united effort of industry, labor, agriculture and
government. In the mounting miracles of science, in the
rapid advances of technology, lie the foundations for almost
countless new industries and for far swifter social progress.
This promise of progress is daily taking more definite
shape and clearer form, as it shakes free of the post-war
mists. — *Earl O. Shreve*

Maturity is achieved when a person accepts life as full
of tension; when he does not torment himself with child-
ish guilt feelings, but avoids tragic adult sins; when he
postpones immediate pleasures for the sake of long-term
values. . . . Our generation must be inspired to search for
that maturity which will manifest itself in the qualities of
tenacity, dependability, co-operativeness and the inner drive
to work and sacrifice for a nobler future of mankind.
— *Joshua L. Liebman*

Lack of will power has caused more failure than lack
of intelligence or ability. — *Flower A. Newhouse*

The teaching of any science, for purposes of liberal
education, without linking it with social progress and teaching its social significance, is a crime against the student
mind. It is like teaching a child how to pronounce words
but not what they mean. — *Vernon Carter*

One principal reason why men are so often useless is, that they divide and shift their attention among a multiplicity of objects and pursuits. — *Emmons*

Laws are always unstable unless they are founded on the manners of a nation; and manners are the only durable and resisting power in a people. — *De Tocqueville*

Many good qualities are not sufficient to balance a single want — the want of money. — *Zimmermann*

Free inquiry, if restrained within due bounds, and applied to proper subjects, is a most important privilege of the human mind; and if well conducted, is one of the greatest friends to truth. But when reason knows neither its office nor its limits, and when employed on subjects foreign to its jurisdiction, it then becomes a privilege dangerous to be exercised. — *D'Aubigne*

Government originated in the attempt to find a form of association that defends and protects the person and property of each with the common force of all. — *Jean Jacques Rousseau*

A leader of men must make decisions quickly . . . be a fighter . . . speak openly, plainly, frankly . . . co-operate, co-ordinate, work with active faith . . . be loyal, true, faithful . . . have a high, intelligent, worthy purpose and ideal. — *Dodge*

How desperately difficult it is to be honest with oneself. It is much easier to be honest with other people. — *Edward F. Benson*

America is the land of, and for, uncommon men not
only because it affords free choice and opportunity for
people to become expert in their chosen occupations, but
also because it has mechanisms and incentives for providing
the tools of production that the skilled must operate if
their skill is to have full fruition in abundant production.

— *Enders M. Voorhees*

All true educators since the time of Socrates and Plato
have agreed that the primary object of education is the attainment of inner harmony, or, to put it into more up-to-
date language, the integration of the personality. Without
such an integration learning is no more than a collection
of scraps, and the accumulation of knowledge becomes a
danger to mental health. — *Sir Alfred Zimmern*

It is better to give love. Hatred is a low and degrading
emotion and is so poisonous that no man is strong enough
to use it safely. The hatred we think we are directing
against some person or thing or system has a devilish way
of turning back upon us. When we seek revenge we administer slow poison to ourselves. When we administer
affection it is astonishing what magical results we obtain.

— *Thomas Dreier*

I would rather be a beggar and spend my money like a
king, than be a king and spend money like a beggar.

— *Robert G. Ingersoll*

Every tomorrow has two handles. We can take hold of
it with the handle of anxiety or the handle of faith. We
should live for the future, and yet should find our life in
the fidelities of the present; the last is only the method of
the first. — *Henry Ward Beecher*

The cause of freedom is identified with the destinies of humanity, and in whatever part of the world it gains ground by and by, it will be a common gain to all those who desire it.   — *Louis Kossuth*

Every man is valued in this world as he shows by his conduct that he wishes to be valued.   — *Bruyére*

If you have something to do that is worthwhile doing, don't talk about it, but do it. After you have done it, your friends and enemies will talk about it.

— *George W. Blount*

You can do what you want to do, accomplish what you want to accomplish, attain any reasonable objective you may have in mind. . . . Not all of a sudden, perhaps, not in one swift and sweeping act of achievement. . . . But you can do it gradually — day by day and play by play — if you *want* to do it, if you *will* to do it, if you *work* to do it, over a sufficiently long period of time.

— *William E. Holler*

The worst sorrows in life are not in its losses and misfortune, but its fears.   — *A. C. Benson*

He that is proud of riches is a fool. For if he be exalted above his neighbors because he hath more gold, how much inferior is he to a gold mine.   — *Jeremy Taylor*

Positiveness is a most absurd foible. If you are in the right, it lessens your triumph; if in the wrong, it adds shame to your defeat.   — *Sterne*

Though you may have known clever men who were
indolent, you never knew a great man who was so; and
when I hear a young man spoken of as giving promise of
great genius, the first question I ask about him always is,
Does he work?   — *Ruskin*

I've never known of an instance in the history of our
company where an executive unloaded responsibilities and
duties on one lower in the ranks, that he did not find himself immediately loaded from above with greater responsibilities.   — *Arthur F. Hall*

We live in deeds, not years; in thoughts, not figures on
a dial. We should count time by heart throbs. He most
lives who thinks most, feels the noblest, acts the best.
                                                    — *Philip James Bailey*

The church of tomorrow must be universal. It cannot
belong to a particular class, race or nation, but must
transcend all such barriers so the brotherhood of man may
be extended among us.   — *Ralph S. Meadowcroft, D.D.*

No society of nations, no people within a nation, no
family can benefit through mutual aid unless good will
exceeds ill will; unless the spirit of co-operation surpasses
antagonism; unless we all see and act as though the other
man's welfare determines our own welfare.
                                                    — *Henry Ford II*

To pardon those absurdities in ourselves which we cannot
suffer in others, is neither better nor worse than to be more
willing to be fools ourselves than to have others so.
                                                    — *Pope*

Regret for time wasted can become a power for good in the time that remains, if we will only stop the waste and the idle, useless regretting. — *Arthur Brisbane*

Doubt is the disease of this inquisitive, restless age. It is the price we pay for our advanced intelligence and civilization — the dim night of our resplendent day. But as the most beautiful light is born of darkness, so the faith that springs from conflict is often the strongest and best.
— *R. Turnbull*

Suspicion is far more apt to be wrong than right; oftener unjust than just. It is no friend to virtue, and always an enemy to happiness. — *H. Ballou*

National progress is the sum of individual industry, energy, and uprightness, as national decay is of individual idleness, selfishness, and vice. — *S. Smiles*

A young man of pleasure is a man of pains. — *Young*

A panic is a sudden desertion of us, and a going over to the enemy of our imagination. — *Bovée*

The function of a modern religion is to accumulate spiritual power in life and for life. We need that power all the time, but if it has not been accumulated it is not there when we need it most. In a world like this, particularly like the one at the present time, can anyone get along just as well without the inspirations of religion? He cannot. Religion keeps us up to the everlasting effort to attain the best life and best things in life. — *Minot Simons, D.D.*

To arrive at perfection, a man should have very sincere
friends or inveterate enemies; because he would be made
sensible of his good or ill conduct, either by the censures of
the one or the admonitions of the other.   — *Diogenes*

All philosophy lies in two words, sustain and abstain.
                                                  — *Epictetus*

In all the affairs of life, social as well as political, courtesies of a small and trivial character are the ones which
strike deepest in the grateful and appreciating heart.
                                                  — *Henry Clay*

When men are most sure and arrogant they are commonly most mistaken, giving views to passion without that
proper deliberation which alone can secure them from the
grossest absurdities.   — *David Hume*

The avaricious man is like the barren sandy ground of
the desert which sucks in all the rain and dew with greedi-
ness, but yields no fruitful herbs or plants for the benefit
of others.   — *Zeno*

The greatest and noblest pleasure which men can have in
this world is to discover new truths; and the next is to
shake off old prejudices.   — *Frederick the Great*

Neither praise nor blame is the object of true criticism.
Justly to discriminate, firmly to establish, wisely to prescribe and honestly to award — these are the true aims and
duties of criticism.   — *Simms*

Education today, more than ever before, must see clearly the dual objectives: Educating for living and educating for making a living. — *James Mason Wood*

Industry, economy, honesty and kindness form a quartet of virtue that will never be improved upon.

— *James Oliver*

Nothing so cements and holds together all the parts of a society as faith or credit, which can never be kept up unless men are under some force or necessity of honestly paying what they owe to one another. — *Cicero*

If frugality were established in the state, if our expenses were laid out rather in the necessaries than the superfluities of life, there might be fewer wants, and even fewer pleasures, but infinitely more happiness. — *Goldsmith*

How narrow our souls become when absorbed in any present good or ill! It is only the thought of the future that makes them great. — *Richter*

It is no great thing to be humble when you are brought low; but to be humble when you are praised is a great and rare attainment. — *St. Bernard*

Our inheritance of well-founded, slowly conceived codes of honor, morals and manners, the passionate convictions which so many hundreds of millions share together of the principles of freedom and justice, are far more precious to us than anything which scientific discoveries could bestow.

— *Winston Churchill*

The wheels of nature are not meant to roll backward;
everything presses on toward Eternity — from the birth
of Time, an impetuous current has set in which bears all
the sons of men toward that interminable ocean.

— *Robert Hall*

You and I must not complain if our plans break down
if we have done our part. That probably means that the
plans of One who knows more than we do have succeeded.

— *Edward E. Hale*

You cannot antagonize and influence at the same time.

— *J. S. Knox*

" Render unto Caesar the things which are Caesar's and
unto God the things which are God's." One would like to
add: Give unto man things which are man's; give man his
freedom and personality, his rights and religion.

— *Pope Pius XII*

Facts, when combined with ideas, constitute the greatest force in the world. They are greater than armaments,
greater than finance, greater than science, business and law
because they constitute the common denominator of all of
them.   — *Carl W. Ackerman*

We have forty million reasons for failure, but not a single
excuse.   — *Rudyard Kipling*

A man's treatment of money is the most decisive test
of his character — how he makes it and how he spends it.

— *James Moffatt*

I believe with all my heart that civilization has produced nothing finer than a man or woman who thinks and practices true tolerance. Some one has said that most of us don't think, we just occasionally rearrange our prejudices. And I suspect that even today, with all the progress we have made in liberal thought, the quality of true tolerance is as rare as the quality of mercy. That men of all creeds have fundamental common objectives is a fact one must learn by the process of education. How to work jointly toward these objectives must be learned by experience.

— *Frank Knox*

To know what one can have and to do with it, being prepared for no more, is the basis of equilibrium.

— *Pearl Buck*

Ideals are the " incentive payment " of practical men. The opportunity to strive for them is the currency that has enriched America through the centuries.

— *Robert E. Hannegan*

Opinions cannot survive if one has no chance to fight for them. — *Thomas Mann*

Take a look at those two open hands of yours. They are tools with which to serve, make friends, and reach out for the best in life. Open hands open the way to achievement. Put them to work today.

— *Wilfred A. Peterson*

The purpose of learning to employ every minute properly is to unclutter our hours, deliver us of feverish activity and earn us true leisure. — *Robert R. Updegraff*

Don't follow any advice, no matter how good, until you feel as deeply in your spirit as you think in your mind that the counsel is wise.   — *David Seabury*

We cannot advance without new experiments in living, but no wise man tries every day what he has proved wrong the day before.   — *James Truslow Adams*

I criticize by creation, not by finding fault.

— *Cicero*

The sacred rights of mankind are not to be rummaged for among old parchments or musty records. They are written, as with a sunbeam, in the whole volume of human nature, by the hand of the Divinity itself, and can never be erased or obscured by mortal power.

— *Alexander Hamilton*

Nature and education are somewhat similar. The latter transforms man, and in so doing creates a second nature.

— *Democritus*

It is necessary to try to surpass one's self always; this occupation ought to last as long as life.

— *Queen Christina*

When a man has not a good reason for doing a thing, he has one good reason for letting it alone.

— *Thomas Scott*

Colors fade, temples crumble, empires fall, but wise words endure.   — *Thorndike*

Your circumstances may be uncongenial, but they shall
not long remain so if you but perceive an Ideal and strive to
reach it. You can not travel within and stand still without.
— James Lane Allen

The American Republic and American business are
Siamese twins; they came out of the same womb at the
same time; they are born in the same principles and when
American business dies, the American Republic will die,
and when the American Republic dies, American business
will die. *— Josiah W. Bailey*

The progress of the industrial age rests on the greater
diversification of labor and the use of more elaborate tools
and machinery which have increased productivity — in
other words, saved labor. . . . In our attempt to cure the
social ills, we should not kill the goose that has laid the
golden eggs. If our society is sick, it is for other reasons
than the conquest by man of the forces of nature.
— John W. Scoville

The man who gets the most satisfactory results is not
always the man with the most brilliant single mind, but
rather the man who can best co-ordinate the brains and
talents of his associates. *— W. Alton Jones*

You may not, cannot, appropriate beauty. It is the wealth
of the eye, and a cat may gaze upon a king.
— Theodore Parker

When we count on chance in lieu of law and labor, we
weaken our healthy attitudes toward work, our fellow men
and our God. *— Ralph W. Sockman, D.D.*

I sincerely believe that the word " relationships " is the key to the prospect of a decent world. It seems abundantly clear that every problem you will have — in your family, in your business, in our nation, or in this world — is essentially a matter of relationships, of interdependence.

— *Clarence Francis*

If what we already know were simply applied to all the agricultural land of the world and the problem of proper distribution were given consideration, the world could feed itself well.   — *Louis Bromfield*

He who, having lost one ideal, refuses to give his heart and soul to another and nobler, is like a man who declines to build a house on the rock because the wind and rain have ruined his house on the sand.   — *Constance Naden*

We have a system which, though far from perfect, is strong with idealism. It gives elbow room for men of all races and all beliefs. It is vital and dynamic. And it works. We have the means of shaping the world in our pattern. If we do, freedom will be assured for all men. The decision is in the hands of this generation. It is a challenge to our political competence. For Western civilization it is the greatest challenge of all time.

— *William O. Douglas*

Nothing is so fatiguing as the eternal hanging on of an uncompleted task.   — *William James*

While man's desires and aspirations stir he cannot choose but err.   — *Goethe*

What priming will do to a pump, information and a sincere, understanding " talking to " will do to an active, impressionable mind — get it started, provoke it to think.

— *Tiorio*

There is an idea abroad among moral people that they should make their neighbors good. One person I have to make good: Myself. But my duty to my neighbor is much more nearly expressed by saying that I have to make him happy if I may.　　— *Robert Louis Stevenson*

There are few of us so blind as not to realize that unless the moral force of religious conviction impels, the goal of truth and lasting international co-operation cannot be attained; there are few of us who do not appreciate the vital truth of the words, " If God does not build the house, those who build it build in vain."　　— *Sumner Welles*

But for money and the need of it, there would not be half the friendship in the world. It is powerful for good if divinely used. Give it plenty of air and it is sweet as the hawthorn; shut it up and it cankers and breeds worms.

— *G. MacDonald*

No thoroughly occupied man was ever yet very miserable.

— *L. E. Landon*

The free expression of opinion, as experience has taught us, is the safety-valve of passion. The noise of the rushing steam, when it escapes, alarms the timid; but it is the sign that we are safe. The concession of reasonable privilege anticipates the growth of furious appetite.

— *Gladstone*

One thing I certainly never was made for, and that is to put principles on and off at the dictation of a party, as a lackey changes his livery at his master's command.

— *Horace Mann*

Democracy is ever eager for rapid progress, and the only progress which can be rapid is progress down hill.

— *Sir James Jeans*

The opinions of men who think are always growing and changing, like living children.   — *Hamerton*

One couldn't carry on life comfortably without a little blindness to the fact that everything has been said better than we can put it ourselves.   — *George Eliot*

I do believe there is many a tear in the heart that never reaches the eyes.   — *Norman MacEwan*

Troubles are usually the brooms and shovels that smooth the road to a good man's fortune; and many a man curses the rain that falls upon his head, and knows not that it brings abundance to drive away hunger.   — *Basil*

Never put much confidence in such as put no confidence in others. A man prone to suspect evil is mostly looking in his neighbor for what he sees in himself. As to the pure all things are pure, even so to the impure all things are impure.   — *Hare*

Young man: Be honest; train yourself for useful work; love God.   — *Milton S. Hershey*

A weak mind is like a microscope, which magnifies trifling things but cannot receive great ones.

— *Lord Chesterfield*

All anger is not sinful, because some degree of it, and on some occasions, is inevitable. But it becomes sinful and contradicts the rule of Scripture when it is conceived upon slight and inadequate provocation, and when it continues long.

— *William Paley*

The disappointment of manhood succeeds the delusion of youth. — *Disraeli*

How many of us are waiting for the opportunity to do some great thing for the betterment of our community, forgetting that the solution of the problem requires only the active intelligent fulfillment of individual civic duty. The only things which are wrong about our Government are the things which are wrong with you and me. Democracy is never a thing done; it is and always will be a goal to be achieved. It means action, not passive acquiescence in things as they are; it requires alertness to duty, a dynamic faith, a willingness to give for the good of all. It can live only as a result of loyalty and devotion to its principles expressed by daily deeds. — *Douglas L. Edmonds*

The toughest thing about success is that you've got to keep on being a success. Talent is only a starting point in business. You've got to keep working that talent.

— *Irving Berlin*

There are two things to aim at in life: first, to get what you want; and, after that, to enjoy it. Only the wisest of mankind achieve the second. — *Logan Pearsall Smith*

The superior man is the providence of the inferior. He is eyes for the blind, strength for the weak, and a shield for the defenseless. He stands erect by bending above the fallen. He rises by lifting others.

— *Robert Ingersoll*

You cannot be buried in obscurity: you are exposed upon a grand theater to the view of the world. If your actions are upright and benevolent, be assured they will augment your power and happiness.

— *Cyrus*

When I'm getting ready to reason with a man, I spend one-third of my time thinking about myself and what I am going to say — and two-thirds thinking about him and what he is going to say.

— *Abraham Lincoln*

Think as you work, for in the final analysis your worth to your company comes not only in solving problems but in anticipating them.

— *H. H. Ross*

Some day, in years to come, you will be wrestling with the great temptation, or trembling under the great sorrow of your life. But the real struggle is here, now, in these quiet weeks. Now it is being decided whether, in the day of your supreme sorrow or temptation, you shall miserably fail or gloriously conquer. Character cannot be made except by a steady, long-continued process.

— *Phillips Brooks*

Undertake something that is difficult; it will do you good. Unless you try to do something beyond what you have already mastered, you will never grow.

— *Ronald E. Osborn*

Chance favors the prepared mind.   — *Louis Pasteur*

Unless each man produces more than he receives, increases his output, there will be less for him and all the others.

— *Bernard M. Baruch*

I hope the day will never come when the American nation will be the champion of the status quo. Once that happens, we shall have forfeited, and rightly forfeited, the support of the unsatisfied, of those who are the victims of inevitable imperfections, of those who, young in years or spirit, believe that they can make a better world and of those who dream dreams and want to make their dreams come true.   — *John Foster Dulles*

To build Utopias in defiance of scientific principles is only a fool's errand. If false hopes are momentarily good for morale, we must ultimately pay for such folly in episodes of disillusionment, cynicism and despair.

— *Merryle Stanley Rukeyser*

It is chiefly upon the lay citizen, informed about science but not its practitioner, that the country must depend in determining the use to which science is put, in resolving the many public policy questions that scientific discoveries constantly force upon us.   — *David E. Lilienthal*

Governments, like clocks, go from the motion men give them, and as governments are made and moved by men, so by them they are ruined also. Therefore governments depend upon men rather then men upon governments.

— *William Penn*

We are all salesmen every day of our lives. We are selling our ideas, our plans, our enthusiasms to those with whom we come in contact. — *Charles M. Schwab*

The race of mankind would perish did they cease to aid each other. We cannot exist without mutual help. All therefore that need aid have a right to ask it from their fellow-men; and no one who has the power of granting can refuse it without guilt. — *Walter Scott*

The search for truth is, as it always has been, the noblest expression of the human spirit. Man's insatiable desire for knowledge about himself, about his environment and the forces by which he is surrounded, gives life its meaning and purpose, and clothes it with final dignity. . . . And yet we know, deep in our hearts, that knowledge is not enough. . . . Unless we can anchor our knowledge to moral purposes, the ultimate result will be dust and ashes — dust and ashes that will bury the hopes and monuments of men beyond recovery. — *Raymond B. Fosdick*

Queer thing, but we always think every other man's job is easier than our own. And the better he does it, the easier it looks. — *Eden Phillpotts*

Family life is the source of the greatest human happiness. This happiness is the simplest and least costly kind, and it cannot be purchased with money. But it can be increased if we do two things: if we recognize and uphold the essential values of family life and if we get and keep control of the process of social change so as to make it give us what is needed to make family life perform its essential functions. — *Robert J. Havighurst*

I know of no safe repository for the ultimate powers of society but the people themselves; and if we think them not enlightened enough to exercise their control with a wholesome discretion, the remedy is not to take it from them, but to increase their discretion by education.

— *Thomas Jefferson*

Some new machinery with adequate powers must be created now if our fine phrases and noble sentiments are to have substance and meaning for our children.

— *James William Fulbright*

In many ways ideas are more important than people — they are much more permanent.   — *C. F. Kettering*

He who would be well taken care of must take care of himself.   — *W. G. Sumner*

By the street of By-and-By, one arrives at the house of Never.   — *Cervantes*

Happiness comes of the capacity to feel deeply, to enjoy simply, to think freely, to risk life, to be needed.

— *Storm Jameson*

To find a career to which you are adapted by nature, and then to work hard at it, is about as near to a formula for success and happiness as the world provides.   One of the fortunate aspects of this formula is that, granted the right career has been found, the hard work takes care of itself.   Then hard work is not hard work at all.

— *Mark Sullivan*

Mere lack of success does not discredit a method, for there are many things that determine and perpetuate our sanctified ways of doing things besides their success in reaching their proposed ends.

— James Harvey Robinson

Before you are five and twenty you must establish a character that will serve you all your life.

— Lord Collingwood

Everybody knows " blue " Monday. Sometimes we see " red." " Black " looks are disconcerting. Often the weak-hearted show the " white " feather or a " yellow " streak. And that " dark brown " taste is not unknown. But if you want to keep in the " pink " of mental condition you mustn't let disturbing riots of color mess up your environment.

— H. E. Townsend

Flash powder makes a more brilliant light than the arc lamp, but you can't use it to light your street corner because it doesn't last long enough. Stability is more essential to success than brilliancy.

— Richard Lloyd Jones

The law of work does seem utterly unfair — but there it is, and nothing can change it; the higher the pay in enjoyment the worker gets out of it, the higher shall be his pay in money also.

— Mark Twain

Most powerful is he who has himself in his own power.

— Seneca

From none but self expect applause.

— Burton

Present suffering is not enjoyable, but life would be worth little without it. The difference between iron and steel is fire, but steel is worth all it costs.

— *Maltbie Babcock*

A well-ordered life is like climbing a tower; the view halfway up is better than the view from the base, and it steadily becomes finer as the horizon expands.

— *William Lyon Phelps*

A man of a right spirit is not a man of narrow and private views, but is greatly interested and concerned for the good of the community to which he belongs, and particularly of the city or village in which he resides, and for the true welfare of the society of which he is a member.

— *Jonathan Edwards*

Indolence is a delightful but distressing state; we must be doing something to be happy. Action is no less necessary than thought to the instinctive tendencies of the human frame.   — *Hazlitt*

There's no thrill in easy sailing when the skies are clear and blue, there's no joy in merely doing things which any one can do. But there is some satisfaction that is mighty sweet to take, when you reach a destination that you thought you'd never make.   — *Spirella*

Many who think that they are taking life seriously are actually only taking themselves seriously. Who takes himself seriously is overconscious of his rights; who takes life seriously is fully conscious of his obligations.

— *Joseph T. O'Callahan*

Upon our children — how they are taught — rests the
fate — or fortune — of tomorrow's world.

— *B. C. Forbes*

Ambition is a lust that is never quenched, but grows
more inflamed and madder by enjoyment.   — *Otway*

Life to me is like a beach covered with lots of pebbles,
the faster we qualify ourselves to pick these pebbles the
richer we will be.   — *Evan A. Sholl*

Each thought that is welcomed and recorded is a nest
egg, by the side of which more will be laid.   — *Thoreau*

There is a vast difference in some instances between what
we really need and that which we think we must have, and
the realization of this truth will greatly lessen the seeming
discomfort in doing without.   — *William M. Peck*

It is probably safe to say that the best brains of the
nation are to be found in industry. This is partly because industry can afford to pay the highest prices for talent,
and also because of the training men receive in that field.
That this fact is not more apparent is due in part to the
reluctance of business men to reveal their accomplishments
to the public, and also because they have directed their
energies in the past almost exclusively to production
problems.   — *Ralph Hendershot*

Rightness expresses of actions, what straightness does
of lines; and there can no more be two kinds of right action
than there can be two kinds of straight lines.

— *Herbert Spencer*

Many people with different backgrounds, cultures, languages, and creeds combine to make a nation. But that nation is greater than the sum total of the individual skills and talents of its people. Something more grows out of their unity than can be calculated by adding the assets of individual contributions. That intangible additional quantity is often due to the differences which make the texture of the nation rich. Therefore, we must never wipe out or deride the differences amongst us — for where there is no difference, there is only indifference.

— Louis Nizer

The practical man is the adventurer, the investigator, the believer in research, the asker of questions, the man who refuses to believe that perfection has been attained. . . . There is no thrill or joy in merely doing that which any one can do. . . . It is always safe to assume, not that the old way is wrong, but that there may be a better way.

— Henry R. Harrower

An ideal is the most practical thing in the world, for it is a force behind action that must be reckoned with by the frankest materialist. *— Edward H. Griggs*

The power in which we must have faith if we would be well, is the creative and curative power which exists in every living thing. *— John Harvey Kellogg*

To the infantryman, his country's military might is only those buddies he can see, and the equipment they have at hand; likewise, to the wage-earner, " free enterprise " is primarily the way his boss treats him and those around him. *— Malcolm Forbes*

Trouble is the next best thing to enjoyment; there is
no fate in the world so horrible as to have no share in either
its joy or sorrows.   — *Longfellow*

The world is rapidly being divided into two camps, the
comradeship of anti-Christ and the brotherhood of Christ.
The lines between these two are being drawn. How long
the battle will be we know not; whether swords will have
to be unsheathed we know not; whether blood will have to
be shed we know not; whether it will be an armed conflict
we know not. But in a conflict between truth and darkness, truth cannot lose.   — *Fulton J. Sheen, D.D.*

The more honesty a man has, the less he affects the air
of a saint.   — *Lavater*

When prosperity comes, do not use all of it.
                                       — *Confucius*

We can get the new world we want, if we want it enough
to abandon our prejudices, every day, everywhere. We
can build this world if we practise now what we said we
were fighting for.   — *Gwen Bristow*

The noblest workers of this world bequeath us nothing
so great as the image of themselves. Their task, be it ever
so glorious, is historical and transient, but the majesty of
their spirit is essential and eternal.   — *George Brown*

Nature is the most thrifty thing in the world; she never
wastes anything; she undergoes change, but there's no
annihilation — the essence remains.   — *T. Binney*

Organization is the art of getting men to respond like thoroughbreds. When you cluck to a thoroughbred, he gives you all of the speed and strength of heart and sinew he has in him. When you cluck to a jackass, he kicks.

— *C. R. House*

Doing for people what they can and ought to do for themselves is a dangerous experiment. In the last analysis, the welfare of the workers depends upon their own initiative. Whatever is done under the guise of philanthropy or social morality which in any way lessens initiative is the greatest crime that can be committed against the toilers. Let social busybodies and professional " public morals experts " in their fads reflect upon the perils they rashly invite under this pretense of social welfare.

— *Samuel Gompers*

An observant man, in all his intercourse with society and the world, constantly and unperceived marks on every person and thing the figure expressive of its value, and therefore, on meeting that person or thing, knows instantly what kind and degree of attention to give it. This is to make something of experience. — *John Foster*

" Honesty is the best policy," " A dollar saved is a dollar earned," " Look before you leap," " A bird in the hand is worth two in the bush," " The laborer is worthy of his hire," may be scoffed at by some intellectuals as trite copybook rules, but nonetheless they sum up the elementary experience of the race in creating and consuming wealth. . . . People may change their minds as often as their coats, and new sets of rules of conduct may be written every week, but the fact remains that human nature has not changed and does not change, that inherent human beliefs stay the same; the fundamental rules of human conduct continue to hold. — *Lammot du Pont*

People forget how fast you did a job — but they remember how well you did it.   — *Howard W. Newton*

It is the social obligation of management to make certain that its executives are functioning at peak performance, both physically and psychologically.   To keep top men from spinning, management must see that executives should: receive periodic medical checkups; receive periodic psychological evaluations; be given an adequate number of assistants of proper ability; have their time pressures reduced through improved selling; be given training in leadership.   — *Dr. Stanley G. Dulsky*

Set me a task in which I can put something of my very self, and it is a task no longer; it is joy; it is art.
                    — *Bliss Carman*

Men are often capable of greater things than they perform.   They are sent into the world with bills of credit, and seldom draw to their full extent.   — *Walpole*

Thinking is the talking of the soul with itself.
                    — *Plato*

No matter how small and unimportant what we are doing may seem, if we do it well, it may soon become the step that will lead us to better things.   — *Channing Pollock*

One realizes the full importance of time only when there is little of it left.   Every man's greatest capital asset is his unexpired years of productive life.
                    — *P. W. Litchfield*

A man is the part he plays among his fellows. He is not isolated; he cannot be. His life is made up of the relations he bears to others — is made or marred by those relations, guided by them, judged by them, expressed in them. There is nothing else upon which he can spend his spirit — nothing else that we can see. It is by these he gets his spiritual growth; it is by these we see his character revealed, his purpose, his gifts. A few (men) act as those who have mastered the secrets of a serious art, with deliberate subordination of themselves to the great end and motive of the play. These have " found themselves," and have all the ease of a perfect adjustment.

— *Woodrow Wilson*

No student ever attains very eminent success by simply doing what is required of him; it is the amount and excellence of what is over and above the required, that determines the greatness of ultimate distinction.

— *Charles Kendall Adams*

The history of the building of the American nation may justly be described as a laboratory experiment in understanding and in solving the problems that will confront the world tomorrow. — *Dr. Nicholas Murray Butler*

The chief end of man, as I see it, is to find security, have liberty to express his abilities, enjoy the love of family and friends, and to secure recognition of his talents, to worship God in his own way, and to participate in a government that will protect him in his exercise of these liberties, and by education and training in the development of the arts and sciences, and the techniques of their application, help him to find his proper place in the scheme of things. — *E. S. Lewis*

For the industrious, thinking, right-living young man the future holds as many rewards as any period in our nation's history.   — *William M. Jeffers*

There are times when minds need to turn to simple things. Perhaps for a few of these nights all of us might do well to leave the briefcases at the office and to read again the pages of the Bible, and to re-read the Declaration of Independence and the Constitution of the United States. We might do well to stay home a few days and walk over the fields, or to stand in the shelter of the barn door and reflect upon the relentless and yet benevolent forces of Mother Nature. The laws of nature are relentless. They can never be disobeyed without exacting a penalty. Yet they are benevolent, for when they are understood and obeyed, nature yields up the abundance that blesses those who understand and obey.   — *Wheeler McMillen*

It is better to create than to be learned; creating is the true essence of life.   — *Niebuhr*

We ought not to look back unless it is to derive useful lessons from past errors, and for the purpose of profiting by dearly bought experience.   — *George Washington*

A great idea is usually original to more than one discoverer. Great ideas come when the world needs them. They surround the world's ignorance and press for admission.
                    — *A. Phelps*

The tallest trees are most in the power of the winds, and ambitious men of the blasts of fortune.   — *William Penn*

Those who attempt to level never equalize. In all societies some description must be uppermost. The levellers, therefore, only change and pervert the natural order of things; they load the edifice of society by setting up in the air what the solidity of the structure requires to be on the ground. — *Burke*

It is of no consequence of what parents a man is born, so he be a man of merit. — *Horace*

Every right has its responsibilities. Like the right itself, these responsibilities stem from no man-made law, but from the very nature of man and society. The security, progress and welfare of one group is measured finally in the security, progress and welfare of all mankind.
— *Lewis Schwellenbach*

A lot of voters always cast their ballot for the candidate who seems to them to be one of the people. That means he must have the same superstitions, the same unbalanced prejudices, and the same lack of understanding of public finances that are characteristic of the majority. A better choice would be a candidate who has a closer understanding and a better education than the majority. Too much voting is based on affability rather than on ability.
— *William Feather*

Executive ability is deciding quickly and getting somebody else to do the work. — *J. G. Pollard*

You may be deceived if you trust too much, but you will live in torment if you do not trust enough.
— *Dr. Frank Crane*

Genius is eternal patience.   — *Michaelangelo*

Great men never make bad use of their superiority; they
see it, and feel it, and are not less modest. The more
they have, the more they know their own deficiencies.
— *Jean Jacques Rousseau*

Every man has a property in his own person; this nobody
has a right to but himself.   — *Locke*

If you can't get enthusiastic about your work, it's time to
get alarmed — something is wrong. Compete with yourself; set your teeth and dive into the job of breaking your
own record. No one keeps up his enthusiasm automatically.
Enthusiasm must be nourished with new actions, new
aspirations, new efforts, new vision. It is one's own fault
if his enthusiasm is gone; he has failed to feed it. If you
want to turn hours into minutes, renew your enthusiasm.
— *Papyrus*

Much of the present difficulty in industrial relations
arises from the fact that too many employers as well as
too many legislators take the Labor Leader more seriously
than he deserves to be taken, while taking the ordinary,
everyday, middle-of-the-road wage-earner less seriously
than he deserves to be taken.   — *Whiting Williams*

For every action there is an equal and opposite reaction.
If you want to receive a great deal, you first have to give
a great deal. If each individual will give of himself to
whomever he can, wherever he can, in any way that he can,
in the long run he will be compensated in the exact proportion that he gives.   — *R. A. Hayward*

Our Creator has put in us hungers that this earth cannot satisfy. We cannot be completely self-contained on earth. Physical sense cannot give us a full life, nor can knowledge alone. No life is full unless it is linked to something that goes on after we are dead. . . . If we have nothing more to live for than just to get ahead in a competitive system, then democracy will go down before other philosophies.   — *Ralph W. Sockman, D.D.*

I prefer credulity to skepticism and cynicism, for there is more promise in almost anything than in nothing at all.
— *Ralph Barton Perry*

Unless we are prepared to search our souls to discover what to say, and then how to say it effectively, we cannot expect to deal successfully with today's domestic and personal problems, not to mention those international issues on which our very lives depend.   — *Everett Case*

Take the course opposite to custom and you will almost always do well   — *Jean Jacques Rousseau*

The time men spend in trying to impress others they could spend in doing the things by which others would be impressed.   — *Frank Romer*

The prudence of the best heads is often defeated by the tenderness of the best of hearts.   — *Henry Fielding*

Nothing inspires confidence in a business man sooner than punctuality, nor is there any habit which sooner saps his reputation than that of being always behind time.
— *W. Mathews*

In vain do they talk of happiness who never subdued an impulse in obedience to a principle. He who never sacrificed a present to a future good, or a personal to a general one, can speak of happiness only as the blind speak of color. — *Horace Mann*

The influence of prayer on the human mind and body is as demonstrable as that of secreting glands. Its results can be measured in terms of increased physical buoyancy, greater intellectual vigor, moral stamina, and a deeper understanding of the realities underlying human relationship. — *Dr. Alexis Carrel*

Our definition of success is unorthodox. We claim that any man who is honest, fair, tolerant, kindly, charitable of others and well behaved is a success, no matter what his station in life. — *Jay E. House*

What is difficulty? Only a word indicating the degree of strength requisite for accomplishing particular objects; a mere notice of the necessity for exertion; a bugbear to children and fools; only a mere stimulus to men. — *Samuel Warren*

Temptation rarely comes in working hours. It is in their leisure time that men are made or marred. — *W. M. Taylor*

Head knowledge is good, but heart knowledge is indispensable. The training of the hands and feet must be added to make a rounded education. We must all learn these days to become spiritual pioneers if we would save the world from chaos. — *E. V. Hammond*

The functions of an executive are to create and enforce policies rather than to work out problems resulting from such policies. — *Louis F. Musil*

Gaiety that sweetens existence and makes it wholesome — a sense of humor, a zest of enjoyment — this is the accompaniment of courage which gives it a supreme value. Something of the high laughter of a Cyrano de Bergerac — the world needs it. — *Dr. Herbert Hichen*

Every man, however obscure, however far removed from the general recognition, is one of a group of men impressible for good, and impressible for evil, and it is in the nature of things that he cannot really improve himself without in some degree improving other men.

— *Dickens*

You may know for a certainty that if your work is becoming uninteresting, so are you; for work is an inanimate thing and can be made lively and interesting only by injecting yourself into it. Your job is only as big as you are. — *George C. Hubbs*

The joy of feeling fit physically is reflected in a clearer and more useful mind. You may read and study forever, but you come to no more important truthful conclusions than these two: 1. Take care of your body (eat and exercise properly), and your mind will improve. 2. Work hard, and be polite and fair, and your condition in the world will improve. No pills, tablets, lotions, philosophies, will do as much for you as this simple formula I have outlined. The formula is not of my invention. Every intelligent man of experience since time began has taught it as a natural fact. — *Ed. Howe*

Oftentimes nothing profits more than self-esteem,
grounded on what is just and right.   — *Milton*

If I had only one sermon to preach it would be a sermon
against pride.   — *Gilbert K. Chesterton*

All higher motives, ideals, conceptions, sentiments in a
man are no account if they do not come forward to
strengthen him for the better discharge of the duties
which devolve upon him in the ordinary affairs of life.
        — *Henry Ward Beecher*

There are plenty of reasons for hope. There need be no
war with Russia, and those who would fight her now, on
the theory that we had better do it and get it over with, are
lightheaded promoters of world destruction.
        — *Dr. Harold W. Dodds*

When a man is pushed, tormented, defeated, he has a
chance to learn something; he has been put on his wits;
on his manhood; he has gained the facts; learns his ignorance; is cured of the insanity of conceit; has got moderation
and real skill.   — *Emerson*

Humanity either makes, or breeds, or tolerates all its
afflictions, great or small.   — *H. G. Wells*

The sweetest and most inoffensive path of life leads
through the avenues of science and learning; and whoever
can either remove any obstruction in this way, or open
up any new prospect, ought, so far, to be esteemed a benefactor to mankind.   — *David Hume*

A man cannot leave a better legacy to the world than a well-educated family.
— *Thomas Scott*

Men must try and try again. They must suffer the consequences of their own mistakes and learn by their own failures and their own successes.
— *Lawson Purdy*

The everyday cares and duties, which men call drudgery, are the weights and counterpoises of the clock of time, giving its pendulum a true vibration and its hands a regular motion; and when they cease to hang upon its wheels, the pendulum no longer swings, the hands no longer move, the clock stands still.
— *Longfellow*

We can be thankful to a friend for a few acres, or a little money; and yet for the freedom and command of the whole earth, and for the great benefits of our being, our life, health, and reason, we look upon ourselves as under no obligation.
— *Seneca*

Waste no tears over the griefs of yesterday.
— *Euripides*

Action and feeling go together and by regulating the action which is under the more direct control of the will, we can regulate the feeling, which is not.
— *William James*

Undertake something that is difficult; it will do you good. Unless you try to do something beyond what you have already mastered, you will never grow.
— *Ronald E. Osborn*

Measure your health by your sympathy with morning and Spring. If there is no response in you to the awakening of nature, if the prospect of an early morning walk does not banish sleep, if the warble of the first bluebird does not thrill you, know that the morning and spring of your life are past. Thus you may feel your pulse.

— Henry Thoreau

Times of general calamity and confusion have ever been productive of the greatest minds. The purest ore is produced from the hottest furnace, and the brightest thunderbolt is elicited from the darkest storm.   *— Colton*

In the deep, unwritten wisdom of life there are many things to be learned that cannot be taught. We never know them by hearing them spoken, but we grow into them by experience and recognize them through understanding. Understanding is a great experience in itself, but it does not come through instruction.   *— Anthony Hope*

Failures are divided into two classes — those who thought and never did, and those who did and never thought.

— John Charles Salak

In spite of the fact that the ladder tapers to one-man rungs at the top, the roomiest part is farthest up.

— Charles R. Gow

True courage is not the brutal force of vulgar heroes, but the firm resolve of virtue and reason.   *— Whitehead*

I've been more bossed by my fortune than it has been bossed by me.   *— John P. Lippett*

The covetous man never has money; the prodigal will
have none shortly. — *Ben Jonson*

This wonder we find in hope, that she is both a flatterer
and a true friend. How many would die did not hope sustain
them; how many have died by hoping too much!
— *Feltham*

Carlyle was right when he said that this life is only a
" gleam of light between two eternities." And still some
folks take it so hectically and so seriously. What's all the
hurry for, anyway? — *Amos Parrish*

No democratic world will work as it should work until we
recognize that we can only enjoy any right so long as we are
prepared to discharge its equivalent duty. This applies
just as much to states in their dealing with one another as
to individuals within the states. — *Anthony Eden*

Reason often makes mistakes, but conscience never does.
— *Josh Billings*

The charities of life are scattered everywhere, enameling
the vales of human beings as the flowers paint the meadows.
They are not the fruit of study, nor the privilege of refine-
ment, but a natural instinct. — *George Bancroft*

Might I give counsel to any man, I would say to him, try
to frequent the company of your betters. In books and in
life, that is the most wholesome society; learn to admire
rightly; the great pleasure of life is that. Note what great
men admire. — *Thackeray*

Better keep yourself clean and bright; you are the window through which you must see the world.

— *George Bernard Shaw*

Whatever strengthens and purifies the affections, enlarges the imagination, and adds spirit to sense, is useful.

— *Shelley*

A people, secure in their jobs, taking pride in their work, and sure of just recognition, will help our society grow to new heights. If all industry should adopt an incentive system, the standard of living of all peoples would be quadrupled; friction between labor and management would disappear, and the satisfaction of all workers would be greatly enhanced.   — *James F. Lincoln*

In a world where so much seems to be hidden by the smoke of falsity and moral degeneration, we Americans must grasp firmly the ideals which have made this country great. We must reaffirm the basic human values that have guided our forefathers. A revival of old-fashioned patriotism and a grateful acknowledgment of what our country has done for us would be good for all our souls.

— *Manton S. Eddy*

Trained and inspired leadership is needed in the troubled world of today. We live in uncertainty and fear. The times call for thinking and straight thinking — one of the goals of true education. Unfortunately, the world so clamors for action that men and women devote little time to thinking. Many believe in second-hand thinking. They find it easier to ascertain and adopt the thoughts of others than to think for themselves.   — *James F. Byrnes*

The history of liberty is the history of the limitation of governmental power, not the increase of it. When we resist . . . concentration of power we are resisting the powers of death, because concentration of power is what always precedes the destruction of human liberties.

— *Woodrow Wilson*

Every job has drudgery, whether it is in the home, in the professional school or in the office. The first secret of happiness is the recognition of this fundamental fact.

— *M. C. McIntosh*

Most of us, swimming against tides of trouble the world knows nothing about, need only a bit of praise or encouragement — and we'll make the goal. Say " Thank you! " whenever you think of it. Say " Nice job! " to that workman who put extra effort into his task. Say " Atta boy! " to the fellow who is struggling through in the face of odds. You'll get a whale of a lot of joy out of life that way. And people will love you. — *Jerome P. Fleishman*

There is a divinity that shapes our ends — but we can help by listening for Its voice. — *Kathleen Norris*

Whether you be man or woman you will never do anything in this world without courage. It is the greatest quality of the mind next to honor. — *James Allen*

The secret of the true love of work is the hope of success in that work; not for the money reward, for the time spent, or for the skill exercised, but for the successful result in the accomplishment of the work itself.

— *Sidney A. Weltmer*

What we can do for another is the test of powers; what
we can suffer for is the test of love.   — *Bishop Westcott*

The world position which our country holds today is
due to the wide vision of the statesmen who founded these
United States and to the daring and indomitable persistence
of the great industrial leaders, together with the myriads
of men who with faith in their leadership have co-operated
to rear the marvelous industrial structure of which our
country is justly so proud.   — *John D. Rockefeller, Jr.*

Our destiny changes with our thought; we shall become
what we wish to become, do what we wish to do, when our
habitual thought corresponds with our desire.

— *Orison Swett Marden*

Whatever is done without ostentation, and without the
people being witnesses of it, is, in my opinion, most praiseworthy: not that the public eye should be entirely avoided,
for good actions desire to be placed in the light; but notwithstanding this, the greatest theater for virtue is conscience.   — *Cicero*

The Ultimate Good desired is better reached by free
trade in ideas — the best test of truth is the power of the
thought to get itself accepted in the competition of the
market.   — *Oliver Wendell Holmes*

To be always intending to live a new life, but never to
find time to set about it; this is as if a man should put off
eating and drinking and sleeping from one day and night to
another, till he is starved and destroyed.   — *Tillotson*

There are times when God asks nothing of his children except silence, patience, and tears. — *C. S. Robinson*

Perfection is attained by slow degrees; it requires the hand of time. — *Voltaire*

Man's knowledge of science has clearly outstripped his knowledge of man. Our only hope of making the atom servant rather than master lies in education, in a broad liberal education where each student within his capacity can free himself from trammels of dogmatic prejudice and apply his educational accoutrement to besetting social and human problems. — *Harry Woodburn Chase*

To re-create strength, rest. To re-create mind, repose. To re-create cheerfulness, hope in God, or change the object of attention to one more elevated and worthy of thought. — *G. Simmons*

Whatever you are by nature, keep to it; never desert your own line of talent. Be what nature intended you for, and you will succeed; be anything else and you will be ten thousand times worse than nothing. — *Sydney Smith*

My father used to say: " Never suspect people. It's better to be deceived or mistaken, which is only human, after all, than to be suspicious, which is common."
— *Stark Young*

Nothing so obstinately stands in the way of all sorts of progress as pride of opinion; while nothing is so foolish and baseless. — *J. G. Holland*

If you make people think they're thinking, they'll love you; but if you really make them think, they'll hate you.

— *Don Marquis*

A barking dog is often more useful than a sleeping lion.

— *Washington Irving*

As a man handles his troubles during the day, he goes to bed at night a General, Captain or Private.　— *Ed. Howe*

The foundations of the world will be shaky until the moral props are restored.　— *Anne O'Hare McCormick*

Every man who observes vigilantly and resolves steadfastly grows unconsciously into genius.

— *Bulwer-Lytton*

Be a life long or short, its completeness depends on what it was lived for.　— *David Starr Jordan*

Because of the law of gravitation the apple falls to the ground.　Because of the law of growth the acorn becomes a mighty oak.　Because of the law of causation, a man is " as he thinketh in his heart."　Nothing can happen without its adequate cause.　— *Don Carlos Musser*

People are much more alike inside than they are on the surface.　— *Verne Burnett*

A small mind is obstinate.　A great mind can lead and be led.　— *Alexander Cannon*

Get the confidence of the public and you will have no difficulty in getting their patronage. Inspire your whole force with the right spirit of service; encourage every sign of the true spirit. So display and advertise wares that customers shall buy with understanding. Treat them as guests when they come and when they go, whether or not they buy. Give them all that can be given fairly, on the principle that to him that giveth shall be given. Remember always that the recollection of quality remains long after the price is forgotten. Then your business will prosper by a natural process.
— *H. Gordon Selfridge*

Nothing is so firmly believed as what we least know.
— *Montaigne*

We must dare to be happy, and dare to confess it, regarding ourselves always as the depositories, not as the authors of our own joy.
— *Amiel*

Why should the Golden Rule be so difficult in business and foreign relations? The happily married treat each other as they wish to be treated. They treat their children better than they wish to be treated themselves. Unless we do unto a friend as we do unto ourselves, we lose a friend. In an emergency we rush to the aid of our neighbor. Is it so great a step to realize that all people everywhere are neighbors?
— *Arthur Dunn*

Our human laws are but the copies, more or less imperfect, of the eternal laws, so far as we can read them.
— *Froude*

The price of wisdom is eternal thought.
— *Frank Birch*

A man too busy to take care of his health is like a mechanic too busy to take care of his tools.

— *Spanish Proverb*

Education makes a people easy to lead, but difficult to drive; easy to govern, but impossible to enslave.

— *Henry Brougham*

Friendships are fragile things, and require as much care in handling as any other fragile and precious thing.

— *Randolph S. Bourne*

The force, the mass of character, mind, heart or soul that a man can put into any work is the most important factor in that work. — *A. P. Peabody*

Opportunities do not come with their values stamped upon them. Every one must be challenged. A day dawns, quite like other days; in it a single hour comes, quite like other hours; but in that day and in that hour the chance of a lifetime faces us. To face every opportunity of life thoughtfully and ask its meaning bravely and earnestly, is the only way to meet the supreme opportunities when they come, whether open-faced or disguised. — *Maltbie Babcock*

Thought is, perhaps, the forerunner and even the mother of ideas, and ideas are the most powerful and the most useful things in the world. — *George Gardner*

If your work is work to you and you don't see beyond that work and see the pleasure in work and the pleasure in service, look out; you are in danger of standing in your present station for a long, long time. — *Milan R. Bump*

Nationalism and internationalism! Both must stand together or the human race will be utterly destroyed. We shall never be able to destroy nationalism and we shall never be able to live without internationalism.

— *Linus R. Fike*

There is only one way to get ready for immortality, and that is to love this life and live it as bravely and faithfully and cheerfully as we can. — *Henry Van Dyke*

We ought not to treat living creatures like shoes or household belongings, which when worn with use we throw away.

— *Plutarch*

It is one thing to wish to have truth on our side, and another to wish sincerely to be on the side of truth.

— *Whately*

You desire a popular art? Begin by having a " people " whose minds are liberated, a people not crushed by misery and ceaseless toil, not brutalized by every superstition and every fanaticism, a people master of itself, and victor in the fight that is being waged today. — *Romain Rolland*

We are apt to love praise, but not to deserve it. But if we would deserve it, we must love virtue more than that.

— *William Penn*

Show me the man you honor, and I will know what kind of a man you are, for it shows me what your ideal of manhood is, and what kind of a man you long to be.

— *Carlyle*

We should not only master questions, but also act upon
them, and act definitely.   — *Woodrow Wilson*

Knowledge comes, but wisdom lingers. It may not be
difficult to store up in the mind a vast quantity of facts
within a comparatively short time, but the ability to form
judgments requires the severe discipline of hard work and
the tempering heat of experience and maturity.
                                        — *Calvin Coolidge*

Our greatest opportunities for advancing productivity
and improving living standards are to be found in the field
of human relationships. Having achieved a better understanding of each other and their common responsibility to
consumers and investors, both management and labor should
do all in their power to educate the American public to
understanding of the simple economic facts that underlie
our industrial and business relationships.
                                        — *Louis Ruthenburg*

A tree that affords thee shade, do not order it to be cut
down.   — *Arabian Proverb*

Everything that looks to the future elevates human nature; for never is life so low or so little as when occupied
with the present.   — *Landor*

The successful producer of an article sells it for more than
it cost him to make, and that's his profit. But the customer
buys it only because it is worth *more* to him than he pays
for it, and that's his profit. No one can long make a profit
producing anything unless the customer makes a profit
using it.   — *Samuel B. Pettengill*

There is nothing keeps longer than a middling fortune, and nothing melts away sooner than a great one. Poverty treads on the heels of great and unexpected riches.

— *Bruyère*

I leave everything to the young men. You've got to give youthful men authority and responsibility if you're going to build up an organization. Otherwise you'll always be the boss yourself and you won't leave anything behind you.

— *A. P. Giannini (70)*

A single conversation across the table with a wise man is worth a month's study of books. — *Chinese Proverb*

If the wealth of this country were distributed, 90 per cent. would be destroyed by the act of distribution. The resulting starvation and anarchy would destroy the rest in less than thirty days. — *J. F. Lincoln*

Self-reverence, self-knowledge, self-control, these three alone lead life to sovereign power. — *Tennyson*

The employer generally gets the employees he deserves.

— *Sir Walter Bilbey*

Sometimes one pays most for the things one gets for nothing. — *Albert Einstein*

When a man begins to understand himself he begins to live. When he begins to live he begins to understand his fellow men. — *Norvin G. McGranahan*

When you hire people who are smarter than you are,
you prove you are smarter than they are.

— *R. H. Grant*

He who is plenteously provided for from within needs but
little from without.   — *Goethe*

The cynic never grows up, but commits intellectual
suicide.   — *Dr. Charles Reynolds Brown*

He that cannot forgive others, breaks the bridge over
which he must pass himself; for every man has need to be
forgiven.   — *Lord Herbert*

Nature has made occupation a necessity to us; society
makes it a duty; habit makes it a pleasure.   — *Capelle*

It is an old saying, and one of fearful and fathomless
import, that we are forming characters for eternity. Forming characters? Whose? Our own or others? Both — and
in that momentous act lies the peril and responsibility of
our existence.   — *Burritt*

Study without reflection is a waste of time; reflection
without study is dangerous.   — *Confucius*

I go walking, and the hills loom above me, range upon
range, one against the other. I cannot tell where one begins
and another leaves off. But when I talk with God He lifts
me up where I can see clearly, where everything has a distinct contour.   — *Mme. Chiang Kai-shek*

In doing one's work primarily for God, the fear of undue restriction is put, sooner or later, out of the question. He pays me and He pays me well. He pays me and He will not fail to pay me. He pays me not merely for the rule of thumb task, which is all that men recognize, but to everything else I bring to my job in the way of industry, good intentions and cheerfulness. If the Lord loveth a cheerful giver, as St. Paul says, we may depend upon it that He loveth a cheerful worker; and where we can cleave the way to His love there we find His endless generosity.

— Basil King

The truest mark of being born with great qualities, is being born without envy.   *— La Rochefoucauld*

They who forgive most, shall be most forgiven.

— Josiah W. Bailey

The whole of the American Dream has been based on the chance to get ahead, for one's self or one's children. Would this country have ever reached the point it has if the individual had always been refused the rewards of his labors and dangers?   *— James Truslow Adams*

Act as though everything you do, rightly or wrongly, accurately or carelessly, may tip the scale of the bigger things of tomorrow for all of us, as indeed every act, potentially, can. Remember: Enemies try to break through at the weakest point. Don't let it be on *your* sector.

— L. G. Elliott

Restlessness and discontent are the first necessities of progress.   *— Thomas A. Edison*

People generally do not appreciate what they do not
suffer for. A thing is held to be cheap if it did not cost
dearly. Honor is lightly worn if it was easily attained.
Inherited liberty is too often carelessly used until it is re-
possessed through sacrifices.

— *Fred Robert Tiffany, D.D.*

The best things in life are never rationed. Friendship,
loyalty, love do not require coupons.

— *George T. Hewitt*

I think it rather fine, this necessity for the tense bracing
of the will before anything worth doing can be done. I
rather like it myself. I feel it is to be the chief thing that
differentiates me from the cat by the fire.

— *Arnold Bennett*

Work your way up or rust your way out.   — *Holton*

A grain of real knowledge, of genuine controllable conviction, will outweigh a bushel of adroitness; and to produce persuasion there is one golden principle of rhetoric not
put down in the books — to understand what you are
talking about.   — *Seeley*

To do what we will, is natural liberty; to do what we
may consistently with the interests of the community to
which we belong, is civil liberty, the only liberty to be desired in a state of civil society.   — *Paley*

All mankind is divided into three classes: Those that are
immovable, those that are movable, and those that move.

— *Arabian Proverb*

Men who have attained things worth having in this world have worked while others idled, have persevered when others gave up in despair, have practiced early in life the valuable habits of self-denial, industry, and singleness of purpose. As a result, they enjoy in later life the success so often erroneously attributed to good luck. — *Grenville Kleiser*

Be sure of the foundation of your life. Know why you live as you do. Be ready to give a reason for it. Do not, in such a matter as life, build an opinion or custom on what you guess is true. Make it a matter of certainty and science. — *Thomas Starr King*

In science, read by preference the newest works; in literature, the oldest. The classics are always modern. — *Lord Lytton*

Most business problems require common sense rather than legal reference. They require good judgment and honesty of purpose rather than reference to the courts. — *Edward N. Hurley*

When a fellow thinks he is putting it over on the boss, the boss is not thinking of putting him over others to boss. —*C. K. Anderson*

Light is the task where many share the toil. — *Homer*

Each man has to seek out his own special aptitude for a higher life in the midst of the humble and inevitable reality of daily existence. Than this, there can be no nobler aim in life. — *Maeterlinck*

Think of your own faults the first part of the night when you are awake, and of the faults of others the latter part of the night when you are asleep.　　*— Chinese Proverb*

The true way to gain much, is never to desire to gain too much. He is not rich that possesses much, but he that covets no more; and he is not poor that enjoys little, but he that wants too much.　　*— Beaumont*

Enthusiasm is the best protection in any situation. Wholeheartedness is contagious. Give yourself, if you wish to get others.　　*— David Seabury*

The easy way is efficacious and speedy — the hard way arduous and long. But as the clock ticks, the easy way becomes harder and the hard way becomes easier. And as the calendar records the years, it becomes increasingly evident that the easy way rests hazardously upon shifting sands, whereas the hard way builds solidly a foundation of confidence that cannot be swept away.　　*— Daniel Rand*

Good management consists in showing *average* people how to do the work of *superior* people.
　　— John D. Rockefeller

The virtues which keep this world sweet and the faithfulness which keeps it steadfast are chiefly those of the average man. The danger of the two-talent man is that he will be content with mediocrity.　　*— W. Russell Bowie*

When a man has put a limit on what he will do, he has put a limit on what he can do.　　*— Charles M. Schwab*

Prejudice and self-sufficiency naturally proceed from in-experience of the world, and ignorance of mankind.
— *Addison*

Spiritual power is a force which history clearly teaches has been the greatest force in the development of men. Yet we have been merely playing with it and never have really studied it as we have the physical forces. Some day people will learn that material things do not bring happiness, and are of little use in making people creative and powerful. Then the scientists of the world will turn their laboratories over to the study of spiritual forces which have hardly been scratched.   — *Charles P. Steinmetz*

We want our children to grow up to be such persons that ill-fortune, if they meet with it, will bring out strength in them, and that good fortune will not trip them up, but make them winners.   — *Edward Sandford Martin*

Family life is too intimate to be preserved by the spirit of justice. It can only be sustained by a spirit of love which goes beyond justice. Justice requires that we carefully weigh rights and privileges and assure that each member of a community receives his due share. Love does not weigh rights and privileges too carefully because it prompts each to bear the burden of the other.   — *Niebuhr*

No man or woman has achieved an effective personality who is not self-disciplined. Such discipline must not be an end in itself, but must be directed to the development of resolute Christian character.   — *John S. Bonnell, D.D.*

This is a world of action, and not for moping and dron-ing in.   — *Dickens*

Within the next few years — a decade perhaps — we
should be in a position to unlock new knowledge about life
and matter so great that wholly new concepts of human life
will follow in the wake of this new knowledge.

— David E. Lilienthal

That man is prudent who neither hopes nor fears anything from the uncertain events of the future.

— Anatole France

We are all manufacturers — making good, making trouble
or making excuses.　　　　　　　　　　　　　*— H. V. Adolt*

A nail is driven out by another nail; habit is overcome
by habit.　　　　　　　　　　　　　　　　　*— Erasmus*

The best insurance policy for the future of an industry is
research, which will help it to foresee future lines of development, to solve its immediate problems, and to improve and
cheapen its products.　　　　　*— Sir Harold Hartley*

You never will be the person you can be if pressure, tension and discipline are taken out of your life.

— Dr. James G. Bilkey

Every generation, no matter how paltry its character,
thinks itself much wiser than the one immediately pre-
ceding it, let alone those that are more remote.

— Schopenhauer

You may not have saved a lot of money in your life, but
if you have saved a lot of heartaches for other folks, you
are a pretty rich man.　　　　　　　　*— Seth Parker*

The old Quaker was right: " I expect to pass through life but once. If there is any kindness, or any good thing I can do to my fellow beings, let me do it now. I shall pass this way but once."
— *W. C. Gannett*

The best security for civilization is the dwelling, and upon properly appointed and becoming dwellings depends, more than anything else, the improvement of mankind.
— *Disraeli*

Many blunder in business through inability or an unwillingness to adopt new ideas. I have seen many a success turn to failure also, because the thought which should be trained on big things is cluttered up with the burdensome detail of little things.
— *Philip S. Delaney*

There is no substitute for accurate knowledge. Know yourself, know your business, know your men.
— *Randall Jacobs*

The glory of the nation rests in the character of her men. And character comes from boyhood. Thus every boy is a challenge to his elders. It is for them that we must win the war — it is for them that we must make a just and lasting peace. For the world of tomorrow, about which all of us are dreaming and planning, will be carried forward by the boys of today.
— *Herbert Hoover*

We are all weak, finite, simple human beings, standing in the need of prayer. None need it so much as those who think they are strong, those who know it not but are deluded by self-sufficiency.
— *Harold Cooke Phillips, D.D.*

Too many of us, when we accomplish what we set out to do, exclaim, " See what I have done! " instead of saying, " See where I have been led."   — *Henry Ford*

Do not be inaccessible. None is so perfect that he does not need at times the advice of others. He is an incorrigible ass who will never listen to any one. Even the most surpassing intellect should find a place for friendly counsel. Sovereignty itself must learn to lean. There are some that are incorrigible simply because they are inaccessible: They fall to ruin because none dares to extricate them. The highest should have the door open for friendship; it may prove the gate of help. A friend must be free to advise, and even to upbraid, without feeling embarrassed.

— *Gracian*

Wealth is not of necessity a curse, nor poverty a blessing. Wholesome and easy abundance is better than either extreme; better for our manhood that we have enough for daily comfort; enough for culture, for hospitality, for Christian charity. More than this may or may not be a blessing. Certainly it can be a blessing only by being accepted as a trust.   — *Raymond Hitchcock*

Our object in traveling should be, not to gratify curiosity, and seek mere temporary amusement, but to learn, and to venerate, to improve the understanding and the heart.

— *Gresley*

No road is too long to the man who advances deliberately and without undue haste; and no honors are too distant for the man who prepares himself for them with patience.

— *Bruyère*

It will be a shock to men when they realize that thoughts that were fast enough for today are not fast enough for tomorrow. But thinking tomorrow's thoughts today is one kind of future life.
— *Christopher Morley*

Honesty isn't any policy at all; it's a state of mind or it isn't honesty.
— *Eugene L'Hote*

I place economy among the first and most important virtues, and public debt as the greatest of dangers. . . . We must make our choice between economy and liberty, or profusion and servitude. If we can prevent the government from wasting the labors of the people under the pretense of caring for them, they will be happy.
— *Thomas Jefferson*

A greater poverty than that caused by lack of money is the poverty of unawareness. Men and women go about the world unaware of the beauty, the goodness, the glories in it. Their souls are poor. It is better to have a poor pocketbook than to suffer from a poor soul.
— *Thomas Dreier*

There should be no inferiors and no superiors for true world friendship.
— *Carlos P. Romulo*

If I wanted to become a tramp, I would seek information and advice from the most successful tramp I could find. If I wanted to become a failure I would seek advice from men who have never succeeded. If I wanted to succeed in all things, I would look around me for those who are succeeding, and do as they have done.
— *Joseph Marshall Wade*

Do not wait for extraordinary circumstances to do good; try to use ordinary situations.   — *Richter*

Judgment of the people is often wiser than the wisest men.
                — *Kossuth*

We are not to judge thrift solely by the test of saving or spending. If one spends what he should prudently save, that certainly is to be deplored. But if one saves what he should prudently spend, that is not necessarily to be commended. A wise balance between the two is the desired end.   — *Owen D. Young*

Pugnacity is a form of courage, but a very bad form.
                — *Sinclair Lewis*

I am wondering what would have happened to me if some fluent talker had converted me to the theory of the eight-hour day and convinced me that it was not fair to my fellow workers to put forth my best efforts in my work. I am glad that the eight-hour day had not been invented when I was a young man. If my life had been made up of eight-hour days I do not believe I could have accomplished a great deal. This country would not amount to as much as it does if the young men of fifty years ago had been afraid that they might earn more than they were paid for.   — *Thomas A. Edison*

Responsibility for the creation of the good world in which the good life may be realized, which the frustrated ages of the past loaded upon the gods, is now being assumed by man. The ideal of this modern drift is the realization of the full joy in living.   — *A. Eustace Haydon*

Do you know that the ready concession of minor points
is a part of the grace of life? — *Henry Harland*

Salesmen should bear in mind that more mature men
who have reached a certain point in business buy rather
than are sold. A real salesman does not attempt to sell
his prospect but instead directs his efforts towards putting
the prospect in a frame of mind so that he will be moved
to action by a given set of facts. — *Roy Howard*

Many of us are like the little boy we met trudging along
a country road with a cat-rifle over his shoulder. " What
are you hunting, buddy? " we asked. " Dunno, sir, I ain't
seen it yet." — *R. Lee Sharpe*

I know that all things considered, the United States of
America, with all of its abuses of democracy and of
liberty itself, is still the garden spot of the world, where
peace, co-operation and constructive effort can and should
prevail always and the cause of a higher Christian civilization advanced. — *George M. Verity*

The full-grown modern human being who seeks but
refuge finds instead boredom and mental dissolution, unless he can be, even in his withdrawal, creative. He can
find the quality of happiness in the strain and travail only
of achievement and growth. And he is conscious of touching the highest pinnacle of fulfilment which his life-urges
demand when his is consumed in the service of an idea,
in the conquest of the goal pursued. — *R. Briffault*

Only those are fit to live who are not afraid to die.
— *Gen. Douglas MacArthur*

The possibilities of modern technology are tremendous. If these possibilities can be realized, no one can doubt that we are on the threshold of gaining a far better standard of living than man has ever known. Never have the rewards of willingness to take a broad view of common interests been greater.   — *Dr. Sumner H. Slichter*

The priceless heritage of the free and independent interchange of thought is not to be kept without ceaseless vigilance. Only by guarding the truth itself can we guard the greatest of all our liberties — the right to proclaim the truth. On that liberty rests the destiny of millions.

— *Lord Southwood*

A fellow doesn't last long on what he has done. He's got to keep on delivering as he goes along.

— *Carl Hubbell*

Besides the practical knowledge which defeat offers, there are important personality profits to be taken. Defeat strips away false values and makes you realize what you really want. It stops you from chasing butterflies and puts you to work digging gold.

— *William Moulton Marston*

The man who wastes to-day lamenting yesterday will waste to-morrow lamenting to-day.   — *Philip M. Raskin*

People who laugh actually live longer than those who don't laugh. Few persons realize that health actually varies according to the amount of laughter.

— *Dr. James J. Walsh*

A man has the right to toot his own horn to his heart's content, so long as he stays in his own home, keeps the windows closed and does not make himself obnoxious to his neighbors.   — *Tiorio*

People are generally better persuaded by the reasons which they have themselves discovered than by those which have come into the mind of others.   — *Pascal*

Curses are like processions; they return to the place from which they came.   — *Ruffini*

And he gave it for his opinion, that whoever could make two ears of corn, or two blades of grass, to grow upon a spot of ground where only one grew before, would deserve better of mankind, and do more essential service to his country, than the whole race of politicians put together.
— *Swift*

Reading maketh a full man; conference a ready man; and writing an exact man; and, therefore, if a man write little, he had need have a great memory; if he confer little, he had need have a present wit; and if he read little, he had need have much cunning, to seem to know that he doth not.   — *Bacon*

There are two things needed in these days; first, for rich men to find out how poor men live; and, second, for poor men to know how rich men work.   — *E. Atkinson*

You can preach a better sermon with your life than with your lips.   — *Goldsmith*

Do today's duty, fight today's temptation; do not weaken and distract yourself by looking forward to things you cannot see, and could not understand if you saw them.   — *Charles Kingsley*

The invectives against capital in the hands of those who have it are double-faced, and when turned about are nothing but demands for capital in the hands of those who have it not, in order that they may do with it just what those who have it are now doing with it.   — *W. G. Sumner*

Necessity of action takes away the fear of the act, and makes bold resolution the favorite of fortune.
                           — *Quarles*

The great menace to the life of an industry is industrial self-complacency.   — *David Sarnoff*

Despise not small things, either for evil or good, for a look may work thy ruin, or a word create thy wealth. A spark is a little thing, yet it may kindle the world.
                           — *M. T. Tupper*

Life is a series of experiences, each one of which makes us bigger, even though sometimes it is hard to realize this. For the world was built to develop character, and we must learn that the setbacks and griefs which we endure help us in our marching onward.   — *Henry Ford*

The fifth freedom, the Freedom of Individual Enterprise, is the keystone of the arch on which the other Four Freedoms rest. This is what freedom means.
                           — *Nicholas Murray Butler*

I would not waste the springtime of my youth in idle dalliance; I would plant rich seeds to blossom in my manhood, and bear fruit when I am old. — *Hillhouse*

It is not likely that posterity will fall in love with us, but not impossible that it may respect or sympathize; so a man would rather leave behind him the portrait of his spirit than a portrait of his face. — *Robert Louis Stevenson*

Statistics are no substitute for judgment.

— *Henry Clay*

In the final analysis, there is no other solution to a man's problems but the day's honest work, the day's honest decisions, the day's generous utterance, and the day's good deed. — *Clare Booth Luce*

It is well when the wise and the learned discover new truths; but how much better to diffuse the truths already discovered amongst the multitudes. Every addition to true knowledge is an addition to human power; and while a philosopher is discovering one new truth, millions of truths may be propagated amongst the people. . . . The whole land must be watered with the streams of knowledge. — *Horace Mann*

Calm self-confidence is as far from conceit as the desire to earn a decent living is remote from greed.

— *Channing Pollock*

The empires of the future are the empires of the mind.

— *Winston Churchill*

False happiness is like false money; it passes for a time
as well as the true, and serves some ordinary occasions;
but when it is brought to the touch, we find the lightness and
alloy, and feel the loss.   — *Pope*

It is an article of faith in my creed to pick the man who
does not take himself seriously, but does take his work
seriously.   — *Michael C. Cahill*

If money is all that a man makes, then he will be poor
— poor in happiness, poor in all that makes life worth
living.   — *Herbert N. Casson*

The first man gets the oyster, the second man gets the
shell.   — *Andrew Carnegie*

Wisdom is the power that enables us to use knowledge
for the benefit of ourselves and others.
                    — *Thomas J. Watson*

One reason why men and women *lose* their heads so often
is that they *use* them so little!   It is the same with everything.   If we have anything that is valuable, it must be put
to some sort of use.   If a man's muscles are neglected, he
soon has none, or rather none worth mentioning.   The
more the mind is used the more flexible it becomes, and the
more it takes upon itself new interests.
                    — *George Matthew Adams*

When you find yourself overpowered, as it were, by melancholy, the best way is to go out and do something kind
to somebody or other.   — *Keble*

If you listen to the neverdo's, it's never done.

— *David Lloyd George*

We are 90% alike, all we peoples, and 10% different.
The trouble is that we forget the 90% and remember the
10% when we criticize others.   — *Sir Charles Higham*

Go outdoors and get rid of nerves.

— *Dr. Frank Crane*

You will find it less easy to uproot faults than to choke
them by gaining virtues. Do not think of your faults,
still less of other's faults. In every person who comes near
you look for what is good and strong; honor that; try to
imitate it, and your faults will drop off like dead leaves
when their time comes.   — *Ruskin*

If we conducted ourselves as sensibly in good times as we
do in hard times, we could all acquire a competence.

— *William Feather*

A salesman, like the storage battery in your car, is constantly discharging energy. Unless he is recharged at
frequent intervals he soon runs dry. This is one of the
greatest responsibilities of sales leadership.

— *R. H. Grant*

Luck means the hardships and privations which you have
not hesitated to endure, the long nights you have devoted
to work. Luck means the appointments you have never
failed to keep; the trains you have never failed to catch.

— *Max O'Rell*

Men have various subjects in which they may excel, or at least would be thought to excel, and though they love to hear justice done to them where they know they excel, yet they are most and best flattered upon those points where they wish to excel and yet are doubtful whether they do or not.   — *Lord Chesterfield*

One cool judgment is worth a thousand hasty councils. The thing to do is to supply light and not heat.
— *Woodrow Wilson*

Associate yourself with men of good quality if you esteem your own reputation; for 'tis better to be alone than in bad company.   — *George Washington*

To be a good American means to understand the simple principles on which our nation was founded, to observe them in our daily life and to fight for them.
— *Newbold Morris*

We win half the battle when we make up our minds to take the world as we find it, including the thorns.
— *Orison S. Marden*

In the history of the world the prize has not gone to those species which specialized in methods of violence, or even in defensive armor. In fact, nature began with producing animals encased in hard shells for defense against the ills of life. It also experimented in size. But smaller animals, without external armor, warm-blooded, sensitive, alert, have cleared those monsters off the face of the earth.
— *Whitehead*

Remember what Simonides said — that he never repented that he had held his tongue, but often that he had spoken. — *Plutarch*

The most precious thing anyone — man or store, anybody or anything — can have is the goodwill of others. It is something as fragile as an orchid. And as beautiful! As precious as a gold nugget — and as hard to find. As powerful as a great turbine, and as hard to build. As wonderful as youth — and as hard to keep.
— *Amos Parrish*

To judge human character rightly, a man may sometimes have very small experience, provided he has a very large heart. — *Bulwer*

Hope is the best possession. None are completely wretched but those who are without hope, and few are reduced so low as that. — *Hazlitt*

The habit of saving is itself an education; it fosters every virtue, teaches self-denial, cultivates the sense of order, trains to forethought, and so broadens the mind.
— *T. T. Munger*

I find in life that most affairs that require serious handling are distasteful. For this reason, I have always believed that the successful man has the hardest battle with himself rather than with the other fellow. To bring one's self to a frame of mind and to the proper energy to accomplish things that require plain hard work continuously is the one big battle that everyone has. When this battle is won for all time, then everything is easy. — *Thomas A. Buckner*

For too many giving is occasional, spasmodic, ill-proportioned. It depends on what is left over when other things have had their full share. Sometimes what it means is that only the small change lying in their pockets goes to the support of good and worthy causes.

— Robert J. McCracken, D.D.

One of the great weaknesses of the American executive has been his indifference to those who misrepresent Business. The average man is too busily at work to reply to those who malign Business. He seems to accept the misrepresentation, libel and calumny as one of the necessary evils of Business, and silently submits until finally the undenied lies grow into general beliefs, with the result that both the public in general and Business in particular suffer.

— Charles E. Carpenter

Truly there is a tide in the affairs of men; but there is no gulf-stream setting forever in one direction.

— James Russell Lowell

I have never met a business man in my life who is not delighted to take on additional employees whenever the demand for his goods and services makes it possible for him to do so.   *— H. W. Prentis, Jr.*

A man is relieved and gay when he has put his heart into his work and done his best; what he has said or done otherwise shall give him no peace.   *— Emerson*

Every person has some splendid traits and if we confine our contacts so as to bring those traits into action, there is no need of ever being bored or irritated or indignant.

— Gelett Burgess

Not what we have, but what we use, not what we see, but what we choose, these are the things that mar or bless the sum of human happiness. — *Joseph Fort Newton*

Failures inspire pity, seldom admiration. The streets of the City of Failure are paved with alibis — some of which are absolutely perfect. — *Harry A. Earnshaw*

No clear-thinking or clear-seeing man or woman can be an apostle of despair. He alone fails who gives up and lies down. To get up each morning with the resolve to be happy; to take anew this attitude of mind whenever the dark or doleful thought presents itself, or whenever the bogeyman stalks into our room or across our path, is to set our own conditions to the events of each day. To do this is to condition circumstances instead of being conditioned by them. — *Ralph Waldo Trine*

Consciousness is the mere surface of our minds, of which, as of the earth, we do not know the inside, but only the crust. — *Schopenhauer*

The smallest actual good is better than the most magnificent promise of impossibilities. — *Macaulay*

If you are pleased at finding faults, you are displeased at finding perfections. — *Lavater*

As are families, so is society. If well ordered, well instructed, and well governed, they are the springs from which go forth the streams of national greatness and prosperity — of civil order and public happiness. — *Thayer*

Worldly fame is but a breath of wind that blows now this way, and now that, and changes name as it changes in direction.   — *Dante*

If you would but exchange places with the other fellow, how much more you could appreciate your own position.
— *Victor E. Gardner*

Public relations work is generally considered to be a relatively new development. Actually, the principles involved are as old as the ages. The 9th Verse of the 14th Chapter of First Corinthians reads: " Except ye utter by the tongue words easy to be understood, how shall it be known what is spoken? For ye shall speak into the air." With the Bible as our authority, how can we public relations people fail?   — *Clifford B. Reeves*

Happy salesmen not only multiply their volume of business and their income, they also multiply themselves.
— *Walter Russell*

The gentleman is solid mahogany; the fashionable man is only veneer.   — *J. G. Holland*

Grin and bear it. You can lighten a problem's weight, if you brighten up and smile. There is more power to a punch delivered in high spirits than one delivered in low spirits.   — *Douglas Fairbanks*

Hope knows not if fear speaks truth, nor fear whether hope be blind as she.   — *Swinburne*

True opinions can prevail only if the facts to which they refer are known; if they are not known, false ideas are just as effective as true ones, if not a little more effective.

— *Walter Lippmann*

A man must not think he can save himself the trouble of being a sensible man and a gentleman by going to his lawyer, any more than he can get himself a sound constitution by going to his doctor.   — *Ed. Howe*

If we have not quiet in our minds, outward comfort will do no more for us than a golden slipper on a gouty foot.

— *Bunyan*

Whoever in trouble and sorrow needs your help, give it to him. Whoever in anxiety or fear needs your friendship, give it to him. It isn't important whether he likes you. It isn't important whether you approve of his conduct. It isn't important what his creed or nationality may be.

— *E. N. West, D.D.*

Since nothing is settled until it is settled right, no matter how unlimited power a man may have, unless he exercises it fairly and justly his actions will return to plague him.

— *Frank A. Vanderlip*

You can't build a triumphant soul on hunger. All the more reason, then, why we who are not hungry nor hopelessly overborne by circumstance should surmount life and carry off a victory in the face of it. And more than pluck is needed to do that, more than just a philosophy believed with the mind. An inner experience of power is needed far beyond ourselves.   — *Harry Emerson Fosdick, D.D.*

No pain, no palm; no thorns, no throne; no gall, no glory;
no cross, no crown.   — *William Penn*

When young men are beginning life, the most important
period, it is often said, is that in which their habits are
formed. That is a very important period. But the period
in which the ideas of the young are formed and adopted is
more important still. For the ideal with which you go
forth to measure things determines the nature, so far as you
are concerned, of everything you meet.

— *Henry Ward Beecher*

Whosoever does not know how to recognize the faults
of great men is incapable of estimating their perfections.
— *Voltaire*

No gain is so certain as that which proceeds from the
economical use of what you already have.
— *Latin Proverb*

A decent man is not responsible for the vice or absurdity
of his profession; and he ought not on that account refuse
to pursue it; it is the custom of the country, there is money
to be got by it, a man must live in the world and make the
best of it, such as it is.   — *Montaigne*

No one is mediocre who has good sense and good sentiments.   — *Joubert*

I am only one, but still I am one; I cannot do everything,
but still I can do something; and because I cannot do
everything I will not refuse to do the something that I
can do.   — *Edward E. Hale*

That pleasure which is at once the most pure, the most elevating and the most intense, is derived, I maintain, from the contemplation of the beautiful.

— *Edgar Allan Poe*

When we build, let us think that we build forever. Let it not be for present delight, nor for present use alone; let it be such work as our descendants will thank us for, and let us think, as we lay stone on stone, that a time is to come when those stones will be held sacred because our hands have touched them, and that men will say as they look upon the labor and wrought substance of them, " See! this our fathers did for us."   — *Ruskin*

The sages do not consider that making no mistakes is a blessing. They believe, rather, that the great virtue of man lies in his ability to correct his mistakes and continually to make a new man of himself.   — *Wang Yang-Ming*

The invisible thing called a Good Name is made up of the breath of numbers that speak well of you.

— *Lord Halifax*

Man is to be trained chiefly by studying and by knowing man.   — *Gladstone*

Science is a first-rate piece of furniture for a man's upper chamber, if he has common sense on the ground floor.

— *Oliver Wendell Holmes*

No man can deliver the goods if his heart is heavier than the load.   — *Frank Irving Fletcher*

An inexhaustible good nature is one of the most precious gifts of heaven, spreading itself like oil over the troubled sea of thought, and keeping the mind smooth and equable in the roughest weather.   — *Washington Irving*

It is good to dream, but it is better to dream and work. Faith is mighty, but action is mightier. Deserving is helpful, but work and desire are invincible.

— *Thomas Robert Gaines*

There is no dependence that can be sure but a dependence upon one's self.   — *John Gay*

You can dissolve everything in the world, even a great fortune, into atoms. And the fundamental principles which govern the handling of a few postage stamps and of millions of dollars are exactly the same. They are the common law of business, and the whole practice of commerce is founded on them. They are so simple that a fool can't learn them; so hard that a lazy man won't.

— *Philip D. Armour*

You can't live on amusement. It is the froth on water — an inch deep and then the mud.   — *G. MacDonald*

What we do upon some great occasion will probably depend on what we already are; and what we are will be the result of previous years of self-discipline.

— *H. P. Liddon*

Merit is never so conspicuous as when coupled with an obscure origin, just as the moon never appears so lustrous as when it emerges from a cloud.   — *Bovée*

There is no law of progress. Our future is in our own hands, to make or to mar. It will be an uphill fight to the end, and would we have it otherwise? Let no one suppose that evolution will ever exempt us from struggles. " You forget," said the Devil, with a chuckle, " that I have been evolving too." — *Dean Inge*

1. Good men are not cheap.

2. Capital can do nothing without brains to direct it.

3. No general can fight his battles alone. He must depend upon his lieutenants, and his success depends upon his ability to secure the right man for the right place.

4. There is no such thing as luck.

5. Most men talk too much. Much of my success has been due to keeping my mouth shut.

6. The young man who wants to marry happily should pick out a good mother and marry one of her daughters — any one will do. — *J. Ogden Armour*

An open mind is all very well in its way, but it ought not to be so open that there is no keeping anything in or out of it. It should be capable of shutting its doors sometimes, or it may be found a little draughty. — *Samuel Butler*

All men seek one goal: success or happiness. The only way to achieve true success is to express yourself completely in service to society. First, have a definite, clear, practical ideal — a goal, an objective. Second, have the necessary means to achieve your ends — wisdom, money, materials and methods. Third, adjust all your means to that end. — *Aristotle*

I could not tread these perilous paths in safety, if I did not keep a saving sense of humor. — *Lord Nelson*

It takes a great deal of boldness mixed with a vast deal
of caution to acquire a great fortune; but then it takes ten
times as much wit to keep it after you have got it as it took
you to make it.   — *Rothschild*

Into the world of fears and hatreds we need to pour a
double portion of the spirit of confidence in the power of
love. " Not peace at any price, but love at all costs." All
our problems today resolve themselves into the problem of
learning to live together.   — *Canon Peter Green*

Imagination disposes of everything; it creates beauty,
justice, happiness, which is everything in this world.
                                            — *Pascal*

The democratic testament derives from Hamilton as well
as from Jefferson. It has two main characteristics. The
first is that the ordinary man believes in himself and in his
ability, along with his fellows, to govern his country. It is
when a people loses its self-confidence that it surrenders
its soul to a dictator or an oligarchy. . . . The second is
the belief, which is fundamental also in Christianity, of the
worth of every human soul — the worth, not the equality.
                                            — *John Buchan*

There is one thing stronger than all the armies in the
world, and that is an Idea whose time has come.
                                            — *Victor Hugo*

Our principles are the springs of our actions; our actions,
the springs of our happiness or misery. Too much care,
therefore, cannot be taken in forming our principles.
                                            — *Skelton*

Every man, at the bottom of his heart, wants to do right. But only he can do right who knows right; only he knows right who thinks right; only he thinks right who believes right. It takes an army of patriotic and order-obeying soldiers to win a war. But only by an army of public-spirited and law-abiding citizens can we hope to win the peace and maintain and remain a great nation. — *Tiorio*

Property is dear to men not only for the sensual pleasure it can afford, but also because it is the bulwark of all they hold dearest on earth, and above all else, because it is the safeguard of those they love most against misery and all physical distress. — *W. G. Sumner*

Those that dare lose a day are dangerously prodigal; those that dare misspend it, desperate.
— *Bishop Joseph Hall*

High ethical standards bring about efficient business methods. — *Watts*

There are two ways to interest a man or arouse his curiosity. One is to tell him something that he didn't know. The other is to remind him of something he has forgotten. — *A. E. N. Gray*

Take interest, I implore you, in those sacred dwellings which are designated by the expressive term, *laboratories*. Demand that they be multiplied and advanced. These are the temples of the future, temples of well-being and happiness . . . where humanity grows greater, stronger, better.
— *Louis Pasteur*

Democracy is eternal and human. It dignifies the human being; it respects humanity.   — *Thomas Mann*

He that would make real progess in knowledge must dedicate his age as well as youth, the latter growth as well as the first fruits, at the altar of truth.   — *Berkeley*

From the glow of enthusiasm I let the melody escape. I pursue it. Breathless I catch up with it. It flies again, it disappears, it plunges into a chaos of diverse emotions. I catch it again, I seize it, I embrace it with delight. . . . I multiply it by modulations, and at last I triumph in the first theme. There is the whole symphony.

— *Beethoven*

The democratic ideal is contradictory to both tyranny and ignorance. Men must be free not only to think, to speak and to worship, but to build within themselves, through education, a preparedness for their later years. Not every man can be a leader, but every man, however limited his natural capacities, can improve in the direction of better choices for himself and his children. If our education is good, then by educating all the people we give every person a better chance.

— *Dr. George D. Stoddard*

Hardship and opposition are the native soil of manhood and self-reliance.   — *Neal*

It will generally be found that men who are constantly lamenting their ill luck are only reaping the consequences of their own neglect, mismanagement, and improvidence, or want of application.   — *S. Smiles*

It is not the place that maketh the person, but the person that maketh the place honorable. — *Cicero*

Politeness is not always the sign of wisdom, but the want of it always leaves room for the suspicion of folly.

— *Landor*

I never knew a man escape failures, in either mind or body, who worked seven days in a week. — *Sir Robert Peel*

It is an undoubted truth that the less one has to do the less time one finds to do it in. One yawns, one procrastinates, one can do it when one will, and, therefore, one seldom does it at all; whereas those who have a great deal of business must (to use a vulgar expression) buckle to it; and then they always find time enough to do it in.

— *Lord Chesterfield*

People who cannot find time for recreation are obliged sooner or later to find time for illness.

— *John Wanamaker*

Man is still responsible. He must turn the alloy of modern experience into the steel of mastery and character. His success lies not with the stars but with himself. He must carry on the fight of self-correction and discipline. He must fight mediocrity as sin and live against the imperative of life's highest ideal. — *Frank Curtis Williams, D.D.*

When you cannot make pure goods and full weight, go to something else that is honest, even if it is breaking stone.

— *James Gamble*

The idea shared by many that life is a vale of tears is just as false as the idea shared by the great majority, the idea to which youth and health and riches incline you, that life is a place of entertainment.   — *Tolstoi*

There are few, if any, jobs in which ability alone is sufficient. Needed, also, are loyalty, sincerity, enthusiasm and team play.   — *Wm. B. Given, Jr.*

Washington and Lincoln were both idealists, and idealism is one of the greatest forces in the world. It makes seeming impossibilities possible and succeeds where prudence fails. But unless the idealist is brave and has the courage to face the truth, his idealism creates nothing.

— *Grenville Kleiser*

Management, in the sense of employer, is merely the agent for the public, the stockholders and the employees. It is management's job to preserve the balance fairly between all these interests, that each may have his fair share without imperiling the continuity of the effort upon which the whole depends.   — *James F. Bell*

Culture, in the deeper issues, is no smooth, placid, academic thing. It is no carefully arranged system of rules and theories. It is the passionate and imaginative instinct for things that are distinguished, heroic and rare. It is the subtilizing and deepening of the human spirit in presence of the final mystery.   — *John Cowper Powys*

Wherever man goes to dwell, his character goes with him.

— *African Proverb*

Talk happiness. The world is sad enough without your
woe.   — *Orison Swett Marden*

Some people bear three kinds of trouble — all they ever
had, all they have now, and all they expect to have.
                                               — *Edward E. Hale*

In modern business it is not the crook who is to be feared
most, it is the honest man who doesn't know what he is
doing.   — *Owen D. Young*

Conscience is a coward, and those faults it has not
strength to prevent, it seldom has justice enough to accuse.
                                               — *Goldsmith*

Liberty, in my opinion, is the only orthodoxy within the
limits of which art may express itself and flourish freely —
liberty that is the best of all things in the life of man, if it
is all one with wisdom and virtue.   — *Arturo Toscanini*

You cannot run away from a weakness. You must sometimes fight it out or perish; and if that be so, why not *now,*
and where you stand?   — *Robert Louis Stevenson*

Aggressive fighting for the right is the greatest sport in
the world.   — *Theodore Roosevelt*

The greatest ability in business is to get along with
others and influence their actions. A chip on the shoulder
is too heavy a piece of baggage to carry through life.
                                               — *John Hancock*

Character is power; it makes friends, draws patronage and support, and opens a sure way to wealth, honor and happiness.   — *J. Howe*

Two things profoundly impress me: The starry heavens above me and the moral law within me.
                                                — *Immanuel Kant*

Have you learned lessons only of those who admired you, and were tender with you, and stood aside for you? Have you not learned great lessons from those who rejected you, and braced themselves against you, or disputed the passage with you?   — *Walt Whitman*

If I were asked to sum up in a single phrase the main purpose of individual life I would express it as the enlargement of personality. Unless an individual can transcend the limits of class, sex, race, age and creed, his personality remains of necessity to that extent incomplete.
                                        — *F. W. Pethick-Lawrence*

Our greatest happiness does not depend on the condition of life in which chance has placed us, but is always the result of a good conscience, good health, occupation, and freedom in all just pursuits.   — *Thomas Jefferson*

Ideas are the roots of creation.   — *Ernest Dimnet*

Security is the priceless product of freedom. Only the strong can be secure, and only in freedom can men produce those material resources which can secure them from want at home and against aggression from abroad.
                                              — *B. E. Hutchinson*

It isn't the size of the dog in the fight, but the size of the fight in the dog, that counts!   *— Harry Howell*

Despite whatever agreement there may be between some of us, let us never forget that we are all working whole-heartedly and humbly for the same goal — a country of peace, abundance and prosperity — for all of our people of all races, of all groups — whoever they may be, wherever they may live.   *— Chester Bowles*

There is little that can withstand a man who can conquer himself.   *— Louis XIV*

I do not despise genius — indeed, I wish I had a basketful of it. But yet, after a great deal of experience and observation, I have become convinced that industry is a better horse to ride than genius. It may never carry any man as far as genius has carried individuals, but industry — patient, steady, intelligent industry — will carry thousands into comfort, and even celebrity; and this it does with absolute certainty.   *— Walter Lippmann*

God does not want us to do extraordinary things: He wants us to do ordinary things extraordinarily well.
                   — Bishop Gore

If there is righteousness in the heart there will be beauty in the character. If there be beauty in the character, there will be harmony in the home. If there is harmony in the home, there will be order in the nation. When there is order in the nation, there will be peace in the world.
                   — Chinese Proverb

Every man should make up his mind that if he expects
to succeed, he must give an honest return for the other
man's dollar.					— E. H. Harriman

Love never looks for faults, and whenever it discovers
them in others it throws over them the mantle of charity
and performs the two-fold miracle of making itself more
beautiful and the one in whom the fault is found more happy.
					— Edward H. Emmett

The true way to be humble is not to stoop till you are
smaller than yourself, but to stand at your real height
against some higher nature that shall show you what the
real smallness of your greatest greatness is.
					— Phillips Brooks

A ship, to run a straight course, can have but one pilot
and one steering wheel. The same applies to the successful
operation of a business. There cannot be a steering wheel
at every seat in an organization.			— Jules Ormont

Be true to the best you know. This is your high ideal.
If you do your best, you cannot do more. Do your best
every day and your life will gradually expand into satisfying
fullness. Cultivate the habit of doing one thing at a time
with quiet deliberateness. Always allow yourself a sufficient
margin of time in which to do your work well. Frequently
examine your working methods to discover and eliminate
unnecessary tension. Aim at poise, repose, and self-control.
The relaxed worker accomplishes most.
					— H. W. Dresser

It is part of the cure to wish to be cured.			— Seneca

An idea, to be suggestive, must come to the individual with the force of a revelation. — *William James*

There is no road too long to the man who advances deliberately and without undue haste; no honors too distant to the man who prepares himself for them with patience. — *Bruyère*

The resource of bigotry and intolerance, when convicted of error, is always the same; silenced by argument, it endeavors to silence by persecution, in old times by fire and sword, in modern days by the tongue. — *G. Simmons*

The way to gain a good reputation is to endeavor to be what you desire to appear. — *Socrates*

The words that a father speaks to his children in the privacy of home are not heard by the world, but, as in whispering galleries, they are clearly heard at the end, and by posterity. — *Richter*

Think wrongly, if you please; but in all cases think for yourself. — *Lessing*

What do I owe to my times, to my country, to my neighbors, to my friends? Such are the questions which a virtuous man ought often to ask himself. — *Lavater*

Gravity must be natural and simple; there must be urbanity and tenderness in it. A man must not formalize on everything. He who does so is a fool; and a grave fool is, perhaps, more injurious than a light fool. — *Cecil*

They who say all men are equal speak an undoubted truth, if they mean that all have an equal right to liberty, to their property, and to their protection of the laws. But they are mistaken if they think men are equal in their station and employments, since they are not so by their talents.

— *Voltaire*

Credit to the fullest the good qualities to be found in others, even though they may far outshine your own.

— *William M. Peck*

There can be no liberty that isn't earned.

— *Robert R. Young*

We must acknowledge that there is such a thing as " the pleasures of sin " — temptation would not be so strong if this were not true. The answer is to make our love of God stronger than all temptation, and in that way to lead the good Christian life.

— *Peter Marshall, D.D.*

Labor is discovered to be the grand conqueror, enriching and building up nations more surely than the proudest battles.

— *Channing*

The customs and fashions of men change like leaves on the bough, some of which go and others come.

— *Dante*

All noise is waste. So cultivate quietness in your speech, in your thoughts, in your emotions. Speak habitually low. Wait for attention and then your low words will be charged with dynamite.

— *Elbert Hubbard*

A decent boldness ever meets with friends.　　— *Homer*

Time stays long enough for anyone who will use it.
　　　　　　　　　　　　　　　　　　　— *Leonardo*

If all our misfortunes were laid in one common heap, whence everyone must take an equal portion, most people would be content to take their own and depart.
　　　　　　　　　　　　　　　　　　　— *Socrates*

The best way to keep good acts in memory is to refresh them with new.　　　　　　　　　　　　　— *Cato*

Behind an able man there are always other able men.
　　　　　　　　　　　　　　　　— *Chinese Proverb*

Cleverness is not wisdom.　　　　　　　　— *Euripides*

We know that man was created, not with an instinct for his own degradation, but imbued with the desire and the power for improvement to which, perchance, there may be no limit short of perfection even here in this life upon earth.
　　　　　　　　　　　　　　　　— *Andrew Carnegie*

I have three chairs in my house; one for solitude, two for friendship and three for society.　　　　— *Thoreau*

Our minds are like our stomachs; they are whetted by the change of their food, and variety supplies both with fresh appetite.　　　　　　　　　　　— *Quintilian*

Right is the only ingredient that can make might lasting in our policy and conduct toward each other, toward minorities and disadvantaged men or people — yes, even toward our enemies. — *R. H. Jackson*

Revenge is always the weak pleasure of a little and narrow mind. — *Juvenal*

That should be considered long which can be decided but once. — *Syrus*

Anything that interferes with individual progress ultimately will retard group progress. — *George H. Houston*

There is not, never has been, and never will be any substitute for productive work. No amount of legislation, no amount of money, borrowed or coined, no economic prestidigitation, governmental or otherwise, can, as such, increase by one iota the wealth of a nation or the standard of living of a people. Existing wealth or property can be and is being redistributed by law, but new wealth can be created only by men and by the man-made machines they guide. — *Philip D. Reed*

The whole story of human and personal progress is an unmitigated tale of denials today — denials of rest, denials of repose and comfort and ease and pleasure — that tomorrow may be richer. — *Carroll*

Real happiness is cheap enough, yet how dearly we pay for its counterfeit. — *H. Ballou*

Greatness has always been a mark to aim at. . . . It is not only inspiring but imperative to " think continually of those who were truly great." Soldiers on forgotten fields of battle, scientists in makeshift laboratories, stubborn idealists fighting to save a lost cause, teachers who would not be intimidated, tireless doctors, the anonymous army of dreamers and doers — all these by their very living fought for everyone. They sacrificed hours of ease for our casual comforts; they gave up safety for our security. Glorifying the heroic spirit of man, they added to our stature.

— *Louis Untermeyer*

Posterity! You will never know how much it cost the present generation to preserve your freedom. I hope you will make good use of it.　　　— *John Quincy Adams*

One fact stands out in bold relief in the history of man's attempts for betterment. That is that when compulsion is used, only resentment is aroused, and the end is not gained. Only through moral suasion and appeal to man's reason can a movement succeed.　　　— *Samuel Gompers*

Happy is he who has laid up in his youth, and held fast in all fortune, a genuine and passionate love for reading.

— *Rufus Choate*

Let the man who has to make his fortune in life remember this maxim: Attacking is the only secret. Dare and the world always yields; or if it beats you sometimes, dare it again and it will succumb.　　　— *Thackeray*

We are born for co-operation, as are the feet, the hands, the eyelids and the upper and lower jaws.

— *Marcus Aurelius*

All persons who bear the blessed title of " parent " have the personal responsibility to see that their children are growing up fully appreciative of the rights of God and their fellowmen.   — *J. Edgar Hoover*

The great scientific discoveries of the past hundred years have been as child's play compared with the titanic forces that will be released when man applies himself to the understanding and mastery of his own nature.

— *Melvin J. Evans*

The prudent, penniless beginner in the world labors for wages for a while, saves a surplus with which to buy tools or land for himself another while, and at length hires another new beginner to help him. This is the just, and generous and prosperous system which opens the way to all, gives hope to all, and consequently energy, and progress, and improvement of conditions to all.   — *Abraham Lincoln*

What a folly it is to dread the thought of throwing away life at once, and yet have no regard to throwing it away by parcels and piecemeal?   — *J. Howe*

Profit is the product of labor plus capital multiplied by management. You can hire the first two. The last must be inspired.   — *Fost*

Produce, produce! Were it but the pitifulest, infinitesimal fraction of a product, produce it in God's name. 'Tis the utmost thou hast in thee? Out with it then! Up, up! " Whatsoever thy hand findeth to do, do it with thy whole might."   —*Carlyle*

If a man empties his purse into his head, no one can take it away from him. An investment in knowledge always pays the best interest. — *Benjamin Franklin*

How majestic is naturalness. I have never met a man whom I really considered a great man who was not always natural and simple. Affectation is inevitably the mark of one not sure of himself. — *Charles G. Dawes*

Nature gives to every time and season some beauties of its own; and from morning to night, as from the cradle to the grave, is but a succession of changes so gentle and easy that we can scarcely mark their progress. — *Dickens*

The world of reality has its limits; the world of imagination is boundless. Not being able to enlarge the one, let us contract the other; for it is from their difference that all the evils arise which render us unhappy.

— *Jean Jacques Rousseau*

Use your gifts faithfully, and they shall be enlarged; practice what you know, and you shall attain to higher knowledge — *Arnold*

He who has injured thee was either stronger or weaker than thee. If weaker, spare him; if stronger, spare thyself. — *Seneca*

It is expedient to have an acquaintance with those who have looked into the world; who know men, understand business, and can give you good intelligence and good advice when they are wanted. — *B. Horne*

The product that will not sell *without* advertising, will not sell profitably *with* advertising.   — *Albert Lasker*

There is no personal charm so great as the charm of a cheerful temperament. It is a great error to suppose this comes entirely by nature — it comes quite as much by culture.   — *Henry Van Dyke*

Try to put well in practice what you already know; and in so doing, you will, in good time, discover the hidden things you now inquire about. Practice what you know, and it will help to make clear what now you do not know.

          — *Rembrandt*

The great gift of conversation lies less in displaying it ourselves than in drawing it out of others. He who leaves your company pleased with himself and his own cleverness is perfectly well pleased with you.   — *Bruyère*

The man who has not learned to say " No " will be a weak if not a wretched man as long as he lives.

          — *A. Maclaren*

Liberty is a thing of the spirit — to be free to worship, to think, to hold opinions, and to speak without fear — free to challenge wrong and oppression with surety of justice.

          — *Herbert Hoover*

Weak arguments are often thrust before my path; but although they are most unsubstantial, it is not easy to destroy them. There is not a more difficult feat known than to cut through a cushion with a sword.   — *Whately*

The everyday cares and duties, which men call drudgery, are the weights and counterpoises of the clock of time, giving its pendulum a true vibration, and its hands a regular motion; and when they cease to hang upon the wheels, the pendulum no longer swings, the hands no longer move, and the clock stands still. — *Longfellow*

To dally much with subjects mean and low, proves that the mind is weak or makes it so. — *Cowper*

Man ought always to have something that he prefers to life; otherwise life itself will seem to him tiresome and void. — *Seume*

Commonsense in an uncommon degree is what the world calls wisdom. — *Coleridge*

Vacillating people seldom succeed. They seldom win the solid respect of their fellows. Successful men and women are very careful in reaching decisions and very persistent and determined in action thereafter. — *L. G. Elliott*

Go make thy garden as fair as thou canst,
Thou workest never alone;
And he whose plot is next to thine
May see it and mend his own.
— *Robert Collyer*

" Nature " will not longer do the work unaided. Nature — if by that we mean blind and non-conscious forces — has, marvelously, produced man and consciousness; they must carry on the task to new results which she alone can never reach. — *Julian Huxley*

If one only wished to be happy, this could be easily accomplished; but we wish to be happier than other people, and this is always difficult, for we believe others to be happier than they are.   — *Montesquieu*

If you wish to travel far and fast, travel light. Take off all your envies, jealousies, unforgiveness, selfishness and fears.   — *Glenn Clark*

A man's strength cannot always be judged by his strongest actions; in many instances he is judged by his weakness.
          — *J. W. A. Henderson*

Whenever you are too selfishly looking out for your own interest, you have only *one* person working for you — yourself. When you help a dozen other people with their problems, you have a *dozen* people working with you.
          — *Wm. B. Given, Jr.*

The fellowship of country roads is a goodly one, and in that fellowship one can find lifelong comrades, passing acquaintances, and a wisdom that can be gained, perhaps, in no other way. It is the wisdom of fields and woods, compounded by the observing eye and the understanding heart; and it is a wisdom that does not grow old, that lasts until a man's hiking days are done, and then it brightens many a fireside hour.   — *Arthur Wallace Peach*

The effects of our actions may be postponed but they are never lost. There is an inevitable reward for good deeds and an inescapable punishment for bad. Meditate upon this truth, and seek always to earn good wages from Destiny.
          — *Wu Ming Fu*

The art of conversation is to be prompt without being stubborn; to refute without argument, and to clothe great matters in a motley garb.　　　　　*— Disraeli*

Life affords no higher pleasure than that of surmounting difficulties, passing from one step of success to another, forming new wishes and seeing them gratified.　He that labors in any great or laudable undertaking has his fatigues first supported by hope and afterward rewarded by joy.
　　　　　　　　　　— Johnson

Lampis the shipowner, on being asked how he acquired his great wealth, replied, " My great wealth was acquired with no difficulty, but my small wealth, my first gains, with much labor."　　　　　　　*— Epictetus*

Co-operation is spelled with two letters — WE.
　　　　　　　　— George M. Verity

If you have genius, industry will improve it; if you have none, industry will supply its place.　　*— Sir J. Reynolds*

A man is simple when his chief care is the wish to be what he ought to be; that is, honestly and naturally human. We may compare existence to raw material.　What it is matters less than what is made of it, as the value of a work of art lies in the flowering of a workman's skill.　True life is possible in social conditions the most diverse, and with natural gifts the most unequal.　It is not fortune or personal advantage, but our turning them to account, that constitutes the value of life.　Fame adds no more than does length of days; quality is the thing.　　　　*— Charles Wagner*

Commonsense does not ask an impossible chessboard, but takes the one before it and plays the game.

— *Wendell Phillips*

There is no wisdom save in truth. Truth is everlasting, but our ideas about truth are changeable. Only a little of the first fruits of wisdom, only a few fragments of the boundless heights, breadths and depths of truth, have I been able to gather. — *Martin Luther*

There are rules to luck, for to the wise not all is accident. Try, therefore, to help luck along. Some are satisfied to stand politely before the portals of Fortune and to await her bidding; better those who push forward, and who employ their enterprise, who on the wings of their worth and valor seek to embrace luck and effectively to gain her favor. And yet, properly seasoned, there is no other way to her but that of virtue and attentiveness; for none has more good luck, or more bad luck, than he has wisdom, or unwisdom.

— *Gracian*

It is better to go down on the great seas which human hearts were made to sail than to rot at the wharves in ignoble anchorage. — *Hamilton Wright Mabie*

Open your mouth and purse cautiously, and your stock of wealth and reputation shall, at least in repute, be great.

— *Zimmermann*

Is not he imprudent, who, seeing the tide making toward him apace, will sleep till the sea overwhelms him?

— *Tillotson*

We should every night call ourselves to an account: What infirmity have I mastered today? What passions opposed? What temptation resisted? What virtue acquired? Our vices will abate of themselves if they be brought every day to the shrift.
— *Seneca*

Natural resources of the world are distributed unequally among different countries and so is the population of the world. Distribution of resources is imperfectly related to the distribution of population, and trade between countries is the principal door to progress for all. It is peculiarly true of trade that the whole is greater than the sum of its parts.
— *John G. Winant*

I attribute the little I know to my not having been ashamed to ask for information, and to my rule of conversing with all descriptions of men on those topics that form their own peculiar professions and pursuits.
— *Locke*

As soon as a man climbs up to a high position, he must train his subordinates and trust them. They must relieve him of all small matters. He must be set free to think, to travel, to plan, to see important customers, to make improvements, to do all the big jobs of Leadership.
— *Herbert N. Casson*

Get to know two things about a man — how he earns his money and how he spends it — and you have the clue to his character, for you have a searchlight that shows up the inmost recesses of his soul. You know all you need to know about his standards, his motives, his driving desires, his real religion.
— *Robert James McCracken, D.D.*

Business is always interfering with pleasure — but it makes other pleasures possible.   — *William Feather*

We shall see but little if we require to understand what we see. How few things can a man measure with the tape of his understanding.   — *Thoreau*

I have three precious things which I hold fast and prize. The first is gentleness; the second is frugality; the third is humility, which keeps me from putting myself before others. Be gentle and you can be bold; be frugal and you can be liberal; avoid putting yourself before others and you can become a leader among men.   — *Lao-Tzu*

Employment, which Galen calls " nature's physician," is so essential to human happiness that indolence is justly considered as the mother of misery.   — *Burton*

Never make a decision yourself, if you don't have to. When one of your men asks you a question, ask him what is the answer. There is only one answer to many questions, and, therefore, this method answers many questions before they are asked. It not only develops your men, but also enables you to measure their ability.   — *Henry L. Doherty*

The American business man cannot consider his work done when he views the income balance in black at the end of an accounting period. It is necessary for him to trace the social incidence of the figures that appear in his statement and prove to the general public that his management has not only been profitable in the accounting sense but salutary in terms of popular benefits.   — *Colby M. Chester*

The sum of behavior is to retain a man's own dignity, without intruding upon the liberty of others.   — *Bacon*

It is folly for an eminent person to think of escaping censure, and a weakness to be affected by it.   All the illustrious persons of antiquity, and indeed of every age, have passed through this fiery persecution.   There is no defense against reproach but obscurity; it is a kind of concomitant to greatness.   — *Addison*

Fear is an acid which is pumped into one's atmosphere. It causes mental, moral and spiritual asphyxiation, and sometimes death; death to energy and all growth.
      — *Horace Fletcher*

Save a part of your income and begin now, for the man with a surplus controls circumstances and the man without a surplus is controlled by circumstances.
      — *Henry H. Buckley*

If the choice is given to us of liberty or security, we must scorn the latter with the proper contempt of free men and the sound judgment of wise men who know that liberty and security are not incompatible in the lives of honest men.
      — *James A. Farley*

Activity back of a very small idea will produce more than inactivity and the planning of genius.
      — *James A. Worsham*

When you cannot make up your mind which of two evenly balanced courses of action you should take — choose the bolder.   — *W. J. Slim*

No one is rich enough to do without a neighbor.

— *Danish Proverb*

When man learns to understand and control his own behavior as well as he is learning to understand and control
the behavior of crop plants and domestic animals, he may be
justified in believing that he has become civilized.

— *E. C. Stakman*

To the young I should offer two maxims: Don't accept
superficial solutions of difficult problems. It is better to do
a little good than much harm. I should not offer anything
more specific; every young person should decide on his or
her own credo.   — *Bertrand Russell*

The expectations of life depend upon diligence; the mechanic that would perfect his work must first sharpen his
tools.   — *Confucius*

No external advantages can supply the place of self-
reliance. The force of one's being, if it has any force, must
come from within. No one can safely imitate another; nor
by following in the footsteps of another can he ever gain
distinction or enjoy prosperity.   — *R. W. Clark*

Faith is to believe what we do not see; and the reward
of this faith is to see what we believe.   — *St. Augustine*

With labor and management working together in common cause — and not against each other — we can build and
produce and prosper, and defeat any threat, from whatever
source, against our own security and the peace of the world.

— *William Green*

We should not lose ourselves in vainglorious schemes for changing human nature all over the planet. Rather, we should learn to view ourselves with a sense of proportion and Christian humility before the enormous complexity of the world in which it has been given us to live.

— George F. Kennan

Stomachs shouldn't be waist baskets.

— P. K. Thomajan

A man to be truly free must accept responsibilities. To be relieved of responsibility means to lose freedom and liberty. Thus it can come about that the real enemy of man can be the state.   *— C. T. A. Sparks, D.D.*

As the essence of courage is to stake one's life on a possibility, so the essence of faith is to believe that the possibility exists.   *— William Salter*

Be not afraid of life. Believe that life is worth living, and your belief will help create the fact.

— William James

Power intoxicates men. When a man is intoxicated by alcohol he can recover, but when intoxicated by power he seldom recovers.   *— James F. Byrnes*

It is an excellent rule to be observed in all discussions, that men should give soft words and hard arguments; that they should not so much strive to silence or vex, as to convince their opponents.   *— Wilkens*

The trouble with worrying so much about your " security " in the future is that you feel so insecure in the present.   — *Harlan Miller*

When a man's desires are boundless, his labors are endless. They will set him a task he can never go through, and cut him out work he can never finish. The satisfaction he seeks is always absent, and the happiness he aims at is ever at a distance.   — *Balguy*

The discipline which corrects the baseness of worldly passions, fortifies the heart with virtuous principles, enlightens the mind with useful knowledge, furnishes it with enjoyment from within itself is of more consequence to real felicity than all the provisions we can make of the goods of fortune.   — *Blair*

Fate often puts all the material for happiness and prosperity into a man's hands just to see how miserable he can make himself with them.   — *Don Marquis*

We learn our virtues from the friends who love us; our faults from the enemy who hates us. We cannot easily discover our real character from a friend. He is a mirror, on which the warmth of our breath impedes the clearness of the reflection.   — *Richter*

Be avaricious of time; do not give any moment without receiving it in value; only allow hours to go from you with as much regret as you give to your gold; do not allow a single day to pass without increasing the treasure of your knowledge and virtue.   — *Le Tourneux*

There is no genius in life like the genius of energy and industry.   — *D. G. Mitchell*

Experience is a jewel, and it had need be so, for it is often purchased at an infinite rate.   — *Shakespeare*

In seeking a definition of democracy this one satisfies me best: democracy is a political expression of deeply felt religion. We are fallible. We certainly haven't attained perfection. But we can strive for it and the virtue is in the striving.   — *Carlos P. Romulo*

It seems to me we can never give up longing and wishing while we are thoroughly alive. There are certain things we feel to be beautiful and good, and we must hunger after them.   — *George Eliot*

'Tis not what man does which exalts him, but what man would do!   — *Robert Browning*

Falsehoods not only disagree with truths, but usually quarrel among themselves.   — *Daniel Webster*

Despite some of the horrors and barbarisms of modern life which appall and grieve us, life in the twentieth century undeniably has — or has the potentiality of — such richness, joy and adventure as were unknown to our ancestors except in their dreams.   — *Arthur H. Compton*

We are very much what others think of us. The reception our observations meet with gives us courage to proceed, or damps our efforts.   — *Hazlitt*

In proportion to the development of his individuality, each person becomes more valuable to others. There is a greater fullness of life about his own existence, and when there is more life in the units there is more in the mass which is composed of them.   — *John Stuart Mill*

Tolerance is the positive and cordial effort to understand another's beliefs, practices and habits without necessarily sharing or accepting them.   — *Joshua L. Liebman*

All men need something to poetize and idealize their life a little — something which they value for more than its use and which is a symbol of their emancipation from the mere materialism and drudgery of daily life.

— *Theodore E. Parker*

Society profits from every useful invention and from all the beneficent creative activities of individuals. The more good things others produce the more there is for us to share. The world profited more from Christopher Columbus' discovery than he did. The world has profited more from the inventions of Thomas A. Edison than he did. We are all beneficiaries of the achievements of the creative and business genius or talents of others.   — *George W. Maxey*

No institution which does not continually test its ideals, techniques and measure of accomplishment can claim real vitality.   — *Milton*

Commonsense and good nature will do a lot to make the pilgrimage of life not too difficult.

— *W. Somerset Maugham*

There is more to life than increasing its speed.
— *Mohandas K. Gandhi*

Do not imagine yourself to have what you have not; but take full account of the excellencies which you possess, and in gratitude remember how you would hanker after them, if you had them not. At the same time take care that in thus hugging them, you do not get into the habit of prizing them so much that without them you would be perturbed.
— *Marcus Aurelius*

Humility leads to strength and not to weakness. It is the highest form of self-respect to admit mistakes and to make amends for them.   — *John J. McCloy*

Sure! Heart's Desire will come true some day. But you must trust and, trusting, you must wait. You've but to vision to clear the brighter way, and see what isn't written on the slate. You must *believe* that happier, bigger things are coming toward you through the trying year. Your ears must hear the rustle of the wings of God's glad messengers, so dry your tears! Our trials are tests; our sorrows pave the way for fuller life when we have earned it so. Give rein to *faith* and hail the brighter day, and you shall come at last real joy to know.   — *Jerome P. Fleishman*

When an archer misses the mark he turns and looks for the fault within himself. Failure to hit the bull's-eye is never the fault of the target. To improve your aim improve yourself.   — *Gilbert Arland*

The effect of great and inevitable misfortune is to elevate those souls which it does not deprive of all virtue.
— *Guizot*

I do not think anybody in the world had so many friends
as I have had. However, I once had an enemy, a determined
enemy, and I have been trying all day to remember his
name.   *— Edward E. Hale*

A college education is not a quantitative body of memo-
rized knowledge salted away in a card file. It is a taste for
knowledge, a taste for philosophy, if you will; a capacity
to explore, to question, to perceive relationships, between
fields of knowledge and experience.

— A. Whitney Griswold

Nobody grows old by merely living a number of years.
People grow old only by deserting their ideals. Years
wrinkle the face, but to give up enthusiasm wrinkles the
soul. Worry, doubt, self-interest, fear, despair — these are
the long, long years that bow the head and turn the growing
spirit back to dust.   *— Watterson Lowe*

Every gathering of Americans — whether a few on the
porch of a crossroads store or massed thousands in a great
stadium — is the possessor of a potentially immeasurable
influence on the future.   *— Dwight D. Eisenhower*

Half of the harm that is done in this world is due to
people who want to feel important . . . they do not mean
to do harm . . . they are absorbed in the endless struggle
to think well of themselves.   *— T. S. Eliot*

If we want to utilize in the proper way and to the fullest
extent the products of man's intellect, we must develop that
part of man's being that is his heart and spirit.

— Ferdinand Pecora

When you approach a problem, strip yourself of preconceived opinions and prejudice, assemble and learn the facts of the situation, make the decision which seems to you to be the most honest, and then stick to it.

— *Chester Bowles*

The best advice I can give to any young man or young woman upon graduation from school can be summed up in exactly eight words, and they are — be honest with yourself and tell the truth. — *James A. Farley*

Adversity has made many a man great who, had he remained prosperous, would only have been rich.

— *Maurice Switzer*

The great scientists, as all great men, have not been concerned with fame. The joy of achievement that comes from finding something new in the universe is by far their greatest joy. A great research scientist is constantly discovering new things in his field. This is his reward. He knows how to spend long years in preparation and long hours in investigation, with no thought of public honor or reward. — *William P. King*

Opinions that are well rooted should grow and change like a healthy tree. — *Irving Batcheller*

" Point of view " must mean more than mere prejudice; it should express conclusions reached by that painful process known as thinking. And when new facts or factors are presented, free men should be as vigilant to change their viewpoints as to confirm them.

— *A. Mortimer Astbury*

You grow up the day you have your first real laugh —
at yourself. — *Ethel Barrymore*

An appealing personality is not something grafted on
from without. It is not like a coat of paint applied to a
building or cosmetics used on the face. It is expressed
through the body, the mind, the heart and the spirit. Although some persons seem to have been born with an ex-
ceptionally appealing personality, no one has a monopoly
on it. — *Edith Johnson*

Our life is what our thoughts make it. A man will
find that as he alters his thoughts toward things and other
people, things and other people will alter towards him.
— *James Allen*

For anything worth having one must pay the price; and
the price is always work, patience, love, self-sacrifice —
no paper currency, no promises to pay, but the gold of real
service. — *John Burroughs*

You can't hold a man down without staying down with
him. — *Booker T. Washington*

Democracy is a way of life. Democracy is sincerity,
friendliness, courage and tolerance. If your life and mine
do not exemplify these characteristics, we do not have the
right to call ourselves full-fledged citizens of the world's
greatest democracy. — *Melvin J. Evans*

Failure is only postponed success as long as courage
" coaches " ambition. The habit of persistence is the
habit of victory. — *Herbert Kaufman*

There are two kinds of discontent in this world; the discontent that works, and the discontent that wrings its hands. The first gets what it wants, and the second loses what it has. There's no cure for the first but success; and there's no cure at all for the second.

— *Gordon Graham*

🌿

Peace is not a relationship of Nations. It is a condition of mind brought about by a serenity of soul. Lasting peace can come only to peaceful people.

— *Horace E. De Lisser*

🌿

Time is the one thing that can never be retrieved. One may lose and regain a friend; one may lose and regain money; opportunity once spurned may come again; but the hours that are lost in idleness can never be brought back to be used in gainful pursuits. Most careers are made or marred in the hours after supper. — *C. R. Lawton*

🌿

When dealing with people, remember you are not dealing with creatures of logic, but with creatures of emotion, creatures bristling with prejudice and motivated by pride and vanity. — *Dale Carnegie*

🌿

I find that a great part of the information I have was acquired by looking up something and finding something else on the way. — *Franklin P. Adams*

🌿

We are forced to measure each moment partly in and of itself, for if everything is justified solely by the future, life becomes rather futile.

— *Malcolm R. Sutherland, Jr.*

Recipe for success: Be polite, prepare yourself for whatever you are asked to do, keep yourself tidy, be cheerful, don't be envious, be honest with yourself so you will be honest with others, be helpful, interest yourself in your job, don't pity yourself, be quick to praise, be loyal to your friends, avoid prejudices, be independent, interest yourself in politics, and read the newspapers.

— Bernard M. Baruch

If business is going to continue to sell through the decades, it must also promote an understanding of what made those products possible, what is necessary to a free market, and what our free market means to the individual liberty of each of us, to be certain that the freedoms under which this nation was born and brought to this point shall endure in the future . . . for America is the product of our freedoms.

— E. F. Hutton

Facts are the basis of policies but they do not create policies; they are only the stuff of which policies are made. Here is where synthesis comes in to build up the facts into useful knowledge which is wisdom, and it is wisdom that alone gives meaning and direction to life.

— Dr. Harold W. Dodds

Great men speak to us only so far as we have ears and souls to hear them; only so far as we have in us the roots, at least, of that which flowers out in them.

— Will Durant

Men who know themselves are no longer fools; they stand on the threshold of the Door of Wisdom.

— Havelock Ellis

We sometimes learn more from the sight of evil than
from an example of good; and it is well to accustom ourselves to profit by the evil which is so common, while that
which is good is so rare. — *Pascal*

The rules which experience suggests are better than those
which theorists elaborate in their libraries.
— *R. S. Storrs*

The belief that youth is the happiest time of life is
founded on a fallacy. The happiest person is the person
who thinks the most interesting thoughts, and we grow
happier as we grow older. — *William Lyon Phelps*

Every man is his own ancestor, and every man his own
heir. He devises his own future, and he inherits his own
past. — *H. F. Hedge*

There are no permanent changes because change itself
is permanent. It behooves the industrialist to research and
the investor to be vigilant. — *Ralph L. Woods*

Imagination, where it is truly creative, is a faculty, not
a quality; its seat is in the higher reason, and it is efficient
only as the servant of the will. Imagination, as too often
understood, is mere fantasy — the image-making power,
common to all who have the gift of dreams.
— *James Russell Lowell*

Idleness among children, as among men, is the root of
all evil, and leads to no other evil more certain than ill
temper. — *H. More*

If the spirit of business adventure is killed, this country
will cease to hold the foremost position in the world.
— *Andrew W. Mellon*

Certain of our blessings can never change. The important things of life will not perish. In whatever brave
new world emerges from this chaos, homes will be created,
good deeds will be done and sacrifices will be made. God
will be reverently worshipped in many a church and chapel.
Hospital, libraries and colleges will be organized and
endowed. The greatest things will endure — faith, hope
and love, and the moral nature in man.
— *Claude M. Fuess*

To think we are able is almost to be so; to determine
upon attainment is frequently attainment itself; earnest
resolution has often seemed to have about it almost a savor
of omnipotence. — *S. Smiles*

If thou art rich, then show the greatness of thy fortune;
or what is better, the greatness of thy soul, in the meekness
of thy conversation; condescend to men of low estate,
support the distressed, and patronize the neglected. Be
great. — *Sterne*

I never met a man I didn't like. — *Will Rogers*

Courage, energy and patience are the virtues which appeal
to my heart. — *Fritz Kreisler*

The only true happiness comes from squandering ourselves for a purpose. — *John Mason Brown*

In modern times, it is only by the power of association
that men of any calling exercise their due influence in the
community.   — *Elihu Root*

To rail at money, to wax indignant against it, is silly.
Money is nothing; its power is purely symbolical. Money
is the sign of liberty. To curse money is to curse liberty —
to curse life, which is nothing, if it be not free.

                                        — *De Gourmont*

Nothing is more unaccountable than the spell that often
lurks in a spoken word. A thought may be present to the
mind, and two minds conscious of the same thought, but
as long as it remains unspoken their familiar talk flows
quietly over the hidden idea.   — *Hawthorne*

We need greater virtues to sustain good than evil fortune.
                                    — *La Rochefoucauld*

Nothing in progression can rest on its original plan. We
might as well think of rocking a grown man in the cradle
of an infant.   — *Burke*

Those who can command themselves command others.
                                            — *Hazlitt*

Thought, not money, is the real business capital, and if
you know absolutely that what you are doing is right,
then you are bound to accomplish it in due season.
                                    — *Harvey S. Firestone*

The sincere alone can recognize sincerity.   — *Carlyle*

To most men experience is like the stern lights of a ship,
which illuminate only the track it has passed.

— Coleridge

Those who enjoy the large pleasures of advanced age
are those who have sacrificed the small pleasures of
youth.　　　　　*— Charles E. Carpenter*

We come nearest to the great when we are great in humility.　　　　　*— Rabindranath Tagore*

Poise is a big factor in a man's success. If I were a
young man just starting out, I would talk things over with
myself as a friend. I would set out to develop poise —
for it can be developed. A man should learn to stand,
what to do with his hands, what to do with his feet, look
his man straight in the eye, dress well and look well and
know he looks well. By dressing well I don't mean ex-
pensively, but neatly and in taste.　　　*— F. Edson White*

Sometimes when I consider what tremendous consequences come from little things — a chance word, a tap
on the shoulder, or a penny dropped on a newsstand — I
am tempted to think . . . there are no little things.

— Bruce Barton

That man lives twice who lives the first life well.

— Herrick

The true danger is when liberty is nibbled away, for
expedients, and by parts.　　　　　*— Burke*

Seeing much, suffering much and studying much, are the three pillars of learning. — *Disraeli*

Be methodical if you would succeed in business, or in anything. Have a work for every moment, and mind the moment's work. Whatever your calling, master all its bearings and details, its principles, instruments and applications. Method is essential if you would get through your work easily and with economy of time. — *W. Mathews*

It never occurs to fools that merit and good fortune are closely united. — *Goethe*

Countries are well cultivated, not as they are fertile, but as they are free. — *Montesquieu*

Intolerance has been the curse of every age and state. — *S. Davies*

Every man is a volume, if you know how to read him. — *Channing*

I know it is more agreeable to walk upon carpets than to lie upon dungeon floors; I know it is pleasant to have all the comforts and luxuries of civilization; but he who cares only for these things is worth no more than a butterfly contented and thoughtless upon a morning flower; and who ever thought of rearing a tombstone to a last-summer's butterfly? — *Henry Ward Beecher*

The real difference between men is energy. A strong will, a settled purpose, an invincible determination, can accomplish almost anything; and in this lies the distinction between great men and little men. — *Fuller*

The secret of a good memory is attention, and attention
to a subject depends upon our interest in it. We rarely
forget that which has made a deep impression on our
minds.   — *Tryon Edwards*

Maxims are to the intellect what laws are to actions:
They do not enlighten, but guide and direct, and though
themselves blind, are protecting.   — *Joubert*

Labor and trouble one can always get through alone, but
it takes two to be glad.   — *Ibsen*

Make the most of yourself, for that is all there is to you.
                                          — *Emerson*

One of the great arts in living is to learn the art of accurately appraising values. Everything that we think,
that we earn, that we have given to us, that in any way
touches our consciousness, has its own value. These values
are apt to change with the mood, with time, or because of
circumstances. We cannot safely tie to any material
value. The values of all material possessions change
continually, sometimes over night. Nothing of this nature
has any permanent set value. The real values are those
that stay by you, give you happiness and enrich you. They
are the human values.   — *George Matthew Adams*

Nothing more completely baffles one who is full of tricks
and duplicity than straightforward and simple integrity
in another.   — *Colton*

Learning makes a man fit company for himself.
                                          — *Young*

The true epic of our times is not " arms and the man,"
but " tools and the man," an infinitely wider kind of epic.
— *Carlyle*

There is but one bond of peace that is both permanent
and enriching: The increasing knowledge of the world in
which experiment occurs.   — *Walter Lippmann*

Your greatness is measured by your kindness —
Your education and intellect by your modesty —
Your ignorance is betrayed by your suspicions and
prejudices —
Your real caliber is measured by the consideration and
tolerance you have for others.   — *Wm. J. H. Boetcker*

Those who have few affairs to attend to are great speakers.
The less men think the more they talk.   — *Montesquieu*

The higher men climb the longer their working day.
And any young man with a streak of idleness in him may
better make up his mind at the beginning that mediocrity
will be his lot. Without immense, sustained effort he will
not climb high. And even though fortune or chance were
to lift him high, he would not stay there. For to keep at
the top is harder almost than to get there. There are no
office hours for leaders.   — *Cardinal Gibbons*

For everything you have missed you have gained something else.   — *Emerson*

Make good habits and they will make you.
— *Parks Cousins*

My general theory is that sound management is merely sound thinking coupled with effective execution. The problems of all businesses are essentially the same. Yet there is some justification for the man who insists that his business is different. It is different. Therefore, while the principles of management are undoubtedly the same throughout business, the applications differ of necessity, and it is in the application of principles which anyone can understand that management proves itself good or bad.

— Herman Nelson

Nothing is ever gained by winning an argument and losing a customer.   *— C. F. Norton*

We moderns with all our pride in our boasted civilization are back where that ancient world was when it first confronted Christ. We are desperately in need of salvation. It is a humiliating experience for an individual or a whole generation to have to acknowledge that it needs to be saved, but only a blind man can fail to see that that is our situation now.   *— Harry Emerson Fosdick, D.D.*

There is no darkness — but ignorance.

— Shakespeare

Everybody ought to do at least two things each day that he hates to do, just for practice.   *— William James*

Good fortune will elevate even petty minds, and give them the appearance of a certain greatness and stateliness, as from their high place they look down upon the world; but the truly noble and resolved spirit raises itself, and becomes more conspicuous in times of disaster and ill fortune.   *— Plutarch*

You cannot raise a man up by calling him down.
                              — *Wm. J. H. Boetcker*

To every problem there is already a solution, whether you know it or not. To every sum in mathematics there is already a correct answer, whether the mathematician has found it or not.

It should be encouraging to you to know that if you are now confronted by any kind of problem, personal or otherwise, there is a way to solve it, and you will find the way as rapidly and as surely as you apply to it the principles of divine truth.

It is possible to make each year bring with it a lasting gift to add to the fullness of experience, to be treasured up, savored, and remembered. They need not be startling, these gifts of the years; they may be things that lie within the reach of all.   — *Grenville Kleiser*

Only those who have the patience to do simple things perfectly will acquire the skill to do difficult things easily.
                              — *Schiller*

The busy world sometimes forgets that we need sympathy in our happiness as well as in our sorrow.
                              — *C. Hanford Henderson*

When the interval between the intellectual classes and the practical classes is too great, the former will possess no influence, the latter will reap no benefit.
                              — *Thomas Buckle*

The father who does not teach his son his duties is equally guilty with the son who neglects them.   — *Confucius*

A politician thinks of the next election; a statesman, of the next generation. — *J. F. Clarke*

The greatest pride, or the greatest despondency, is the greatest ignorance of one's self. — *Spinoza*

Life never becomes a habit to me. It's always a marvel. — *Katherine Mansfield*

It is the paradox of life that the way to miss pleasure is to seek it first. The very first condition of lasting happiness is that a life should be full of purpose, aiming at something outside self. As a matter of experience, we find that true happiness comes in seeking other things, in the manifold activities of life, in the healthful outgoing of all human powers. — *Hugh Black*

Let us read with method, and propose to ourselves an end to what our studies may point. The use of reading is to aid us in thinking. — *Edward Gibbon*

If we begin with certainties, we shall end in doubts; but if we begin with doubts, and are patient in them, we shall end in certainties. — *Bacon*

Men are often capable of greater things than they perform. They are sent into the world with bills of credit, and seldom draw to their full extent. — *Walpole*

A man who has committed a mistake and doesn't correct it is committing another mistake. — *Confucius*

Well arranged time is the surest mark of a well arranged mind.   — *Pitman*

There is nothing so useful to man in general, nor so beneficial to particular societies and individuals, as trade. This is that alma mater, at whose plentiful breast all mankind are nourished.   — *Henry Fielding*

Many men who spend an hour a day in physical exercises to keep fit refuse to spend an hour a week in the cultivation of their morals and their ethics. We have put so much stress on developing muscles and so little emphasis on developing our souls that our children are beginning to doubt if we have any souls at all.

— *Allen E. Claxton, D.D.*

Set the course of your lives by the three stars — sincerity, courage, unselfishness. From these flow a host of other virtues. . . . He who follows them and does not seek success, will attain the highest type of success, that which lies in the esteem of those among whom he dwells.

— *Dr. Monroe E. Deutsch*

People seldom improve when they have no other model but themselves to copy after.   — *Goldsmith*

Selfishness is the root and source of all natural and moral evils.   — *Emmons*

The man who cannot enjoy his own natural gifts in silence, and find his reward in the exercise of them, will generally find himself badly off.   — *Goethe*

It is not only what we do, but also what we do not do,
for which we are accountable.   — *Molière*

Half the secret of getting along with people is consideration of their views; the other half is tolerance in one's own
views.   — *Daniel Frohman*

Courage and perseverance have a magical talisman, before
which difficulties disappear and obstacles vanish into air.
                              — *John Quincy Adams*

Γ

The worth of a state, in the long run, is the worth of the
individuals composing it.   — *John Stuart Mill*

Γ

The pulpit will not fulfill its function by merely thunder-
ing " Thou shalt nots." The church, together with the
home, the school and all community agencies must provide
constructive and creative activities for parents as well as for
youth.   — *Ralph W. Sockman, D.D.*

Γ

Life, with all its sorrows, cares, perplexities and heart-
breaks, is more interesting than bovine placidity, hence
more desirable. The more interesting it is, the happier it is.
                              — *William Lyon Phelps*

Γ

Such as thy words are, such will thine affections be esteemed; and such as thine affections, will be thy deeds;
and such as thy deeds will be thy life.   — *Socrates*

Every moment of resistance to temptation is a victory.
                              — *Faber*

We protract the career of time by employment, we lengthen the duration of our lives by wise thoughts and useful actions. Life to him who wishes not to have lived in vain is thought and action. — *Zimmermann*

The eyes of other people are the eyes that ruin us. If all but myself were blind, I should want neither fine clothes, fine houses, nor fine furniture. — *Benjamin Franklin*

In the scientific world I find just that disinterested devotion to great ends that I hope will spread at last through the entire range of human activity. — *H. G. Wells*

Where secrecy or mystery begins, vice or roguery is not far off. — *Johnson*

He that fancies himself very enlightened, because he sees the deficiencies of others, may be very ignorant, because he has not studied his own. — *Bulwer*

Every violation of truth is a stab at the health of human society. — *Emerson*

Learning without thought is labor lost; thought without learning is perilous. — *Confucius*

I had six honest serving men — they taught me all I knew: Their names were Where and What and When — and Why and How and Who. — *Kipling*

The farther we get away from the land, the greater our insecurity. — *Henry Ford*

The origin of civilization is man's determination to do
nothing for himself which he can get done for him.

— *H. C. Bailey*

Silence and reserve suggest latent power. What some
men think has more effect than what others say.

— *Lord Chesterfield*

When thought is too weak to be simply expressed, it's
clear proof that it should be rejected.   — *Vauvanargues*

We do not choose our own parts in life, and have nothing
to do with those parts. Our duty is confined to playing
them well.   — *Epictetus*

Economy is half the battle of life; it is not so hard to
earn money as to spend it well.   — *Spurgeon*

Experience has convinced me that there is a thousand
times more goodness, wisdom, and love in the world than
men imagine.   — *Gehles*

Nothing can be proposed so wild or so absurd as not to
find a party, and often a very large party, to espouse it.

— *Cecil*

Men are not to be judged by their looks, habits, and
appearances; but by the character of their lives and con-
versations, and by their works. It is better to be praised
by one's own works than by the words of another.

— *L'Estrange*

Better be unborn than untaught, for ignorance is the root of misfortune.
— *Plato*

It is well for us to remember that America is what it is today because alone of all the countries of the world, we have expanded under those Siamese twins, political and economic freedom.
— *W. Alton Jones*

Men who do things without being told draw the most wages.
— *Edwin H. Stuart*

We are told that there are no new frontiers to conquer, but this is the attitude of those who despair today, who despaired yesterday, and who will still be at it during the rest of their lives. We dare not follow such an attitude of mind. It has been well stated " that the pioneer is a creature not of time but of spirit."
— *Myers Y. Cooper*

I have always observed that to succeed in the world one should appear like a fool but be wise.
— *Montesquieu*

He that will not reason is a bigot; he that cannot reason is a fool; and he that dares not reason is a slave.
— *Sir William Drummond*

Protestant, Roman Catholic and Jewish leaders should set one example to the world by getting together in conference and co-operation instead of resorting to controversy and conflict.
— *Ralph W. Sockman, D.D.*

To live in hearts we leave behind is not to die.
— *Campbell*

The social problems raised by science must be faced and solved by the social sciences and the humanities. . . . If, in the long run, science is going to continue to create rather than destroy, it must be supplemented by the knowledge and wisdom to be gained from the other branches of the curriculum. For it should not be forgotten that the sacred human rights which we fought Hitler to preserve, stem from the teachings of these subjects to which we confess allegiance, but which we rarely understand completely or follow sincerely.   *— Harold W. Dodds*

Suspicion is no less an enemy to virtue than to happiness. He that is already corrupt is naturally suspicious, and he that becomes suspicious will quickly be corrupt.

— Johnson

The successful people are the ones who can think up stuff for the rest of the world to keep busy at.

— Don Marquis

The outstanding characteristic of the relationship between the subordinate and his superiors is his dependence upon them for the satisfaction of his needs.

— Douglas McGregor

Great men are very apt to have great faults; and the faults appear the greater by their contrast with their excellencies.   *— G. Simmons*

Man must be disappointed with the lesser things of life before he can comprehend the full value of the greater.

— Bulwer

Kind looks, kind words, kind acts, and warm hand-shakes — these are secondary means of grace when men are in trouble and are fighting their unseen battles.

— *John Hall*

🥀

Do not attempt to do a thing unless you are sure of yourself; but do not relinquish it simply because someone else is not sure of you. — *Stewart E. White*

🥀

Those who compare the age in which their lot has fallen with a golden age which exists only in imagination may talk of degeneracy and decay, but no man who is correctly informed as to the past will be disposed to take a morose or desponding view of the present. — *Thomas Macaulay*

🥀

Perseverance is more prevailing than violence; and many things which cannot be overcome when they are together yield themselves up when taken little by little.

— *Plutarch*

🥀

It is a hard rule of life, and I believe a healthy one, that no great plan is ever carried out without meeting and overcoming endless obstacles that come up to try the skill of man's hand, the quality of his courage, and the endurance of his faith. — *Donald Douglas*

🥀

The best leaders are those most interested in surrounding themselves with assistants and associates smarter than they are — being frank in admitting this — and willing to pay for such talents. — *Amos Parrish*

🥀

That state is best ordered when the wicked have no command, and the good have. — *Pittacus*

The worst obstructionist in any community is not the
man who is opposed to doing anything, but the man who
will not do what he can because he cannot do what he would
like to do.   — *J. L. Long*

The record seems to show that free enterprise is the
only system of government in the world that is not on trial.
If it is on trial, why is America being called upon to save
the world from economic chaos?   — *Walter S. Gifford*

We shall have " better business " when everyone realizes
that while it pays to invest money in their industries and
develop natural resources, it pays still higher dividends to
improve mankind and develop human resources.
                                        — *H. E. Steiner*

The difference between failure and success is doing a thing
nearly right and doing it exactly right.
                                        — *Edward C. Simmons*

It's what each of us sows, and how, that gives to us
character and prestige. Seeds of kindness, goodwill, and
human understanding, planted in fertile soil, spring up
into deathless friendships, big deeds of worth, and a memory
that will not soon fade out. We are all sowers of seeds —
and let us never forget it!
                                        — *George Matthew Adams*

Those unacquainted with the world take pleasure in intimacy with great men; those who are wiser fear the
consequences.   — *Horace*

Cannot our ethical system be taught upon a non-sectarian basis in all schools, squaring it up with the sciences to the end that our boys and girls, when they emerge, are not ripe fruit for the disbelieving skeptics and the intellectual exhibitionists? — *Andrew V. Clements*

Little progress can be made by merely attempting to repress what is evil; our great hope lies in developing what is good. — *Calvin Coolidge*

He that sympathizes in all the happiness of others, perhaps himself enjoys the safest happiness; and he that is warned by the folly of others has perhaps attained the soundest wisdom. — *Colton*

One cool judgment is worth a thousand hasty counsels. — *Woodrow Wilson*

Happy the man who has learned the cause of things and has put under his feet all fear, inexorable fate, and the noisy strife of the hell of greed. — *Virgil*

Solitary reading will enable a man to stuff himself with information, but without conversation his mind will become like a pond without an outlet — a mass of unhealthy stagnature. It is not enough to harvest knowledge by study; the wind of talk must winnow it and blow away the chaff. Then will the clear, bright grains of wisdom be garnered, for our own use or that of others. — *William Matthews*

More than half the difficulties of the world would be allayed or removed by the exhibition of good temper. — *Sir Arthur Helps*

A warning is like an alarm clock: If you don't pay any
heed to its ringing, some day it will go off and you won't
hear it.   — *Harris*

A man would do well to carry a pencil in his pocket, and
write down the thoughts of the moment.   Those that come
unsought for are commonly the most valuable, and should
be secured, because they seldom return.   — *Bacon*

We must not let go manifest truths because we cannot
answer all questions about them.   — *Jeremy Collier*

Bad laws are the worst sort of tyranny.   — *Burke*

Nothing in this world is so good as usefulness.   It binds
your fellow creatures to you, and you to them; it tends
to the improvement of your own character and gives you a
real importance in society, much beyond what any artificial
station can bestow.   — *B. C. Brodie*

Confidence is a plant of slow growth in an aged bosom.
                                           — *William Pitt*

Wealth brings with it its own checks and balances.   The
basis of political economy is noninterference.   The only
safe rule is found in the self-adjusting meter of demand
and supply.   Open the doors of opportunity to talent and
virtue and they will do themselves justice, and property will
not be in bad hands.   In a free and just commonwealth,
property rushes from the idle and imbecile to the industrious, brave and persevering.   — *Emerson*

All who have meditated on the art of governing mankind have been convinced that the fate of empires depends on the education of youth. — *Aristotle*

It is well to think well; it is divine to act well.
— *Horace Mann*

Benjamin Franklin went through life an altered man because he once paid too dearly for a penny whistle. My concern springs usually from a deeper source, to wit, from having bought a whistle when I did not want one.
— *Robert Louis Stevenson*

Self-defense is Nature's oldest law. — *John Dryden*

Order is the sanity of the mind, the health of the body, the peace of the city, the security of the state. As the beams to a house, as the bones to the body, so is order to all things. — *Southey*

Every man who loves his country, or wishes well to the best interests of society, will show himself a decided friend not only of morality and the laws, but of religious institutions, and honorably bear his part in supporting them.
— *J. Hawes*

It is well to read everything of something, and something of everything. — *Henry Brougham*

Profit is the ignition system of our economic engine.
— *Charles Sawyer*

When a man is wrong and won't admit it, he always gets angry. — *Haliburton*

Better be despised for too anxious apprehensions, than ruined by too confident security. — *Burke*

Religion, properly understood, should be largely independent of seasons and places. Religion should not surrender to control by alternations of climate. There is something lacking in a religion which the summertime can destroy. — *Philip S. Watters, D.D.*

Everything for which democracy stands is based on religious faith. Neither enlightened self-interest nor practical ethics can make an effective substitute.
— *Elbert D. Thomas*

The well-meaning people who talk of education as if it were a substance distributable by coupon in large or small quantities never exhibit any understanding of the truth that you cannot teach anybody anything that he does not want to learn. — *George Sampson*

The wise man does not expose himself needlessly to danger, since there are few things for which he cares sufficiently; but he is willing, in great crises, to give even his life — knowing that under certain conditions it is not worth while to live. — *Aristotle*

What we do best or most perfectly is what we have most thoroughly learned by the longest practice, and at length it falls from us without our notice, as a leaf from a tree.
— *Thoreau*

We cannot all be masters. — *Shakespeare*

No man is worth his salt who is not ready at all times to risk his body, to risk his well-being, to risk his life, in a great cause. — *Theodore Roosevelt*

Morale is faith in the man at the top.
— *Albert S. Johnstone*

By eating what is sufficient man is enabled to work; he is hindered from working and becomes heavy, idle, and stupid if he takes too much. As to bodily distempers occasioned by excess, there is no end of them.
— *T. Jones*

Truth will rise above falsehood as oil above water.
— *Cervantes*

Justice is as strictly due between neighbor nations as between neighbor citizens. — *Benjamin Franklin*

Thought is the first faculty of man; to express it is one of his first desires; to spread it, his dearest privilege.
— *Abbé Raynal*

There exists a passion for comprehension, just as there exists a passion for music. That passion is rather common in children, but gets lost in most people later on. Without this passion there would be neither mathematics nor natural science. — *Albert Einstein*

Unintelligent people always look for a scapegoat.

— *Ernest Bevin*

In the lottery of life there are more prizes drawn than blanks, and to one misfortune there are fifty advantages. Despondency is the most unprofitable feeling a man can indulge in. — *De Witt Talmage*

Thoughts lead on to purposes; purposes go forth in action; actions form habits; habits decide character; and character fixes our destiny. — *Tryon Edwards*

The conscience of children is formed by the influences that surround them; their notions of good and evil are the result of the moral atmosphere they breathe. — *Richter*

" Man " is the principal syllable in Management.

— *C. T. McKenzie*

When the dictators and the opportunists are gone, the cross will still stand before us and something in us will say, " That is the real thing." — *Ralph W. Sockman, D.D.*

I would have a man generous to his country, his neighbors, his kindred, his friends, and most of all his poor friends. Not like some who are most lavish with those who are able to give most to them. — *Pliny*

To will and not to do when there is opportunity, is in reality not to will; and to love what is good and not to do it, when it is possible, is in reality not to love it.

— *Swedenborg*

In all the affairs of life let it be your great care, not to hurt your mind, or offend your judgment. And this rule, if observed carefully in your deportment, will be a mighty security to you in your undertakings.   *— Epictetus*

There is no witness so terrible — no accuser so powerful as conscience which dwells within us.   *— Sophocles*

There are different kinds of curiosity; one of interest, which causes us to learn that which would be useful to us; and the other of pride, which springs from a desire to know that of which others are ignorant.   *— La Rochefoucauld*

Debt is the secret foe of thrift, as vice and idleness are its open foes. The debt-habit is the twin brother of poverty.   *— T. T. Munger*

The man that makes a character, makes foes.

  — Young

Thinking, for many, is life's most painful activity. For the fortunate others, there's not much in life that approaches it.   *— Carth Cate*

No one grows old by living — only by losing interest in living.   *— Marie Ray*

Agreement makes us soft and complacent; disagreement brings out our strength. Our real enemies are the people who make us feel so good that we are slowly, but inexorably, pulled down into the quicksand of smugness and self-satisfaction.   *— Sydney J. Harris*

I firmly believe that the army of persons who urge
greater centralization of authority and greater dependence
upon the federal treasury, are really more dangerous to our
form of government than any external threat that can possibly be arrayed against us. — *Dwight D. Eisenhower*

Back of ninety-nine out of one hundred assertions that
a thing cannot be done is nothing but the unwillingness to
do it. — *William Feather*

Freedom without obligation is anarchy; freedom with
obligation is democracy. — *Earl Riney*

Successful salesmanship is 90% preparation and 10%
presentation. — *Bertrand R. Canfield*

In making a living today, many no longer leave room for
life. — *Joseph Sizoo, D.D.*

To talk about the need for perfection in man is to talk
about the need for another species. The essence of man
is imperfection. Imperfection and blazing contradictions
— between mixed good and evil, altruism and selfishness,
co-operativeness and combativeness, optimism and fatalism,
affirmation and negation. — *Norman Cousins*

Woman knows what Man has too long forgotten, that
the ultimate economic and spiritual unit of any civilization
is still the family. — *Clare Booth Luce*

The trouble with some of us is that we have been inocu-
lated with small doses of Christianity which keep us from
catching the real thing. — *Dr. Leslie D. Weatherhead*

Most of us never recognize opportunity until it goes to work in our competitor's business.　　　*— P. L. Andarr*

Falsehood often lurks upon the tongue of him, who, by self-praise, seeks to enhance his value in the eyes of others.
— James Gordon Bennett

The great accomplishments of man have resulted from the transmission of ideas and enthusiasm.
— Thomas J. Watson

One hand cannot applaud alone.　　*— Arabian Proverb*

There is no kind of peace which may be purchased on the bargain counter.　　*— Carey Williams*

Wisdom is knowing when to speak your mind and when to mind your speech.　　*— Evangel*

All genuine progress results from finding new facts. No law can be passed to make an acre yield 300 bushels. God has already established the laws. It is for us to discover them, and to learn the facts by which we can obey them.
— Wheeler McMillen

Of all the forces that make for a better world, none is so indispensable, none so powerful, as hope. Without hope men are only half alive. With hope they dream and think and work.　　*— Charles Sawyer*

Thinking is one thing no one has ever been able to tax.
— *Charles F. Kettering*

The United States is the richest, and, both actually and potentially, the most powerful state on the globe. She has much to give to the world; indeed, to her hands is chiefly entrusted the shaping of the future. If democracy in the broadest and truest sense is to survive, it will be mainly because of her guardianship.
— *Lord Tweedsmuir*

Civilization ceases when we no longer respect and no longer put into their correct places the fundamental values, such as work, family and country; such as the individual, honor and religion.
— *R. P. Lebret*

Shun idleness. It is a rust that attaches itself to the most brilliant metals.
— *Voltaire*

He who sacrifices his conscience to ambition burns a picture to obtain the ashes.
— *Chinese Proverb*

Pride is a deeply rooted ailment of the soul. The penalty is misery; the remedy lies in the sincere, life-long cultivation of humility, which means true self-evaluation and a proper perspective toward past, present and future.
— *Robert Gordis*

He who allows his day to pass by without practicing generosity and enjoying life's pleasures is like a blacksmith's bellows — he breathes but does not live.
— *Sanskrit Proverb*

Every man is to be respected as an absolute end in himself; and it is a crime against the dignity that belongs to him as a human being, to use him as a mere means for some external purpose. *— Immanuel Kant*

Someone said of nations — but it might well have been said of individuals, too — that they require of their neighbors " something sufficiently akin to be understood, something sufficiently different to provoke attention, and something sufficiently great to command admiration."

— Phoebe Low

The glow of one warm thought is to me worth more than money. *— Thomas Jefferson*

Faith is indispensable and the world at times does not seem to have quite enough of it. It has and can accomplish what seems to be the impossible. Wars have been started and men and nations lost for the lack of faith. Faith starts from the individual and builds men and nations. America was built by and on the faith of our ancestors.

— G. A. Sandberg

Whatever necessity lays upon thee, endure; whatever she commands, do. *— Goethe*

Did you ever hear of a man who had striven all his life faithfully and singly toward an object, and in no measure obtained it? If a man constantly aspires, is he not elevated? Did ever a man try heroism, magnanimity, truth, sincerity, and find that there was no advantage in them — that it was a vain endeavor? *— Thoreau*

There is no power on earth more formidable than the
truth.   — *M. Runbeck*

I tell you that as long as I can conceive something better
than myself I cannot be easy unless I am striving to
bring it into existence or clearing the way for it.
                                    — *George Bernard Shaw*

This is no time for ease and comfort. It is the time to
dare and endure.   — *Winston Churchill*

Happiness is not so much in having or sharing. We
make a living by what we get, but we make a life by what
we give.   — *Norman MacEwan*

Life is very interesting, if you make mistakes.
                                    — *Georges Carpentier*

My reading of history convinces me that most bad government results from too much government.
                                        — *Thomas Jefferson*

To live is to function. That is all there is in living.
                                — *Oliver Wendell Holmes*

He who will not reason, is a bigot; he who cannot is a
fool; and he who dares not, is a slave.
                                    — *William Drummond*

A hated government does not long survive.   — *Seneca*

If you would win a man to your cause, first convince him that you are his true friend. Therein is a drop of honey that catches his heart, which, say what he will, is the greatest highroad to his reason, and which when once gained, you will find but little trouble in convincing his judgment of the justice of your cause, if, indeed, that cause be really a just one. On the contrary, assume to dictate to his judgment, or to command his action, or to make him as one to be shunned or despised, and he will retreat within himself, close all the avenues to his head and heart; and though your cause be naked truth itself, transformed to the heaviest lance, harder than steel and sharper than steel can be made, and though you throw it with more than Herculean force and precision, you shall be no more able to pierce him than to penetrate the hard shell of a tortoise with a rye straw. — *Abraham Lincoln*

A life of ease is a difficult pursuit. — *Cowper*

It takes a lot of thought and effort and downright determination to be agreeable. — *Ray D. Everson*

I believe that the ultimate object of all activities in a republic should be the development of the manhood of its citizens. — *John D. Rockefeller, Jr.*

A miser grows rich by seeming poor; an extravagant man grows poor by seeming rich. — *Shakespeare*

A career, like a business, must be budgeted. When it is necessary, the budget can be adjusted to meet changing conditions. A life that hasn't a definite plan is likely to become driftwood. — *David Sarnoff*

There is a single reason why 99 out of 100 average business men never become leaders. That is their *unwillingness to pay the price of responsibility*. By the price of responsibility I mean hard driving, continual work . . . the courage to make decisions, to stand the gaff . . . the scourging honesty of *never fooling yourself about yourself*. You travel the road to leadership heavily laden. While the nine-to-five-o'clock worker takes his ease, you are " toiling upward through the night." Laboriously you extend your mental frontiers. Any new effort, the psychologists say, wears a new groove in the brain. And the grooves that lead to the heights are not made between nine and five. They are burned in by midnight oil.

— *Owen D. Young*

Life is too short to be little.   — *Disraeli*

As the gardener, by severe pruning, forces the sap of the tree into one or two vigorous limbs, so should you stop off your miscellaneous activity and concentrate your force on one or a few points.   — *Emerson*

Prejudice, ignorance, bitterness and, above all, selfishness are the great obstacles to peace in people, groups and nations.   — *Joseph A. Tytheridge, D.D.*

These three things — work, will, success — fill human existences. Will opens the door to success, both brilliant and happy. Work passes these doors, and at the end of the journey success comes in to crown one's efforts.

— *Louis Pasteur*

The proper study of mankind is man.   — *Pope*

Many receive a criticism and think it is fine; think they got their money's worth; think well of the teacher for it, and then go on with their work just the same as before. That is the reason much of the wisdom of Plato is still locked up in the pages of Plato.   *— Robert Henri*

The man who trusts men will make fewer mistakes than he who distrusts them.   *— Cavour*

On the occasion of every accident that befalls you, remember to turn to yourself and inquire what power you have for turning it to use.   *— Epictetus*

There is one rule for industrialists and that is: Make the best quality of goods possible at the lowest cost possible, paying the highest wages possible.   *— Henry Ford*

I believe the intelligent and consistent practice of the Christian faith can solve any personal problem. This conviction is based on hundreds of modern people who have passed through our conference rooms in a church at the heart of New York City. People must be taught to realize that in faith they have a mechanism and power by which they can actually live victorious, happy and successful lives.
   — Norman Vincent Peale, D.D.

The interesting and inspiring thing about America is that she asks nothing for herself except what she has a right to ask for humanity itself.   *— Woodrow Wilson*

Prosperity cannot be divorced from humanity.
   — Calvin Coolidge

Ideals are like stars; you will not succeed in touching them with your hands. But like the seafaring man on the desert of waters, you choose them as your guides, and following them you will reach your destiny.

— *Carl Schurz*

Strange is our situation here upon earth. Each of us comes for a short visit, not knowing why, yet sometimes seeming to divine a purpose.

From the standpoint of daily life, however, there is one thing we do know: that man is here for the sake of other men — above all for those upon whose smile and well-being our own happiness depends, and also for the countless unknown souls with whose fate we are connected by a bond of sympathy. Many times a day I realize how much my own outer and inner life is built upon the labors of my fellow men, both living and dead, and how earnestly I must exert myself in order to give in return as much as I have received. My peace of mind is often troubled by the depressing sense that I have borrowed too heavily from the work of other men.

— *Albert Einstein*

Great men are they who see that spiritual is stronger than any material force; that thoughts rule the world.

— *Emerson*

We are told by some that we are slaves. If being a slave means doing only what we have to do, then most of us are in truth slaves, but he who does more than he is required to do becomes at once free. He is his own master. How often do we hear it said, " It was not my work." Too often we fix our minds almost entirely upon what we are going to get and give no thought at all as to what we are going to give in return.

— *A. W. Robertson*

Good breeding sums up in its instinctive attitude all the
efforts a man has made towards perfection, aye, and all that
his ancestors have made before him. It is unconscious, the
simple acting out of a sound, wholesome nature.

— *C. Hanford Henderson*

Lord, grant that I may always desire more than I can
accomplish.   — *Michelangelo*

Our common future is badly served when the eloquence of
our attacks on the other fellow exceeds the energy with
which we co-operate with them.   — *Clarence Francis*

Reproach is infinite, and knows no end
    So voluble a weapon is the tongue;
Wounded, we wound; and neither side can fail
    For every man has equal strength to rail.

— *Homer*

The price of power is responsibility for the public good.
                                         — *Winthrop W. Aldrich*

Business is religion, and religion is business. The man
who does not make a business of his religion has a religious
life of no force, and the man who does not make a religion
of his business has a business life of no character.

— *Maltbie Babcock*

A good man and a wise man may, at times, be angry with
the world, and at times grieved for it; but no man was ever
discontented with the world if he did his duty in it.

— *Southey*

In business the earning of profit is something more than
an incident of success. It is an essential condition of success; because the continued absence of profit itself spells
failure. But while loss spells failure, large profits do not
connote success. Success must be sought in business also in
excellence of performance; and in business, excellence of
performance manifests itself, among other things, in the
advancing of methods and processes; in the improvement
of products; in more perfect organization, eliminating friction as well as waste; in bettering the condition of the
workingmen, developing their faculties and promoting their
happiness; and in the establishment of right relations
with customers and with the community.

— *Louis D. Brandeis*

It is not enough to be busy; so are the ants. The question is: What are we busy about?   — *Thoreau*

Pressure is on us by the nature of the job. Performance
releases pressure.   — *Fisher*

Make the most of today. Translate your good intentions into actual deeds. Know that you can do what ought
to be done. Improve your plans. Keep a definite goal of
achievement constantly in view. Realize that work well and
worthily done makes life truly worth living.

— *Grenville Kleiser*

The measure of a man's real character is what he would
do if he knew he would never be found out.

— *Macaulay*

Work is often the father of pleasure.   — *Voltaire*

Laughter and tears are meant to turn the wheels of the same sensibility; one is windpower, and the other water-powered, that is all. — *Oliver Wendell Holmes*

I feel an earnest and humble desire, and shall do till I die, to increase the stock of harmless cheerfulness.
— *Charles Dickens*

The sooner we come to understand that things can be done without our assistance, the sooner we reach our philosophy of life. — *Anderson M. Baten*

The world is my country, all mankind are my brethren, and to do good is my religion. — *Thomas Paine*

Real friendship is a slow grower and never thrives unless engrafted upon a stock of known and reciprocal merit.
— *Lord Chesterfield*

The hearts of men are chilled by the threat of the cold war and by the touch of a still icier pessimism which is blood brother to despair. Men who are without faith and, therefore, cannot hope, are inclined to yield to the pressure of circumstances and events and give up their liberties, seeking security and warmth in peace at any price and in freedom from molestation.
— *Thomas A. Donnellan, D.D.*

Tsze-King asked, " Is there one word which may serve as a rule of practice for all one's life? "
The Master said, " Is not reciprocity such a word? What you do not want done to yourself, do not do to others."
— *Confucius*

Most men take least notice of what is plain, as if that were of no use; but puzzle their thoughts, and lose themselves in those vast depths and abysses which no human understanding can fathom.   — *Sherlock*

Thoughts, even more than overt acts, reveal character.
                                        — *W. S. Plumer*

Be rather bountiful than expensive; do good with what thou hast, or it will do thee no good.   — *William Penn*

A human being who is absolutely dependent upon his own muscles can just barely keep himself alive under favorable circumstances; and to raise himself above the animals he must in some way supplement his own feeble strength.   Civilization came into existence because certain strong groups of people used the muscles of men and women of weaker groups for this purpose; if there were no machines to-day there would be no art, literature, science, leisure, or comfort for anyone without slavery.
                                        — *F. A. Merrick*

Those who can command themselves command others.
                                        — *Hazlitt*

He that sips of many arts, drinks of none.   — *Fuller*

Keeping your clothes well pressed will keep you from looking hard pressed.   — *Coleman Cox*

He who promises runs in debt.   — *Talmud*

Man cannot be satisfied with mere success. He is concerned with the terms upon which success comes to him. And very often the terms seem more important than the success.   — *Charles A. Bennett*

Where necessity ends, curiosity begins; and no sooner are we supplied with everything that nature can demand than we sit down to contrive artificial appetites.

— *Johnson*

It is not size that counts in business. Some companies with $500,000 capital net more profits than other companies with $5,000,000. Size is a handicap unless efficiency goes with it.   — *Herbert N. Casson*

I never could believe that Providence had sent a few men into the world, ready booted and spurred to ride, and millions ready saddled and bridled to be ridden.

— *Richard Rumbold*

In a free country there is much clamor with little suffering; in a despotic state there is little complaint but much suffering.   — *Caruot*

Whoever admits that he is too busy to improve his methods has acknowledged himself to be at the end of his rope. And that is always the saddest predicament which anyone can get into.   — *J. Ogden Armour*

God gives every bird its food, but he does not throw it into the nest.   — *J. G. Holland*

Be sure to find a place for intellectual and cultural interests outside your daily occupation. It is necessary that you do so if this business of living is not to turn to dust and ashes in your mouth. Moreover, do not overlook the claims of religion as the explanation of an otherwise unintelligible world. It is not the fast tempo of modern life that kills but the boredom, a lack of strong interest and failure to grow that destroy. It is the feeling that nothing is worth while that makes men ill and unhappy.
— *Dr. Harold W. Dodds*

Prayer, like radium, is a luminous and self-generating form of energy.   — *Alexis Carrel*

Time is
Too slow for those who Wait,
Too swift for those who Fear,
Too long for those who Grieve;
Too short for those who Rejoice;
But for those who Love,
Time is Eternity.   — *Henry Van Dyke*

All our institutions rest upon business. Without it we should not have schools, colleges, churches, parks, playgrounds, pavements, books, libraries, art, music, or anything else that we value.   — *Cassius E. Gates*

A precedent embalms a principle.   — *Disraeli*

In the same degree that we overrate ourselves, we shall underrate others; for injustice allowed at home is not likely to be correct abroad.   — *Washington Allston*

The only method by which people can be supported is out of the effort of those who are earning their own way. We must not create a deterrent to hard work.

— *Robert A. Taft*

There are certain times when most people are in a disposition of being informed, and 'tis incredible what a vast good a little truth might do, spoken in such seasons.

— *Pope*

Technical progress is the real hope for the future of the country; political reform cannot do anything for us. The engineer is engaged in a war of human liberation; his technique is different. The political reformer fights against ambition and initiative; the engineer is fighting against slavery. It is better for all to live well with a few rich than for all to live in slavery on a lower level.

— *Glenn Frank*

A man's true greatness lies in the consciousness of an honest purpose in life, founded on a just estimate of himself and everything else, on frequent self-examinations, and a steady obedience to the rule which he knows to be right, without troubling himself about what others may think or say, or whether they do or do not that which he thinks and says and does.

— *Marcus Aurelius*

All social life, stability, progress, depend upon each man's confidence in his neighbor, a reliance upon him to do his duty.

— *A. Lawrence Lowell*

Advertising is one of the few callings in which it is advisable to pay attention to some one else's business.

— *Howard W. Newton*

It is the individual citizen's understanding of facts that counts in a democracy. In totalitarian states, only a few people have to know the significance of facts. Here in America everyone has to know what facts mean.

— Paul A. Wagner

Opportunities are greater to-day than ever before in history. Young people graduating from our schools have greater chances for health, happiness and prosperity than had the children of any previous generation. A little money will do more to-day in setting up a young man or woman in business than it would ever do heretofore. There is a greater demand to-day for people of character than at any time in the history of America. Industry, intelligence, imagination and persistence are great gold mines.

— Roger W. Babson

Nothing is really work unless you would rather be doing something else.   *— Chub De Wolfe*

War is partially the result of the greed of men, of imperialistic ambitions, the desire to reach out and possess what others possess. We have seen the hatred of one people for another, notably the persecution of the Jews. Such hatred, however, as well as the cruelty and unkindness that may exist below the veneer of our civilization, are transitory.   *— Alfred Grant Walton, D.D.*

Formal education is but an incident in the lifetime of an individual. Most of us who have given the subject any study have come to realize that education is a continuous process ending only when ambition comes to a halt.

— Col. R. I. Rees

Adoption and continuation of policies that incorporate a maximum of " forward thinking " should be the most vital single consideration of all executives.

— *Charles Presbrey*

Teach our children the wholesome ideals of America today — and the threat of vicious Communism will be dead tomorrow. — *Martin Vanbee*

To profit from good advice requires more wisdom than to give it. — *Churton Collins*

Christ had something to say about economics. He said, " Lay not up your treasures on earth, but lay them up in heaven." Today, because we have laid up no treasure in heaven, we are in danger of losing what we have laid up on earth. Unless we rebuild God in our hearts we will never rebuild and reconstruct the world.

— *Humphrey Beever, D.D.*

The crossroads of trade are the meeting place of ideas, the attrition ground of rival customs and beliefs; diversities beget conflict, comparison, thought; superstitions cancel one another, and reason begins. — *Will Durant*

It would do the world good if every man in it would compel himself occasionally to be absolutely alone. Most of the world's progress has come out of such loneliness.

— *Bruce Barton*

I am the inferior of any man whose rights I trample underfoot. — *Horace Greeley*

Happy the man who has learned the cause of things and has put under his feet all fear, inexorable fate, and the noisy strife of the hell of greed.   — *Virgil*

No one has learned the meaning of life until he has surrendered his ego to the service of his fellow men.

— *Beran Wolfe*

I have found it helpful to keep constantly in mind that there are really two entries to be made for every transaction — one in terms of immediate dollars and cents, the other in terms of goodwill.   — *Ralph Hitz*

TEN COMMANDMENTS FOR VICTORY

1. Obey orders always, honestly, cheerfully and conscientiously!

2. Do your duty on time all the time!

3. Practice self-control and self-denial always!

4. Be considerate of others; be willing to give before you take!

5. Be neat and clean in person as well as in speech!

6. Don't find fault, lest you find time for little else!

7. Whatever you do, do it just a little bit better than anyone else!

8. Resolve to win, always on the alert for Victory!

9. Be true to yourself, your comrades, your God and your country!

10. Be faithful and dependable, ever mindful of your sacred privilege in serving America!

— *Major Manfred Pakas*

By merit, not favoritism, shall we attain our ends.

— *Plout*

It is happily and kindly provided that in every life there are certain pauses, and interruptions which force consideration upon the careless, and seriousness upon the light; points of time where one course of action ends and another begins.
— *Johnson*

To succeed, a business must occupy a field of public usefulness by producing a good article at the lowest price consistent with fair treatment of all those concerned with its production, distribution and consumption.
— *Walter C. Teagle*

RULES FOR BUSINESS SUCCESS

1. Carefully examine every detail of the business.
2. Be prompt.
3. Take time to consider and then decide quickly.
4. Dare to go forward.
5. Bear your trouble patiently.
6. Maintain your integrity as a sacred thing.
7. Never tell business lies.
8. Make no useless acquaintances.
9. Never try to appear something more than you are.
10. Pay your debts promptly.
11. Learn how to risk your money at the right time.
12. Shun strong liquor.
13. Employ your time well.
14. Do not reckon on chance.
15. Be polite to everyone.
16. Never be discouraged.
17. Work hard and you will succeed.
— *Rothschild*

An idea a day will keep the sheriff away.
— *Don E. Roseman*

There is very definitely something that each of us can do to help strengthen the United Nations. If enough of us will do it, the results can be decisive. Each of us . . . in his own home . . . in his own community can help to develop public interest, understanding and support for what the United Nations is trying to do. Once an informed and enlightened public interest is aroused, no government on the face of the earth — I don't care what its form may be — can be indifferent to its pressure. National policies are the sum total of the informed public thinking of citizens.
— *Angus S. Mitchell*

The hardest thing to find is the independent business man who knows how to get all the factors working together, and who can so organize them that he can pay the bills out of the receipts. That everlasting problem spoils a good many business enterprises. I think I could run almost any business if somebody would pay the bills. I talk to a great many radical clubs. They say that capital exploits labor, that all the capitalist does is to hire some labor, underpay it, sell it at a high price and pocket the difference. Sometimes I say to them, " Now, if that is all there is to do, why don't some of you do that and make money yourself? The reason you don't is because you can't." If there are one hundred radicals present, I am pretty safe in saying that there isn't one man among them who can hire any kind of labor, pay the current wages, and get a product that he can sell for enough to pay the wages. — *Thomas N. Carver*

Be so that thy conduct can become law universal.
— *Immanuel Kant*

The future belongs to those who are virile, to whom it is a pleasure to live, to create, to whet their intelligence on that of the others. — *Sir Henri Deterding*

If the Golden Rule is to be preached at all in these modern days, when so much of our life is devoted to business, it must be preached specially in its application to the conduct of business.   *— F. S. Schenck*

To be absolutely certain about something, one must know everything or nothing about it.   *— Olin Miller*

Health is most worth while to conserve. I do not mean simply the abounding vigor of youth, with abundance of fresh air and exercise and with its reserves which seem to mock the warnings of elders. I mean, rather, the sustained and protected strength which is based on the conservation of physical resources and gives promise of a long life well lived. In our onward journey the ranks are rapidly thinned by the passing out of those who have had their brief stay and were soon done. When their notes matured they were unable to meet them. Nothing is sadder than these physical bankruptcies, which deprive men and women of opportunities when, with the capital of experience well invested, they should have the most ample returns.

— Charles Evans Hughes

If ever this free people, if this Government itself is ever utterly demoralized, it will come from this incessant human wriggle and struggle for office, which is but a way to live without work.   *— Abraham Lincoln*

If you load responsibility on a man unworthy of it he will always betray himself.   *— August Heckscher*

A prudent question is one-half of wisdom.   *— Bacon*

The greatest asset of any nation is the spirit of its people, and the greatest danger that can menace any nation is the breakdown of that spirit — the will to win and the courage to work.   — *George B. Cortelyou*

But if you should take the bond of goodwill out of the universe no house or city could stand, nor would even the tillage of the fields abide. If that statement is not clear, then you may understand how great is the power of friendship and of concord from a consideration of the results of enmity and disagreement. For what house is so strong, or what state so enduring that it cannot be utterly overthrown by animosities and division?   — *Cicero*

The American economic story, despite defects and drawbacks and dreams turned nightmares, is such a good and strong and persuasive story that it needs no attempt to conceal or gloss over blemishes and imperfections. It can stand on its own with its virtues and deficiencies fully displayed. Like Cromwell's face, the U.S. economy is best portrayed " warts and all."   — *Herbert Harris*

Nine requisites for contented living:
Health enough to make work a pleasure. Wealth enough to support your needs. Strength to battle with difficulties and overcome them. Grace enough to confess your sins and forsake them. Patience enough to toil until some good is accomplished. Charity enough to see some good in your neighbor. Love enough to move you to be useful and helpful to others. Faith enough to make real the things of God. Hope enough to remove all anxious fears concerning the future.   — *Goethe*

Don't judge a man by his opinion of himself.
                    — *J. L. Schnadig*

It is now evident to all men of spiritual discernment that healing of the world's woes will not come through this or that social or political theory; not through violent changes in government, but in the still small voice that speaks to the conscience and the heart.   — *Arthur J. Moore, D.D.*

No person was ever honored for what he received. Honor has been the reward for what he gave.

— *Calvin Coolidge*

The way to get ahead is to start now. If you start now, you will know a lot next year that you don't know now and that you would not have known next year if you had waited.

— *William Feather*

All the world is a store, and all the people in it are sales-people. That is to say, every one of us human beings is trying to transfer an idea from his own head into some other brain. And *that* is the essence of salesmanship.

— *Arthur Brisbane*

Don't be fooled by the calendar. There are only as many days in the year as you make use of. One man gets only a week's value out of a year while another man gets a full year's value out of a week.   — *Charles Richards*

Budgets are not merely affairs of arithmetic, but in a thousand ways go to the root of prosperity of individuals, the relation of classes and the strength of kingdoms.

— *Gladstone*

Charity is injurious unless it helps the recipient to become independent of it.   — *John D. Rockefeller, Jr.*

It is beyond the vision or ability of any human being to foretell what will follow partial socialization of industry and a governmental supervision over practically all business. . . . I feel, however, that we can assume that we will never go back to the old order of things; that we will find that this is simply the first chapter of a new book and that no one can as yet foretell the trend of the chapters or acts that are to follow.   — *George M. Verity*

When anger rises, think of the consequences.
— *Confucius*

In the harsh face of life faith can read a bracing gospel.
— *Robert Louis Stevenson*

Whatever you do, you need courage. Whatever course you decide upon, there is always someone to tell you you are wrong. There are always difficulties arising which tempt you to believe that your critics are right. To map out a course of action and follow it to an end, requires some of the same courage which a soldier needs. Peace has its victories, but it takes brave men to win them.
— *Emerson*

Walter B. Pitkin has written a book on " Life Begins at Forty." I rise to offer a substitute, Mr. Pitkin, " Life Begins Each Morning." Whether one is twenty, forty or sixty; whether one has succeeded, failed or just muddled along; whether yesterday was full of sun or storm, or one of those dull days with no weather at all, Life Begins Each Morning! . . . Each night of life is a wall between to-day and the past. Each morning is the open door to a new world — new vistas, new aims, new tryings.
— *Leigh Mitchell Hodges*

When ancient opinions and rules of life are taken away, the loss cannot possibly be estimated. From that moment we have no compass to govern us, nor can we know distinctly to what port to steer.   — *Burke*

Life comes before literature, as the material always comes before the work. The hills are full of marble before the world blooms with statues.   — *Phillips Brooks*

A helping word to one in trouble is often like a switch on a railroad track — an inch between wreck and smooth-rolling prosperity.   — *Henry Ward Beecher*

A man who dares to waste one hour of life has not discovered the value of life.   — *Darwin*

The progress of democracy seems irresistible, because it is the most uniform, the most ancient and the most permanent tendency which is to be found in history.   — *De Tocqueville*

To accept good advice is but to increase one's own ability.   — *Goethe*

The business that considers itself immune to the necessity for advertising sooner or later finds itself immune to business.   — *Derby Brown*

We are apt to say that money talks, but it speaks a broken, poverty-stricken language. Hearts talk better, clearer and with wider intelligence.
    — *William Allen White*

What a man knows should find expression in what he
does.   The chief value of superior knowledge is that it leads
to a performing manhood.   — *Bovée*

We always like those who admire us, but we do not always
like those whom we admire.   — *La Rochefoucauld*

Sufficient to each day are the duties to be done and the
trials to be endured.   God never built a Christian strong
enough to carry today's duties and tomorrow's anxieties
piled on the top of them.   — *T. L. Cuyler*

Great occasions do not make heroes or cowards; they
simply unveil them to the eyes of men.   Silently and im-
perceptibly, as we wake or sleep, we grow strong or we
grow weak, and at last some crisis shows us what we have
become.   — *Bishop Westcott*

Industry prospers when it offers people articles which
they want more than they want anything they now have.
The fact is that people never buy what they need.   They
buy what they want.   — *Charles F. Kettering*

Put off thy cares with thy clothes; so shall thy rest
strengthen thy labor, and so thy labor sweeten thy rest.
                                             — *Quarles*

It is well to learn caution by the misfortunes of others.
                                             — *Syrus*

You can't escape the responsibility of tomorrow by evading it today.   — *Abraham Lincoln*

The business man who has faith is not very likely to go wrong. He is going to steer his ship of commerce through the troubled waters of misfortune, perhaps even adversity, with a serenity born of the consciousness that nothing can harm him permanently so long as he sees clearly and acts wisely. There will be many hands eager to retard his progress. Slander will raise its ugly head from many little by-ways along his path. Ill health may come; the loss of loved ones; the crippling of his finances; the striking down of his most cherished hopes; and yet — the man who has Faith — who believes that right is right will triumph. — *Jerome P. Fleishman*

Man's capacities have never been measured. Nor are we to judge of what he can do by any precedents, so little has been tried. — *Thoreau*

How is it possible to expect that mankind will take advice when they will not so much as take warning?

— *Swift*

Industry has been regarded in the past as a way to make a living. I believe it is the great new realization of Business America that industry can be something far finer and bigger, a way to make a life. — *E. T. Trigg*

While just government protects all in their religious rites, true religion affords government its surest support.

— *George Washington*

Haste and rashness are storms and tempests, breaking and wrecking business; but nimbleness is a full, fair wind, blowing it with speed to the haven. — *Fuller*

THOUGHT

You say " I think " ten times a day
  Or fifteen times, or twenty
And even more. Well, anyway
  You sure repeat it plenty.
But pause and ponder half a wink
  And start your brain-cells clinking;
" I think " you say, but do you Think
  Or only Think you're thinking?

How often is the thing you've thought
  Out of Yourself created
And not a dictum you've been taught
  And simply imitated?
Into a reverie you sink
  And like an owl you're blinking,
But do you actually Think,
  Or only Think you're thinking?

" I think," you say — and ladle out
  Some fusty old opinion
That probably was known about
  In Pharaoh's dominion.
Do new ideas ever slink
  Into your cranium's chinking?
I wonder — do you really think
  Or only Think you're thinking?

Traditions, customs, fill your head
  And some of them have virtue,
But most of them have long been dead
  They fester there and hurt you.
Son, chuck that clutter in the drink,
  Wake up — don't sit there blinking!
Wake up! And then perhaps you'll Think
  And not just Think you're thinking!

— *Berton Braley*

I can complain because rose bushes have thorns or rejoice because thorn bushes have roses. It's all how you look at it.   — J. Kenfield Morley

The acquiring of culture is the developing of an avid hunger for knowledge and beauty.

— Jesse Lee Bennett

Without labor there is no rest, nor without fighting can the victory be won.   — Thomas à Kempis

If we are to achieve a victorious standard of living today we must look for the opportunity in every difficulty instead of being paralyzed at the thought of the difficulty in every opportunity.   — Walter E. Cole

You can never have a greater or a less dominion than over yourself.   — L. da Vinci

Not the truth of which one supposes himself possessed, but the effort he has made to arrive at truth, makes the worth of the man. For not by the possession, but by the investigation, of truth are his powers expanded. Possession makes us easy, indolent, proud. If God held all Truth shut in his right hand, and in his left nothing but the ever-restless instinct for truth, and should say to me, Choose! I should bow humbly to his *left* hand, and say, " Father, give."   — Lessing

There are glimpses of heaven to us in every act, or thought, or word, that raises us above ourselves.

— A. P. Stanley

We communicate happiness to others not often by great acts of devotion and self-sacrifice, but by the absence of fault-finding and censure, by being ready to sympathize with their notions and feelings, instead of forcing them to sympathize with ours.   — *Clarke*

You will never " find " time for anything. If you want time, you must make it.   — *Charles Bixton*

It must be obvious to those who take the time to look at human life that its greatest values lie not in getting things, but in doing them, in doing them together, in all working toward a common aim, in the experience of comradeship, of warmhearted 100 per cent human life.

— *W. T. Grant*

The man who questions opinion is wise; the man who quarrels with facts is a fool.   — *Frank A. Garbutt*

Wondrous is the strength of cheerfulness, and its power of endurance — the cheerful man will do more in the same time, will do it better, will persevere in it longer, than the sad or sullen.   — *Carlyle*

Never regard study as a duty, but as the enviable opportunity to learn to know the liberating influence of beauty in the realm of the spirit for your own personal joy and to the profit of the community to which your later work belongs.   — *Albert Einstein*

Our thought is the key which unlocks the doors of the world.   — *Samuel McC. Crothers*

We tend to think and feel in terms of the art we like; and if the art we like is bad then our thinking and feeling will be bad. And if the thinking and feeling of most of the individuals composing a society is bad, is not that society in danger?
— *Aldous Huxley*

The multitude which is not brought to act as unity, is confusion. That unity which has not its origin in the multitude is tyranny.
— *Pascal*

Though a taste of pleasure may quicken the relish of life, an unrestrained indulgence leads to inevitable destruction.
— *Dodsley*

A true man never frets about his place in the world, but just slides into it by the gravitation of his nature, and swings there as easily as a star.
— *E. H. Chapin*

The great need today in every phase of our social, economical and political life is *understanding*. It has always been so, but today the need is even greater.
— *Charles R. Hook*

Our business is not only with eternity but with time, to build up on earth the kingdom of God, to enable man to live worthily and not merely to die in hope.
— *Lord Tweedsmuir*

Never seem wiser or more learned than the company you are with. Treat your learning like a watch and keep it hidden. Do not pull it out to count the hours, but give the time when you are asked.
— *Lord Chesterfield*

The greatest asset of any nation is the spirit of its people, and the greatest danger that can menace any nation is the breakdown of that spirit — the will to win and the courage to work.   — *George B. Cortelyou*

The doctrine of human equality reposes on this: that there is no man really clever who has not found that he is stupid. There is no big man who has not felt small. Some men never feel small; but these are the few men who are.   — *Gilbert K. Chesterton*

The educated man is a man with certain subtle spiritual qualities which make him calm in adversity, happy when alone, just in his dealings, rational and sane in the fullest meaning of that word in all the affairs of life.

— *Ramsay MacDonald*

GOOD RULES TO FOLLOW

Learn to get along with people.
Learn to exhibit more patience than any other man you know.
Learn to respect other men's ideas and opinions.
Learn to think problems through to the end.
Learn to try to put yourself in the other fellow's place.
Be democratic.
Be loyal.
Cultivate cheerfulness.
WORK.   — *Harry J. Klingler*

The highest use of capital is not to make more money, but to make money do more for the betterment of life.

— *Henry Ford*

The bravest are the tenderest. The loving are the daring.

— *Longfellow*

A man's ledger does not tell what he is, or what he is worth. Count what is in man, not what is on him, if you would know what he is worth — whether rich or poor.
— *Henry Ward Beecher*

A dose of poison can do its work but once, but a bad book can go on poisoning minds for generations.
— *W. John Murray*

Hold yourself responsible for a higher standard than anybody else expects of you. Never excuse yourself. Never pity yourself. Be a hard master to yourself — and be lenient to everybody else.
— *Beecher*

A man with nothing to do does far more strenuous "labor" than any other form of work. To be enforced to be idle is terribly difficult and even a small proportion of your day wasted is worse than working many hours overtime. But my greatest pity is for the man who dodges a job he knows he should do. He is a shirker; and boy! what punishment he takes . . . from himself.
— *E. R. Collcord*

With the worship of God must go denial of self. These are the two wings for flight. Pride of any kind will be rooted out, and also desire for power over others. Not until it is rooted out can the economic potentials be developed properly and made available for all. Love of God and love of the brethren are the true preparation and discipline for life.
— *Bernard C. Newman, D.D.*

Every man carries with him the world in which he must live.
— *F. Marion Crawford*

There is no such thing as a little country. The greatness
of a people is no more determined by their number than
the greatness of a man is determined by his height.

— *Victor Hugo*

Forget yourself in your work. If your employer sees that
you are more concerned about your own interests than
about his, that you are fussy about getting credit for every
little or big thing you do, then you are apt to be passed by
when a responsible job has to be filled. . . . Don't worry
about how big an increase in your salary you can contrive
to get. Don't let your mind dwell on money at all, if you
can help it. Throw yourself, body, soul, and spirit, into
whatever you are doing. . . . The truth is that in every
organization, no matter how large or how small, someone
is taking notice of any employee who shows special ability.

— *Harry B. Thayer*

War would end if the dead could return.   — *Baldwin*

Example teaches better than precept. It is the best
modeler of the character of men and women. To set a
lofty example is the richest bequest a man can leave behind
him.   — *S. Smiles*

Custom governs the world; it is the tyrant of our feelings
and our manners and rules the world with the hand of a
despot.   — *J. Bartlett*

Character development is the great, if not the sole, aim
of education.   — *O'Shea*

The trade-unionist has the same limitation imposed upon him as the capitalist. He cannot advance his interests at the expense of society. — *Ramsay MacDonald*

The races of mankind would perish did they cease to aid each other. From the time that the mother binds the child's head till the moment that some kind assistant wipes the brow of the dying, we cannot exist without mutual help.
— *Walter Scott*

We don't thank God enough for much that He has given us. Our prayers are too often the beggar's prayer, the prayer that asks for something. We offer too few prayers of thanksgiving and of praise. — *Robert E. Woods, D.D.*

Personal liberty will prove a poor and shrunken thing incapable of satisfying our aspirations if it does not exact as its minimum requirement that there shall be the preservation of opportunity for the growth of personality.
— *Cardoza*

Depression, gloom, pessimism, despair, discouragement, these slay ten human beings to every one murdered by typhoid, influenza, diabetes or pneumonia. If tuberculosis is the great white plague, fear is the great black plague. Be cheerful. — *Dr. Frank Crane*

Parents wonder why the streams are bitter, when they themselves have poisoned the fountain. — *Locke*

Every difficulty slurred over will be a ghost to disturb your repose later on. — *Chopin*

The genius of America is production; and a large percentage of our productive enterprises are headed by men who have come up from the worker's bench.

— *William S. Knudsen*

To live in the presence of great truths and eternal laws, to be led by permanent ideals — that is what keeps a man patient when the world ignores him, and calm and unspoiled when the world praises him.

— *Dr. A. Peabody*

All my life people have been coming to me with plans to make over society and its institutions. Many of these plans have seemed to me good. Some have been excellent. All of them have had one fatal defect. They have assumed that human nature would behave in a certain way. If it would behave in that way these plans would work, but if human nature would behave in that way these plans would not be necessary, for in that case society and its institutions would reform themselves.   — *Elihu Root*

An intelligent plan is the first step to success. The man who plans knows where he is going, knows what progress he is making and has a pretty good idea when he will arrive. Planning is the open road to your destination. If you don't know where you are going, how can you expect to get there?   — *Basil S. Walsh*

When enthusiasm is inspired by reason; controlled by caution; sound in theory; practical in application; reflects confidence; spreads good cheer; raises morale; inspires associates; arouses loyalty, and laughs at adversity, it is beyond price.   — *Coleman Cox*

There is not enough love, obviously, in our religious exercises; we try to buy ourselves into good relationship with God. We bow Him out of our lives in normal things and then think we can ingratiate ourselves by a few religious exercises on Sunday. The attitude seems to be: Lord, I'll do my part and you do Yours but let's not become too intimate in the process.

— *William Ward Ayer, D.D.*

Eighty percent of our criminals come from unsympathetic homes. — *Hans Christian Andersen*

Money never starts an idea; it is the idea that starts the money. — *W. J. Cameron*

I have long been profoundly convinced that in the very nature of things, employers and employees are partners, not enemies; that their interests are common, not opposed; that in the long run the success of each is dependent upon the success of the other. If the labor movement will do its share in outlawing industrial warfare; substituting partnership therefor; if more men of broad vision and high purpose respond to the opportunity for constructive leadership which labor unionism offers, well may it be that the trade union movement will enjoy the glory and honor of ushering in industrial peace. — *John D. Rockefeller, Jr.*

That nation is worthless that will not, with pleasure, venture all for its honor. — *Schiller*

Fortune is for all; judgment is theirs who have won it for themselves. — *Aeschylus*

In all the affairs of human life, social as well as political,
courtesies of a small and trivial character are the ones that
strike deepest to the grateful and appreciating heart.

— *Henry Clay*

Could we see when and where we are to meet again, we
would be more tender when we bid our friends goodbye.

— *Ouida*

Laboring toward distant aims sets the mind in a higher
key and puts us at our best.   — *C. H. Parkhurst. D.D.*

One ought to read just as inclination takes him, for what
he reads as a task will do him little good.   — *Johnson*

Surely there must be some place where the great minds of
Shelley, Homer and Spinoza go after death. The denial
of immortality does not square with intelligence. Adolph S.
Ochs, shortly before his death, said that he believed that
he was more than an animal and that he did not believe
that this life is the end. Our bodies change and in the end
crumble. It is a house of clay. But inside there is a
spiritual duplicate. As we have borne the image of the
earthly, so shall we bear the image of the heavenly.

— *Malcolm James MacLeod, D.D.*

To those who have lived long together, everything heard
and everything seen recalls some pleasure communicated,
some benefit conferred, some petty quarrel or some slight
endearment. Esteem of great powers, or amiable qualities
newly discovered may embroider a day or a week, but a
friendship of twenty years is interwoven with the texture
of life.   — *Johnson*

Don't flatter yourself that friendship authorizes you to say disagreeable things to your intimates. The nearer you come into relation with a person, the more necessary do tact and courtesy become. Except in cases of necessity, which are rare, leave your friend to learn unpleasant things from his enemies; they are ready enough to tell him.

— *Oliver Wendell Holmes*

The five evidences of education are as follows:
1. Correctness and precision of speech.
2. Refined and gentle manners.
3. The power and habit of reflection.
4. The power of growth.
5. The possession of efficiency — the power to do.

— *Nicholas Murray Butler*

Very few big executives want to be surrounded by " yes " men. Their greatest weakness often is the fact that " yes " men build up around the executive a wall of fiction, when what the executive wants most of all is plain facts.

— *Burton Bigelow*

Genius begins great works; labor alone finishes them.

— *Joubert*

One great use of words is to hide our thoughts.

— *Voltaire*

Employment gives health, sobriety, and morals. Constant employment and well-paid labor produce, in a country like ours, general prosperity, content, and cheerfulness.

— *Daniel Webster*

The science of legislation is like that of medicine in one respect; viz.: that it is far more easy to point out what will do harm, than what will do good. — *Colton*

No matter how busy you are you usually find time to see to it that your automobile is kept in repair. You would never think of starting out if your automobile brakes, motor or gears were not functioning properly. But, how about your body? Has it ever occurred to you that you should have it checked up at least once every year? How do you know whether or not your vital organs are functioning properly? The man who submits himself to his family doctor for regular examination will rarely need to worry about his health. His physician will advise the proper diet, exercise, recreation, etc. If his advice is followed much trouble may be averted; many serious conditions can be halted in their early stages. — *Dr. John L. Rice*

No matter what the form of a government, there are in fact only two kinds of government possible. Under one system, the state is everything and the individual is an incident. Under that system, the individual is a subject, rather than a citizen. Under that system, the individual has no rights, though they may be termed such; he has only privileges. Under that system, the state is the reservoir of all rights, all privileges, all powers. But this system our forefathers rejected. They declared that all just government derives its powers from the consent of the governed. They affirmed the dignity and the sanctity of the individual. . . . They elected a man-made state, not a state-made man. — *Frank M. Dixon*

If a man will begin with certainties, he will end with doubts; but if he will be content to begin with doubts, he will end in certainties. — *Bacon*

Don't expect to be paid a dollar an hour for your working hours when you then use your leisure hours as though they were not worth five cents a dozen.

— *Henry L. Doherty*

He that is good for making excuses is seldom good for anything else. — *Benjamin Franklin*

The errors of faith are better than the best thoughts of unbelief. — *Thomas Russell*

Any fact is better established by two or three good testimonies than by a thousand arguments. — *Emmons*

In a balanced organization, working towards a common objective, there is success. — *T. L. Scrutton*

There is far too much talk about making life easy. It is all right to take the pain and bitterness out of struggle; but were you to take the struggle out, there would be no adequate chance for young Americans. — *Paul Shoup*

Wood burns because it has the proper stuff in it; and a man becomes famous because he has the proper stuff in him. — *Goethe*

We have an obligation to other people, to our neighbor and to our country. But the man who stops there has lost the purpose of his life below. Please bear in mind we are not created for time, but for eternity. God is the sure Tax-Gatherer. Yet how many refuse to pay tribute to Him.

— *Thomas Lester Graham, D.D.*

Political freedom goes hand in hand with religious freedom. Wherever religion is free men can no longer be kept in chains. Religious freedom means liberty for all, with special favors to none.   *— John S. Bonnell, D.D.*

Every day sees humanity more victorious in the struggle with space and time.   *— Guglielmo Marconi*

All things come to him who waits — provided he knows what he is waiting for.   *— Woodrow Wilson*

There can be no friendship where there is no freedom. Friendship loves a free air, and will not be fenced up in straight and narrow enclosures.   *— William Penn*

No one could ever meet death for his country without the hope of immortality.   *— Cicero*

The most agreeable thing in life is worthy accomplishment. It is not possible that the idle tramp is as contented as the farmers along the road who own their own farms, and whose credit is good at the bank in town. When the tramps get together at night, they abuse the farmers, but do not get as much satisfaction out of it as do the farmers who abuse the tramps. The sounder your argument, the more satisfaction you get out of it.   *— Ed. Howe*

The future can be anything we want it to be, providing we have the faith and that we realize that peace, no less than war, requires " blood and sweat and tears."
        — Charles F. Kettering

We never seem to know what anything means until we
have lost it. The full significance of these words, property,
ease, health — the wealth of meaning that lies in epithets,
parent, child, friend, we never know until they are taken
away; till in place of the bright, visible being, comes the
awful and desolate shadow where nothing is — where we
stretch out our hands in vain, and strain our eyes upon dark
and dismal vacuity. — *O. Dewey*

Though not always called upon to condemn ourselves, it is
always safe to suspect ourselves. — *Whately*

There never was a person who did anything worth doing
who did not receive more than he gave.
— *Henry Ward Beecher*

For me, hard work represents the supreme luxury of life.
— *Albert M. Greenfield*

When a millionaire is a million times more happy than
the owner of a single dollar, folks will have a real kick
coming. — *Josh Harper*

Immense power is acquired by assuring yourself in your
secret reveries that you were born to control affairs.
— *Andrew Carnegie*

When electricity was invented people became discontent
with oil lamps. And so our missionaries employ this
sound business principle: " Show the people something
better and they'll want it."
— *Horace W. B. Donegan, D.D.*

Life is a romantic business. It is painting a picture, not
doing a sum; but you have to make the romance, and it
will come to the question how much fire you have in
your belly.   — *Oliver Wendell Holmes*

Nothing in life is to be feared. It is only to be understood.   — *Marie Curie*

The first step in debt is like the first step in falsehood,
involving the necessity of going on in the same course,
debt following debt, as lie follows lie.   — *S. Smiles*

Censure is the tax a man pays to the public for being
eminent.   — *Swift*

When bad men combine, the good must associate; else
they will fall, one by one, in unpitied sacrifice, in a contemptible struggle.   — *Burke*

The first step, my son, which we make in this world, is
the one on which depends the rest of our days.
                                                    — *Voltaire*

He conquers twice who conquers himself in victory.
                                                    — *Syrus*

Those who are greedy of praise prove that they are poor
in merit.   — *Plutarch*

They know enough who know how to learn.
                                                — *Henry Adams*

Money alone is only a mean; it presupposes a man to use it. The rich man can go where he pleases, but perhaps please himself nowhere. He can buy a library or visit the whole world, but perhaps has neither patience to read nor intelligence to see. . . . The purse may be full and the heart empty. He may have gained the world and lost himself; and with all his wealth around him . . . he may live as blank a life as any tattered ditcher.

— Robert Louis Stevenson

We are not here to play, to dream, to drift;
We have hard work to do and loads to lift;
Shun not the struggle — face it, 'tis God's gift.

— Shaftesbury

If we devote our time disparaging the products of our business rivals, we hurt business generally, reduce confidence, and increase discontent.   *— Edward N. Hurley*

I do not prize the word cheap. It is not a word of inspiration. It is the badge of poverty, the signal of distress. Cheap merchandise means cheap men and cheap men mean a cheap country.   *— William McKinley*

There can be no peace when there is not God in the hearts of men. When you drive the devil out of the human heart the stream of life will be sweet, happy and peaceful.

— Charles Clifford Peale, D.D.

If one advances confidently in the direction of his dreams, and endeavors to live the life which he has imagined, he will meet with a success unexpected in common hours.

— Thoreau

Mere words are cheap and plenty enough, but ideas that rouse and set multitudes thinking come as gold from the mines. — *A. Owen Penny*

The future that we study and plan for begins today.
— *Chester O. Fischer*

Only he who can see the invisible can do the impossible.
— *Frank L. Gaines*

Purpose is what gives life a meaning.
— *C. H. Parkhurst, D.D.*

One may as well be asleep as to read for anything but to improve his mind and morals, and regulate his conduct.
— *Sterne*

Hope is a flatterer, but the most upright of all parasites; for she frequents the poor man's hut, as well as the palace of his superior. — *Shenstone*

Man has been called " the representative product of the universe "; and we will do well to remember that in this position his actions represent the worst of which nature is capable as well as the best. — *L. V. Jacks*

Always do right. This will gratify some people and astonish the rest. — *Mark Twain*

A boy who isn't handicapped is handicapped.
— *E. L. Cord*

When we control business in the public interest we are also bound to encourage it in the public interest or it will be a bad thing for everybody and worst of all for those on whose behalf the control is nominally exercised.

— Theodore Roosevelt

All that we know we have absorbed from our own experiences, or rearranged in our minds from observing other people, or reasoned out either consciously or unconsciously from thought-data given by inheritance or gathered from our own previous trends of thinking in moments past. The way we are going to think tomorrow depends largely on what we are thinking today. *— David Leslie Brown*

The workingman must not lose sight of the fact that the principle of brotherhood is applicable to all men, regardless of capital or poverty. *— John Lewis Zacker, D.D.*

If you never break a promise, if you always pay the money you owe exactly on the day it is due, nobody will know but that you are worth a billion. And you will be just as good a risk as a man worth a billion, for all that he could do would be to pay promptly on the due date.

— Hamilton Fish

One of the eternal conflicts out of which life is made up is that between the efforts of every man to get the most he can for his services and that of society disguised under the name of capital to get his services for the least possible return. *— Oliver Wendell Holmes*

Conceit may puff a man up, but can never prop him up.

— Ruskin

No evil is without its compensation. The less money,
the less trouble; the less favor, the less envy. Even in
those cases which put us out of wits, it is not the loss itself,
but the estimate of the loss that troubles us.   — Seneca

People who never had enough thrift and forethought to
buy and pay for property in the first place seldom have
enough to keep the property up after they have gained it in
some other way.   — Thomas Nixon Carver

How shall we learn to know ourselves? By reflection?
Never; but only through action. Strive to do thy duty;
then shalt thou know what is in thee.   — Goethe

Labor is life; from the inmost heart of the worker rises
his God-given force, the sacred celestial life-essence
breathed into him by Almighty God.   — Carlyle

Social problems can no longer be solved by class warfare
any more than international problems can be solved by wars
between nations. Warfare is negative and will sooner or
later lead to destruction, while goodwill and co-operation
are positive and supply the only safe basis for building a
better future.   — J. Nansen

One of the secrets of life is to keep our intellectual
curiosity acute.   — William Lyon Phelps

It is an accepted law of ethics that punishment in
the Court of Conscience, unlike that in Courts of Law, lessens with each repeated and unrebuked offense.
                    — Joseph S. Auerbach

We shall never have more time. We have, and have always had, all the time there is. No object is served in waiting until next week or even until to-morrow. Keep going day in and out. Concentrate on something useful. Having decided to achieve a task, achieve it at all costs.
— *Arnold Bennett*

Never mind your happiness; do your duty.
— *Will Durant*

It is nothing to give pension and cottage to the widow who has lost her son; it is nothing to give food and medicine to the workman who has broken his arm, or the decrepit woman wasting in sickness. But it is something to use your time and strength to war with the waywardness and thoughtlessness of mankind; to keep the erring workman in your service till you have made him an unerring one, and to direct your fellow-merchant to the opportunity which his judgment would have lost. — *John Ruskin*

Unless a capacity for thinking be accompanied by a capacity for action, a superior mind exists in torture.
— *Benedetto Croce*

To be well informed, one must read quickly a great number of merely instructive books. To be cultivated, one must read slowly and with a lingering appreciation the comparatively few books that have been written by men who lived, thought, and felt with style.
— *Aldous Huxley*

Goodwill is the one and only asset that competition cannot undersell nor destroy. — *Marshall Field*

Nothing great in science has ever been done by men, whatever their powers, in whom the divine afflatus of the truth-seeker was wanting.   — *Thomas Huxley*

Be not penny-wise; riches have wings; sometimes they fly away of themselves, and sometimes they must be set flying to bring in more.   — *Bacon*

Great trials seem to be a necessary preparation for great duties.   — *Thomson*

If you think of " standardization " as the best that you know today, but which is to be improved tomorrow — you get somewhere.   — *Henry Ford*

What the future holds for us, depends on what *we* hold for the future. Hard working " todays " make high-winning " tomorrows."   — *William E. Holler*

It is man's motive that counts for righteousness, not his outer act alone.   — *Blanche Huntsinger*

Some persons are always ready to level those above them down to themselves, while they are never willing to level those below them up to their own position. But he that is under the influence of true humility will avoid both these extremes. On the one hand, he will be willing that all should rise just so far as their diligence and worth of character entitle them to; and on the other hand, he will be willing that his superiors should be known and acknowledged in their place, and have rendered to them all the honors that are their due.   — *Jonathan Edwards*

I do not know how wicked American millionaires are, but as I travel about and see the results of their generosity in the form of hospitals, churches, public libraries, universities, parks, recreation grounds, art museums and theatres I wonder what on earth we should do without them.

— *William Lyon Phelps*

Everything can be improved. — *C. W. Barron*

'Tis not the dying for a faith that's so hard; 'tis the living up to it that is difficult. — *Thackeray*

The abundant life of which we have heard so much recently does not come to those who have all obstacles removed from their paths by others. It develops from within and is rooted in strong mental and moral fiber. To look to government to supply all material safeguards is to sound the doom of the great American tradition. If America is to go forward, we must develop in our colleges ideals of courage, industry, and independence.

— *Dr. William Mather Lewis*

The illusion that times that were are better than those that are, has probably pervaded all ages.

— *Horace Greeley*

Complete adaptation to environment means death. The essential point in all response is the desire to control environment. — *John Dewey*

I am a man of peace. God knows how I love peace. But I hope I shall never be such a coward as to mistake oppression for peace. — *Louis Kossuth*

The active part of man consists of powerful instincts,
some of which are gentle and continuous; others violent
and short; some baser, some nobler, and all necessary.

— F. W. Newman

We need fewer philosophies and more philosophers.

— Frank Romer

I believe the true road to preeminent success in any line
is to make yourself master of that line.

— Andrew Carnegie

Few things are more striking than the fact that while
the best are nearly powerless to effect changes, the worst are
so potent.   *— Watts*

If today's average American is confronted with an hour
of leisure, he is likely to palpitate with panic. An hour
with nothing to do! So he jumps into a dither and into a
car, and starts driving off fiercely in pursuit of diversion.
. . . I thank heaven I grew up in a small town, in a horse-
and-buggy era, when we had, or made, time to sit and
think, and often just to sit. . . . We " catch " a train.
We " grab " a bite of lunch. We " contact " a client.
Everything has to be active and electric. . . . We need less
leg action and more acute observation as we go. Slow down
the muscles and stir up the mind.   *— Don Herold*

It is not the ship so much as the skillful sailing that as-
sures the prosperous voyage.   *— George William Curtis*

Common sense is the favorite daughter of reason.

— H. W. Shaw

You all have powers you never dreamed of. You can
do things you never thought you could do. There are no
limitations in what you can do except the limitations in
your own mind as to what you cannot do. Don't think you
cannot. Think you *can*. — *Darwin P. Kingsley*

If you are poor, work. If you are burdened with seemingly unfair responsibilities, work. If you are happy, work.
Idleness gives room for doubts and fears. If disappointments come, keep right on working. If sorrow overwhelms
you and loved ones seem not true, work. If health is
threatened, work. When faith falters and reason fails,
just work. When dreams are shattered and hope seems
dead, work. Work as if your life were in peril. It really is.
No matter what ails you, work. Work faithfully — work
with faith. Work is the greatest remedy available for both
mental and physical afflictions. — *Korsaren*

I have brought myself by long meditation to the conviction that a human being with a settled purpose must accomplish it, and that nothing can resist a will which will
stake even existence upon its fulfillment. — *Disraeli*

Freedom must always be exercised under discipline, and
post-war higher education will, I believe, rededicate itself
to the high purpose of social and civic devotion to a unified,
outgoing, outgiving, democratic America.
— *Dr. Robert Gordon Sproul*

The experience of a century and a half has demonstrated
that our system of free government functions best when the
maximum degree of information is made available to our
people. In fact, free and candid discussion of vexing problems is the bedrock of democracy and it may be our surest
safeguard for peace. — *Brien McMahon*

The highest purpose of intellectual cultivation is to give
a man a perfect knowledge and mastery of his own inner
self.   — *Novalis*

Whatever crushes individuality is despotism, by whatever
name it may be called.   — *John Stuart Mill*

If we are to build for lasting peace, we must abandon
the nineteenth-century conception that the road to peace
lies through a nicely poised balance of power. Again and
again cold experience has taught us that no peace dependent
upon a balance of power lasts. If we would build upon
twentieth-century reality, we must throw the balance of
power theory out of the window.   — *Francis B. Sayre*

Look well to the hearthstone; therein all hope for
America lies.   — *Calvin Coolidge*

Peace is not the elimination of the causes of war. Rather
it is a mastery of great human forces and the creation of
an environment in which human aims may be pursued
constructively.   — *James H. Case, Jr.*

CAST OF CHARACTERS

I Won't is a tramp,
I Can't is a quitter,
I Don't Know is lazy,
I Wish I Could is a wisher,
I Might is waking up,
I Will Try is on his feet,
I Can is on his way,
I Will is at work,
I Did is now the boss.   — *Earl Cassel*

THE MAN YOU ARE

It isn't the man that you might have been
  Had the chance been yours again,
Nor the prize you wanted but didn't win
  That weighs in the measure of men.
No futile " if " or poltroon " because "
  Can rowel your stock to par.
The world cares naught for what never was —
  It judges by what you are.

It isn't the man that you hope to be,
  If fortune and fate are kind,
That the chill, keen eyes of the world will see
  In weighing your will and mind.
The years ahead are a chartless sea,
  And tomorrow's a world away;
It isn't the man that you'd like to be,
  But the man that you are today.

There's little worth in the phantom praise
  Of a time that may never dawn,
And less in a vain regret for days
  And deeds long buried and gone.
There's little time on this busy earth
  To argue the why and how.
The game is yours if you prove your worth,
  And prove it here and now!   — *Ted Olsen*

A friend is a present you give yourself.
          — *Robert Louis Stevenson*

Hating hard work can get to be such an obsession that
you won't let it pile up.   — *H. C. Brown*

Knowledge and human power are synonymous, since the
ignorance of the cause frustrates the effect.   — *Bacon*

The most urgent necessity in human life is to be able to
face life victoriously. For many — the number is appalling
— are living mentally, physically, morally and spiritually
defeated.   — F. A. Wickett

There is no truth to be gathered from all history more
certain, or more momentous, than this:
That civil liberty cannot long be separated from religious
liberty without danger and, ultimately, without destruction
of both.
Wherever religious liberty exists, it will, first or last, bring
in and establish civil liberty.
Wherever the State establishes one Church, suppressing
all others, the State Church will, first or last, become the
engine of despotism, and overthrow, unless it be itself overthrown, every vestige of political right.   — Joseph Story

The manufacturer who waits in the woods for the world
to beat a path to his door is a great optimist. But the
manufacturer who shows his " mousetraps " to the world
keeps the smoke coming out of his chimney.
                                             — O. B. Winters

Act nothing in furious passion. It's putting to sea in a
storm.   — Fuller

The fact is, nothing comes; at least, nothing good. All
has to be fetched.   — Charles Buxton

It is a very easy thing to devise good laws; the difficulty
is to make them effective. The great mistake is that of
looking on all men as virtuous, or thinking that they can be
made so by laws; and consequently the greatest art of a
politician is to render vices serviceable to the cause of
virtue.   — Lord Bolingbroke

A good man likes a hard boss. I don't mean a nagging boss or a grouchy boss. I mean a boss who insists on things being done right and on time; a boss who is watching things closely enough so that he knows a good job from a poor one. Nothing is more discouraging to a good man than a boss who is not on the job, and who does not know whether things are going well or badly.

— William Feather

The thoughts that come often unsought, and, as it were, drop into the mind, are commonly the most valuable of any we have, and therefore should be secured, because they seldom return again. *— Locke*

TEN SUCCESS RULES

Put success before amusement.
Learn something every day.
Cut free from routine.
Concentrate on net profits.
Make your services known.
Never worry over trifles.
Shape your decisions quickly.
Acquire skill and technique.
Deserve loyalty and co-operation.
Value character above all.

— Herbert N. Casson

Laws are not invented; they grow out of circumstances.

— Azarias

Prejudice, which sees what it pleases, cannot see what is plain. *— A. DeVere*

If you choose to represent the various parts in life by holes upon a table, of different shapes — some circular, some triangular, some square, some oblong, — and the persons acting these parts by bits of wood of similar shapes, we shall generally find that the triangular person has got into the square hole, the oblong into the triangular, and a square person has squeezed himself into the round hole. The officer and the office, the doer and the thing done, seldom fit so exactly that we can say they were almost made for each other.   — *Sydney Smith*

We haven't taken time to begin to learn about the world through which we are passing. . . . I predict that our liberal arts faculties will more and more be giving refresher courses to graduates and to non-graduates alike. . . . It is time that the word " commencement " be given a new educational content for the graduating classes of our great universities.   — *Charles Seymour*

The more people who own little businesses of their own, the safer our country will be, and the better off its cities and towns; for the people who have a stake in their country and their community are its best citizens.
        — *John Hancock*

The man whom Heaven appoints to govern others, should himself first learn to bend his passions to the sway of reason.   — *Thomson*

Nature imitates herself. A grain thrown into good ground brings forth fruit; a principle thrown into a good mind brings forth fruit. Everything is created and conducted by the same Master — the root, the branch, the fruits — the principles, the consequences.   — *Pascal*

Life is like a game of cards. Reliability is the ace, industry the king, politeness the queen, thrift the jack: commonsense is playing to best advantage the cards you draw And every day, as the game proceeds, you will find the ace, king, queen, jack in your hand and opportunity to use them. — *Ed. Howe*

Conditions never get so bad in this country but that a man who works can get business. — *Lawrence P. Fisher*

Get all you can without hurting your soul, your body, or your neighbor. Save all you can, cutting off every needless expense. Give all you can. Be glad to give, and ready to distribute; laying up in store for yourselves a good foundation against the time to come, that you may attain eternal life. — *John Wesley*

As to people saying a few idle words about us, we must not mind that any more than the old church steeple minds the rooks cawing about it. — *Eliot*

Politicians think that by stopping up the chimney they can stop its smoking. They try the experiment, they drive the smoke back, and there is more smoke than ever; but they do not see that their want of common sense has increased the evil they would have prevented. — *Borne*

Education has now become the chief problem of the world, its one holy cause. The nations that see this will survive, and those that fail to do so will slowly perish. . . . There must be re-education of the will and of the heart as well as of the intellect, and the ideals of service must supplant those of selfishness and greed. — *G. Stanley Hall*

Schools need not preach political doctrine to defend
democracy.   If they shape men capable of critical thought
and trained in social attitudes, that is all that is necessary.
                                        — *Albert Einstein*

" Theirs not to make reply, theirs not to reason why,"
may be a good enough motto for men who are on their way
to be shot.   But from such men expect no empires to be
builded, no inventions made, no great discoveries brought
to light.   — *Bruce Barton*

If we make religion our business, God will make it our
blessedness.   — *H. G. J. Adam*

No power is strong enough to be lasting if it labors under
the weight of fear.   — *Cicero*

When a fool has made up his mind the market has
gone by.   — *Spanish Proverb*

Fear is an insidious virus.   Given a breeding place in
our minds, it will permeate the whole body of our work; it
will eat away our spirit and block the forward path of our
endeavors.   Fear is the greatest enemy of progress.   Progress
moves ever on, and does not linger to consider microscop-
ically the implications of each particular action.   Only
small and over-cautious minds see the shadows of lurking
enemies and dangers everywhere, and shrink away from the
increased efforts needed to overcome them.   Fear is met
and destroyed with courage.   Again and again, when the
struggle seems hopeless and all opportunity lost — some
man or woman with a little more courage, a little more effort,
brings victory.   — *James F. Bell*

It is the height of absurdity to sow little but weeds in the first half of one's lifetime and expect to harvest a valuable crop in the second half.

— *Percy H. Johnston*

It is a psychological law that whatever we desire to accomplish we must impress upon the subjective or subconscious mind; that is, we must register a vow with ourselves, we must make our resolution with vigor, with faith that we can do the thing we want to do; we must register our conviction with such intensity that the great creative forces within us will tend to realize them. Our impressions will become expressions just in proportion to the vigor with which we register our vows to accomplish our ambitions, to make our visions realities.   — *Orison Swett Marden*

Opportunity is as scarce as oxygen; men fairly breathe it and do not know it.   — *Doc Sane*

The three great essentials to achieve anything worth while are, first, hard work; second, stick-to-itiveness; third, common sense.   — *Thomas A. Edison*

We are either progressing or retrograding all the while; there is no such thing as remaining stationary in this life.

— *J. F. Clarke*

It were happy if we studied nature more in natural things; and acted according to nature, whose rules are few, plain, and most reasonable.   — *William Penn*

Not doing more than the average is what keeps the average down.   — *Wm. M. Winans*

Prudence is no doubt a valuable quality, but prudence
which degenerates into timidity is very seldom the path to
safety.   — *Viscount Cecil*

Today the treacherous, unexplored areas of the world
are not in continents or the seas; they are in the minds and
hearts of men.   — *Allen E. Claxton, D.D.*

The uprisings of 1789 cost Louis XVI some prerogatives,
but four years later a valueless currency cost him his head.
Germany's inflation of the 1920s laid the foundation upon
which Hitler built. Indeed, a runaway inflation is the goal
of revolutionists. The maxim of that apostle of revolution,
Lenin, was " Debauch the currency! "
                                   — *Edgar M. Queeny*

The dissemination of information is one of the cornerstones of modern civilization.   — *John F. Budd*

There are two ways of meeting difficulties: you alter the
difficulties, or you alter yourself to meet them.
                                   — *Phyllis Bottome*

To believe a business impossible is the way to make it so.
How many feasible projects have miscarried through
despondency, and been strangled in their birth by a cowardly
imagination.   — *Jeremy Collier*

It's an old adage that the way to be safe is never to be
secure. . . . Each one of us requires the spur of insecurity
to force us to do our best.   — *Dr. Harold W. Dodds*

One of the most hopeful portents of the times does not appear in any index of rising commodity prices — car loadings — bank deposits — or business volume — though it actuates all of them. It is the human factor — the stamina, the resourcefulness, the daring of the men to whom business looks for leadership.

If adversity put business leadership to rigorous test — it also provided a rigorous course of training. If it took off the fat — it toughened the spirit.   — *P. W. Litchfield*

When men speak ill of thee, live so as nobody may believe them.   — *Plato*

A Morning Resolve

I will this day try to live a simple, sincere, and serene life; repelling promptly every thought of discontent, anxiety, discouragement, impurity, and self-seeking; cultivating cheerfulness, magnanimity, charity, and the habit of holy silence; exercising economy in expenditure, carefulness in conversation, diligence in appointed service, fidelity to every trust, and a childlike trust in God.

— *John H. Vincent*

If men would consider not so much wherein they differ, as wherein they agree, there would be far less of uncharitableness and angry feeling in the world.   — *Addison*

Free and fair discussion will ever be found the firmest friend to truth.   — *G. Campbell*

Let the motive be in the deed and not in the event. Be not one whose motive for action is the hope of reward.

— *Kreeshna*

Civilization requires slaves. Human slavery is wrong, insecure and demoralizing. On mechanical slavery, on the slavery of the machine, the future of the world depends.

— *Oscar Wilde*

Individuals may form communities, but it is institutions alone that can create a nation. — *Disraeli*

I do not believe in that word Fate. It is the refuge of every self-confessed failure. — *Andrew Soutar*

Exaggeration is a blood relation to falsehood and nearly as blamable. — *H. Ballou*

As A Man Grows Older

He values the voice of experience more and the voice of prophecy less.

He finds more of life's wealth in the common pleasures — home, health, children.

He thinks more about worth of men and less about their wealth.

He begins to appreciate his own father a little more.

He boasts less and boosts more.

He hurries less, and usually makes more progress.

He esteems the friendship of God a little higher.

— *Roy L. Smith*

The difference between a " wise guy " and a wise man is *plenty!* — *Galen Starr Ross*

When the Master of the universe has points to carry in his government he impresses his will in the structure of minds. — *Emerson*

When business is not all that it should be there is a
temptation to sit back and say, " Well, what's the use!
We've done everything possible to stir up a little business
and there is nothing doing so what's the use of trying! "
There is always a way. There was a way in and there is
a way out. And success comes to the man who grits his
teeth, squares his jaw, and says, " There is a way for me
and, by jingo, I'll find it." The stagnator gathers green
scum, finally dries up and leaves an unsightly hollow.

—Clifford Sloan

Limit to strength?
There is no limit to strength.
Limit to courage?
There is no limit to courage.
Limit to suffering?
There is no limit to suffering.

— D'Annunzio

The man who saves time by galloping loses it by missing
his way; the shepherd who hurries his flock to get them
home spends the night on the mountain looking for the
lost; economy does not consist in haste, but in certainty.

— Ramsay MacDonald

To live is not to learn, but to apply.   *— Legouvé*

The suppression of unnecessary offices, of useless estab-
lishments and expenses, enabled us to discontinue our internal taxes. These, covering our land with officers, and
opening our doors to their intrusions, had already begun
that process of domiciliary vexation which, once entered, is
scarcely to be restrained from reaching, successively, every
article of property and produce.   *— Thomas Jefferson*

The world is moving so fast now-a-days that the man who says it can't be done is generally interrupted by someone doing it.   — *Elbert Hubbard*

I believe in the supreme worth of the individual and in his right to life, liberty and the pursuit of happiness.

I believe that every right implies a responsibility; every opportunity, an obligation; every possession, a duty.

I believe that the law was made for man and not man for the law; that government is the servant of the people and not their master.

I believe in the dignity of labor, whether with head or hand; that the world owes no man a living but that it owes every man an opportunity to make a living.

I believe that thrift is essential to well-ordered living and that economy is a prime requisite of a sound financial structure, whether in government, business or personal affairs.

I believe that truth and justice are fundamental to an enduring social order.

I believe in the sacredness of a promise, that a man's word should be as good as his bond; that character — not wealth or power or position — is of supreme worth.

I believe that the rendering of useful service is the common duty of mankind and that only in the purifying fire of sacrifice is the dross of selfishness consumed and the greatness of the human soul set free.

I believe in an all-wise and all-loving God, named by whatever name, and that the individual's highest fulfillment, greatest happiness and widest usefulness are to be found in living in harmony with His will.

I believe that love is the greatest thing in the world; that it alone can overcome hate; that right can and will triumph over might.   — *John D. Rockefeller, Jr.*

What is defeat? Nothing but education; nothing but the first step to something better.   — *Wendell Phillips*

The ability to form friendships, to make people believe in you and trust you is one of the few absolutely fundamental qualities of success. Selling, buying, negotiating are so much smoother and easier when the parties enjoy each other's confidence. The young man who can make friends quickly will find that he will glide instead of stumble through life. — *John J. McGuirk*

If your capacity to acquire has outstripped your capacity to enjoy, you are on the way to the scrap-heap.

— *Glen Buck*

The spectacle of a nation praying is more awe-inspiring than the explosion of an atomic bomb. The force of prayer is greater than any possible combination of man-made or man-controlled powers because prayer is man's greatest means of tapping the infinite resources of God.

— *J. Edgar Hoover*

Many people take no care of their money till they come nearly to the end of it, and others do just the same with their time. — *Goethe*

Mankind — in far too many places — is hungry. We can and must help. For hunger is no ally of freedom. The economic machinery of the world is stalled and damaged as a result of the war. The machinery must be repaired and started again. We have tools and parts. We have what is just as important — the " know-how." . . . We can supply that " know-how " and guidance to make effective the aid we provide. For this aid is in our tradition — a tradition rooted in freedom and progess.

— *John W. Snyder*

When a nation gives birth to a man who is able to produce a great thought, another is born who is able to understand and admire it.   — *Joubert*

There are nettles everywhere, but smooth, green grasses are more common still; the blue of heaven is larger than the cloud.   — *E. B. Browning*

Think like a man of action and act like a man of thought.
                    — *Henri Bergson*

In a world of checks and balances, the most successful man often is the one who stores up " credits " for the future rather than the one who insists on a daily quota of praise, reward and compensation for all he gives or does. There may seem to be injustices and inequities as we go along in living, but very often, in looking back, hardships and heartaches have turned out to be disguised blessings, hardening us for a crisis or a job or a condition which otherwise we might have been unable to handle creditably.
                    — *Edgar Paul Hermann*

Great and dramatic changes have taken place in the world. Old values, old ways of thinking, have changed — to give way to new and pressing problems that tax all our optimism and purpose, and that call for the best we can contribute to the work of the world. But one fact stands out clear and challenging: The sound, basic principles of personal progress and success have not changed. They have been modified and accelerated in their operation — given new directions, perhaps — but still the greatest rewards go to those who can give most.   — *L. G. Elliott*

Earn a little, and spend a little — less.
                    — *John Stevenson*

Business is a great game. I play it very hard and in as sportsmanlike a way as I know how, and I feel that at the end of the day I have got the fullest reward. I am an enthusiast in business. Besides ambition, business demands courage, judgment, imagination and organizing ability. But it has no use for self-satisfaction or for mental laziness — the first crime in the list.   — *H. Gordon Selfridge*

He who stops being better stops being good.
                              — *Oliver Cromwell*

There is nothing quite so dead as a self-centered man — a man who holds himself up as a self-made success, and measures himself by himself and is pleased with the result.
                              — *Wesley G. Huber, D.D.*

There isn't a plant or a business on earth that couldn't stand a few improvements — and be better for them. Someone is going to think of them. Why not beat the other fellow to it?   — *Roger W. Babson*

Character and personal force are the only investments that are worth anything.   — *Walt Whitman*

A single solitary philosopher may be great, virtuous and happy in the depth of poverty, but not a whole people.
                              — *Iselin*

A man is sane morally at thirty, rich mentally at forty, wise spiritually at fifty — or never!
                              — *Dr. William Osler*

It is the age that forms the man, not the man that forms
the age. Great minds do indeed react on the society which
has made them what they are, but they only pay with interest what they have received.   — *Macaulay*

Losses are comparative, imagination only makes them
of any moment.   — *Pascal*

If it is not in the interest of the public it is not in the
interest of business.   — *Joseph H. Defrees*

The world has never been so rich in helpers as it is
today, and consequently never have there been people so
happy and so blessed in their lives. Volunteers for human
service seem to spring from the ground. It would be difficult to point out a more encouraging fact for the world's
future.   — *Minot Simons, D.D.*

The great task of the peace is to work morals into it.
The only sort of peace that will be real is one in which
everybody takes his share of responsibility. World organizations and conferences will be of no value unless there
is improvement in the relation of men to men.
                              — *Sir Frederick Eggleston*

Communism is obsessed with a hatred of ways of life
other than its own and is afraid that unless these are swept
away they will eventually overcome it.
                              — *Cyril Forster Garbett, D.D.*

Who bravely dares must sometimes risk a fall.
                              — *Smollett*

Education

To be at home in all lands and all ages; to count Nature
as a familiar acquaintance and Art an intimate friend; to
gain a standard for the appreciation of other men's work
and the criticism of one's own; to carry the keys of the
world's library in one's pocket, and feel its resources behind
one in whatever task he undertakes; to make hosts of
friends among the men of one's own age who are the leaders
in all walks of life; to lose oneself in general enthusiasms
and co-operate with others for common ends. . . .

— William De Witt Hyde

There are many persons that smile on hearing talk of
building a better world and say that the world cares nothing
for that. These persons have lost faith in people and God
because of their own mistakes.   *— John S. Bonnell, D.D.*

A man may be ungrateful, but the human race is not so.

— Milton

The human body is made up of some four hundred
muscles, evolved through centuries of physical activity.
Unless these are used, they will deteriorate. The business
executive should look for ways of using his muscles, naturally, each day. Instead of always using his desk bells,
he should occasionally do an office errand himself. He
might, with profit, walk one way or part way to his office
instead of riding; or walk up or down a flight or two of
stairs instead of invariably using the elevator. He should
cultivate muscle hunger.   *— Dr. Eugene Lyman Fisk*

We look forward to the time when the Power of Love will
replace the Love of Power. Then will our world know the
blessings of Peace.   *— Gladstone*

The progress of the world depends upon the men who walk in the fresh furrows and through the rustling corn; upon those whose faces are radiant with the glare of furnace fires; upon the delvers in mines, and the workers in shops; upon those who give to the Winter air the ringing music of the axe; upon those who battle with the boisterous billows of the sea; upon the inventors and discoverers; upon the brave thinkers.   — *Robert Ingersoll*

Of course the one who gains the most from the contest is the player himself, and no one can long be a player if he is a poor sport and fails to do his best. Let the game be tennis, golf, baseball, or football, or the bigger game called life, whatever it is we must do our best because it keeps up the spirit — and that's what we need more than anything else. And if I keep up my spirit, and by example help to pull my neighbor out of his slump then my life has not been a failure. I am a success!   — *Malcolm W. Bingay*

No two things differ more than hurry and dispatch. Hurry is the mark of a weak mind, dispatch of a strong one. A weak man in office, like a squirrel in a cage, is laboring eternally, but to no purpose, and is in constant motion without getting on a job; like a turnstile, he is in everybody's way, but stops nobody; he talks a great deal, but says very little; looks into everything but sees nothing; and has a hundred irons in the fire, but very few of them are hot, and with those few that are, he only burns his fingers.
                                            — *Colton*

Only free people can hold their purpose and their honor steady to a common end, and prefer the interests of mankind to any narrow interest of their own.
                                    — *Woodrow Wilson*

In some respects the world is in the same situation that
it was in after the fall of the Roman empire. There is an
even greater need for a religious revival now because pagan-
ism has become sophisticated. — *Barbara Ward*

The man who cannot believe in himself cannot believe
in anything else. The basis of all integrity and character is
whatever faith we have in our own integrity.
— *Roy L. Smith*

No sacrifice short of the sacrifice of individual liberty,
individual self-respect, and individual enterprise is too great
a price to pay for permanent peace. — *Clark H. Minor*

When boasting ends, there dignity begins. — *Young*

It is good to dream, but it is better to dream and work.
Faith is mighty, but action with faith is mightier. Desiring
is helpful, but work and desire are invincible.
— *Thomas Robert Gaines*

Education is anything that we do for the purpose of
taking advantage of the experience of some one else.
— *Lyman Bryson*

War will disappear, like the dinosaur, when changes in
world conditions have destroyed its survival value.
— *Robert A. Millikan*

Neutrality, as a lasting principle, is an evidence of weakness. — *Louis Kossuth*

Freedom from fear simply cannot be attained by political fiat or international agreement. Fear is a personal emotion and it can be controlled or conquered only by individual persons.   — *Franklin P. Cole, D.D.*

You can never expect too much of yourself in the matter of giving yourself to others.   — *Theodore C. Speers, D.D.*

The great difference between the real statesman and the pretender is, that the one sees into the future, while the other regards only the present; the one lives by the day, and acts on expedience; the other acts on enduring principles and for immortality.   — *Burke*

The chains of habit are too weak to be felt until they are too strong to be broken.   — *Johnson*

Political economy is only the economy of human aggregates, and its laws are laws which we may individually recognize. What is required for their elucidation is not long arrays of statistics nor the collocation of laboriously ascertained facts, but that sort of clear thinking which, keeping in mind the distinction between the part and the whole, seeks the relations of familiar things, and which is as possible for the unlearned as for the learned.
                              — *Henry George*

Not on one string are all life's jewels strung.
                              — *William Morris*

He's no failure. He's not dead yet.   — *W. L. George*

What is a minority? The chosen heroes of this earth have been in a minority. There is not a social, political, or religious privilege that you enjoy today that was not bought for you by the blood and tears and patient suffering of the minority. It is the minority that have stood in the van of every moral conflict, and achieved all that is noble in the history of the world. — *John Ballantine Gouch*

We would accomplish many more things if we did not think of them as impossible. — *C. Malesherbes*

The end crowns all; and that old common arbitrator, time, will one day end it. — *Shakespeare*

We want the spirit of America to be efficient; we want American character to be efficient; we want American character to display itself in what I may, perhaps, be allowed to call spiritual efficiency — clear disinterested thinking and fearless action along the right lines of thought. — *Woodrow Wilson*

In science, as in common life, we frequently see that a novelty in system, or in practice, cannot be duly appreciated till time has sobered the enthusiasm of its advocates. — *Maud*

My share of the work of the world may be limited, but the fact that it is work makes it precious. Darwin could work only half an hour at a time; but in many diligent half-hours he laid anew the foundations of philosophy. Green, the historian, tells us that the world is moved not only by the mighty shoves of the heroes, but also by the aggregate of the tiny pushes of each honest worker. — *H. Kellogg*

FOUNDATION STONES

In building a firm foundation for Success, here are a few stones to remember:

1. The wisdom of preparation.
2. The value of confidence.
3. The worth of honesty.
4. The privilege of working.
5. The discipline of struggle.
6. The magnetism of character.
7. The radiance of health.
8. The forcefulness of simplicity.
9. The winsomeness of courtesy.
10. The attractiveness of modesty.
11. The inspiration of cleanliness.
12. The satisfaction of serving.
13. The power of suggestion.
14. The buoyancy of enthusiasm.
15. The advantage of initiative.
16. The virtue of patience.
17. The rewards of co-operation.
18. The fruitfulness of perseverance.
19. The sportsmanship of losing.
20. The joy of winning.   — *Rollo C. Hester*

This world has cares enough to plague us; but he who meditates on others' woe, shall, in that meditation, lose his own.   — *Cumberland*

The circumstances of the world are so variable, that an irrevocable purpose or opinion is almost synonymous with a foolish one.   — *W. H. Seward*

The art of conversation is to be prompt without being stubborn; to refute without argument, and to clothe great matters in a motley garb.   — *Disraeli*

Equality is one of the most consummate scoundrels that ever crept from the brain of a political juggler — a fellow who thrusts his hand into the pocket of honest industry or enterprising talent, and squanders their hard-earned profits on profligate idleness or indolent stupidity.

— *Paulding*

Should one look through a red glass at a white lily, he would seem to see a red lily. But there would be no red lily. So it is with humanity's problems. They consist of false mental pictures. — *M. D. Garbrick*

No leader can make a happy, humane, workable society out of a stubborn lot of individualists who are more conscious of their rights than of their responsibilities, who accept a low moral standard in business and family life, who want more than they need, and are motivated by fear and greed, some of them forcing their will through blocs of special interests which are prejudicial to the welfare of the whole society. — *Samuel M. Shoemaker, D.D.*

No liberal man would impute a charge of unsteadiness to another for having changed his opinion. — *Cicero*

When business embarks on a rampage which does not help humanity to live and GROW — when it pushes *beyond* this range of usefulness and overproduces human needs — or when it falls behind and outlives its usefulness — it runs into trouble of some kind. And when the business tree is crowded with these dead or dying branches, the tree as a whole begins to suffer. We run into a business depression or plunge into industrial war to shake the rotten branches down. — *V. C. Kitchen*

The lesson which wars and depressions have taught is that if we want peace, prosperity and happiness at home we must help to establish them abroad. — *Hugo L. Black*

The toxin of fatigue has been demonstrated; but the poisons generated by evil temper and emotional excess over non-essentials have not yet been determined, although without a doubt they exist. Explosions of temper, emotional cyclones, and needless fear and panic over disease or misfortune that seldom materialize, are simply bad habits. By proper ventilation and illumination of the mind it is possible to cultivate tolerance, poise and real courage without being a bromide-taker. — *Metchnikoff*

How men long for celebrity! Some would willingly sacrifice their lives for fame, and not a few would rather be known by their crimes than not known at all.
— *Sinclair*

Dreaming is an act of pure imagination, attesting in all men a creative power, which, if it were available in waking, would make every man a Dante or a Shakespeare.
— *H. F. Hedge*

No peace is good unless educators and the church are allowed to speak and unless they conduct themselves so that they will be listened to. Not only a military office of intelligence is needed but a spiritual and intellectual intelligence service as well. — *Carl J. Hambro, D.D.*

After we have recognized that we are all undeserving creatures who have received the love of God, who can but respond and show it in his own life?
— *Edgar F. Romig*

Ten Pointers

1. Be yourself. Cultivate desirable qualities.
2. Be alert. Look for opportunities to express yourself.
3. Be positive. Determine your goal and the route to it.
4. Be systematic. Take one step at a time.
5. Be persistent. Hold to your course.
6. Be a worker. Work your brain more than your body.
7. Be a student. Know your job.
8. Be fair. Treat the other man as you would be treated.
9. Be temperate. Avoid excess in anything.
10. Be confident. Have faith that cannot be weakened.

— Everett W. Lord

Only in quiet waters things mirror themselves undistorted.
Only in a quiet mind is adequate perception of the world.

— Hans Margolius

Until someone has lighted on the secret of making men's minds more accurate, all the progress that can be made in the discovery of truth will not prevent their reasoning falsely; and the further anyone attempts to speed them beyond the common notions, the more he will lay them open to error. *— Vauvanargues*

The antidote for crime should be administered in childhood, by the parents. The problem is not fundamentally that of the improper child so much as it is that of the improper home. *— Justice John W. Hill*

Experience is not what happens to a man. It is what a man does with what happens to him.

— Aldous Huxley

The most precious thing anyone — man or store, anybody or anything — can have is the goodwill of others. It
is something as fragile as an orchid. And as beautiful!
As precious as a gold nugget — and as hard to find. As
powerful as a great turbine — and as hard to build. As
wonderful as youth — and as hard to keep.

— Amos Parrish

Neither patents, processes nor secrets are any longer
assurance of success. The men responsible for the financing
of industry have come to recognize that scientific methods
have largely leveled down the advantages between one
product and another. There are no longer any secrets in
business — at least not in the most successful business.

— Bruce Barton

Some people are so afraid to die that they never begin
to live.   *— Henry Van Dyke*

When the great finals come, each one will be asked five
questions:
First: What did you accomplish in the world with the
power that God gave you?
Second: How did you help your neighbor and what did
you do for those in need?
Third: What did you do to serve God?
Fourth: What did you leave in the world that was worth
while when you came from it?
Last: What did you bring into this new world which will
be of use here?   *— J. Stanley Durkee*

Economy is in itself a source of great revenue.

— Seneca

To most people loneliness is a doom. Yet loneliness is the very thing which God has chosen to be one of the schools of training for His very own. It is the fire that sheds the dross and reveals the gold.

— *Bernard M. Martin, D.D.*

Kindness in ourselves is the honey that blunts the sting of unkindness in another. — *Landor*

If well thou hast begun, go on; it is the end that crowns us, not the fight. — *Herrick*

While actions are always to be judged by the immutable standard of right and wrong, the judgments we pass upon men must be qualified by considerations of age, country, station and other accidental circumstances; and it will then be found that he who is most charitable in his judgment is generally the least unjust. — *Southey*

It is hardly possible to suspect another without having in one's self the seeds of the baseness the other is accused of.

— *Stanislaus*

Method will teach you to win time. — *Goethe*

It is great happiness to be praised of them who are most praiseworthy. — *Sir P. Sidney*

Never hurry; take plenty of exercise; always be cheerful, and take all the sleep you need, and you may expect to be well. — *J. F. Clarke*

WHAT KIND OF A CHAP ARE YOU?

Are you one of the chaps who can take his raps
    And still not hit the floor;
Who'll stick by the gun till his task is done
    And then look 'round for more?

Do you grin at your work or sulk and shirk
    When the job seems hard to do;
Are you there with the grit to do your bit;
    Can the boss depend on you?

Is your conscience clear, with nothing to fear
    As you punch the clock each night;
When you leave the job, do your pulses throb
    With the thought of a task done right?

Is it pleasure or dread when you pillow your head
    And think of the coming day;
Do you breathe a prayer for strength to bear
    Does your job mean simply pay?

Just pause a bit and see if you fit
    In the class that's pictured here —
For it's never too late to clean the slate
    And start on a record clear.

                                        — *Frank A. Collins*

Time ripens all things; no man is born wise.

                                        — *Cervantes*

In this world of unequal things and irregularities we
should follow the Master's advice. He went about encouraging. He wasn't a fault-finder. He was a faith finder — a
finder of human power and of human excellence.

                                        — *Karl Reiland, D.D.*

TRADE

As we pay others, so we are paid,
Life gives us back just what we give;
And so, goodwill controls success,
But trade that we may truly live.
Sales may be made in money, yes,
But they are always made to men;
And so, goodwill controls success,
Bringing folks back to buy again.
He profits most whose every sale,
Creates a friend whose kindly thought
Serves to perpetuate the tale,
Of what and where and why he bought.

— *Furrow*

The best advice on the art of being happy is about as
easy to follow as advice to be well when one is sick.

— *Madame Swetchine*

The only way for a rich man to be healthy is by exercise
and abstinence, to live as if he were poor.

— *Sir W. Temple*

Men of age object too much, consult too long, adventure
too little, repeat too soon, and seldom drive business home
to the full period, but content themselves with a mediocrity
of success. — *Francis Bacon*

Pleasure is a necessary reciprocal: no one feels, who does
not at the same time give it. To be pleased, one must
please. What pleases you in others, will in general please
them in you. — *Lord Chesterfield*

Some of the greatest thinking has been done by those who cared little for riches — Pasteur, Edison, Jane Addams — and who shall say that theirs was not the richer life? Today, the world knows the poetry of Shakespeare, the music of Wagner, the art of Rembrandt; but who knows even the names of the money barons of their day — or cares to know? If you want your name to live after you, you'll not give all your thought to money. But, whether you want to make money, or write a book, or build a bridge, or run a streetcar — or do anything else successfully — you'll do well to remember that in all the world there is no word more important than — " *Think!* "   — *Edwin Baird*

When we have done our best, we should wait the result in peace.   — *J. Lubbock*

Resolved, to live with all my might while I do live. Resolved, never to lose one moment of time, to improve it in the most profitable way I possibly can. Resolved, never to do anything which I should despise or think meanly of in another. Resolved, never to do anything out of revenge. Resolved, never to do anything which I should be afraid to do if it were the last hour of my life.

— *Jonathan Edwards*

'Tis looking downward makes one dizzy.

— *Robert Browning*

Cleverness is serviceable for everything, sufficient for nothing.   — *Amiel*

The devil never tempted a man whom he found judiciously employed.   — *Spurgeon*

Wisdom does not show itself so much in precept as in life — in firmness of mind and a mastery of appetite. It teaches us to do as well as to talk, and to make our words and actions all of a color. — *Seneca*

Genuine morality is preserved only in the school of adversity; a state of continuous prosperity may easily prove a quicksand to virtue. — *Schiller*

We exaggerate misfortune and happiness alike. We are never either so wretched or so happy as we say we are. — *Balzac*

If we are ever to enjoy life, now is the time — not to-morrow, nor next year, nor in some future life after we have died. The best preparation for a better life next year is a full, complete, harmonious, joyous life this year. Our beliefs in a rich future life are of little importance unless we coin them into a rich present life. Today should always be our most wonderful day. — *Thomas Dreier*

In time of great anxiety we can draw power from our friends. We should at such times, however, avoid friends who sympathize too deeply, who give us pity rather than strength. Like so many unwise parents, such friends — well meaning, though they be — give " set lessons in fear " rather than in courage. It is said that Napoleon before one of his great battles used to invite his marshals to file past his tent, where he grasped their hands in silence. Certain friends, like Napoleon, can give us a sense of triumphing power. — *D. Lupton*

It is the growling man who lives a dog's life. — *Coleman Cox*

1. Do more than exist, live.
2. Do more than touch, feel.
3. Do more than look, observe.
4. Do more than read, absorb.
5. Do more than hear, listen.
6. Do more than listen, understand.
7. Do more than think, ponder.
8. Do more than talk, say something.

— John H. Rhoades

We can achieve the utmost in economies by engineering knowledge; we can conquer new fields by research; we can build plants and machines that shall stand among the wonders of the world; but unless we put the right man in the right place — unless we make it possible for our workers and executives alike to enjoy a sense of satisfaction in their jobs, our efforts will have been in vain.

— E. R. Stettinius, Jr.

Responsibility walks hand in hand with capacity and power.   *— J. G. Holland*

Who does more earnestly long for a change than he who is uneasy in his present circumstances? And who run to create confusions with so desperate a boldness as those who have nothing to lose, hope to gain by them?

— Sir T. More

The intellectual content of religions has always finally adapted itself to scientific and social conditions after they have become clear. . . . For this reason I do not think that those who are concerned about the future of a religious attitude should trouble themselves about the conflict of science with traditional doctrines.   *— John Dewey*

MENTAL HEALTH RULES

1. HAVE A HOBBY: Acquire pursuits which absorb your interest; sports and " nature " are best.

2. DEVELOP A PHILOSOPHY: Adapt yourself to social and spiritual surroundings.

3. SHARE YOUR THOUGHTS: Cultivate companionship in thought and in feeling. Confide, confess, consult.

4. FACE YOUR FEARS: Analyze them; daylight dismisses ghosts.

5. BALANCE FANTASY WITH FACT: Dream but also do; wish but build; imagine but ever face reality.

6. BEWARE ALLURING ESCAPES: Alcohol, opiates and barbitals may prove faithless friends.

7. EXERCISE: Walk, swim, golf — muscles need activity.

8. LOVE, BUT LOVE WISELY: Sex is a flame which uncontrolled may scorch; properly guided, it will light the torch of eternity.

9. DON'T BECOME ENGULFED IN A WHIRLPOOL OF WORRIES: Call early for help. The doctor is ready for your rescue.

10. TRUST IN TIME: Be patient and hopeful, time is a great therapist. — *Dr. Joseph Fetterman*

When the peoples of a nation are filled with God's spirit and seek His guidance they will have it; and, having it, they will select leaders who are like-minded and will direct them into God's paths. — *Joseph I. Chapman, D.D.*

The true interest of Americans is mutual interest. The doctrines that put race against race, group against group, class against class and worker against employer all are false doctrines. They are preached only by assassins of progress who are economic parasites or political pirates. We want to recreate an America in which their falsehoods cannot prevail, where the energies of men and women shall be devoted to constructive efforts. — *Wheeler McMillen*

Love work.
Turn a deaf ear to slander.
Be considerate in correcting others.
Do not be taken up by trifles.
Do not resent plain speaking.
Meet offenders half-way.
Be thorough in thought.
Have an open mind.
Do your duty without grumbling.

— *Marcus Aurelius*

A man of courage is also full of faith.   — *Cicero*

Many of us are like the little boy we met trudging along a country road with a cat-rifle over his shoulder. " What are you hunting, buddy? " we asked. " Dunno, sir, I ain't seen it yet."   — *R. Lee Sharpe*

The first lesson of life is to burn our own smoke; that is, not to inflict on outsiders our personal sorrows and petty morbidness, not to keep thinking of ourselves as exceptional cases.   — *James Russell Lowell*

A new type of management is required in this new business era — one that realizes that responsibility begins rather than ends when the goods reach the shipping platform. First of all, such management will concern itself primarily with the manufacture of customers rather than the manufacture of the product alone. Management must resort to logical analysis more than to precedent. A keen understanding of human beings will permit management to secure unusual results.   — *Howard E. Blood*

We love peace, but not peace at any price. There is a peace more destructive of the manhood of living man, than war is destructive of his body. Chains are worse than bayonets.
— *Jerrold*

The most thoroughly wasted of all days is that on which one has not laughed. — *Chamfort*

The man who graduates to-day and stops learning to-morrow is uneducated the day after.
— *Newton D. Baker*

It is well to read up everything within reach about your business; this not only improves your knowledge, your usefulness and your fitness for more responsible work, but it invests your business with more interest, since you understand its functions, its basic principles, its place in the general scheme of things. — *Daniel Willard*

In men whom men condemn as ill
I find so much of goodness still;
In men whom men pronounce divine
I find so much of sin and blot,
I hesitate to draw the line
Between the two, when God has not.
— *Joaquin Miller*

I have a feeling — as compelling as a religious conviction — that if industry will constantly pass on to the worker and the customer all the savings of labor-saving machinery and invention, rather than siphon them off into the pools of watered securities, it will by that process keep distribution and production in balance and go as far toward Utopia as our poor human natures will go or be driven.
— *Samuel B. Pettengill*

For strength to bear is found in duty alone,
And he is blest indeed who learns to make
The joy of others cure his own heartache.

— *Drake*

When a man tells you that he knows the exact truth about
anything you are safe in inferring that he is an inexact
man.   — *Bertrand Russell*

A long time ago a noted specialist said that his secret of
success as a physician was keeping the patient's head cool
and his feet warm. And it is just now becoming generally
known that a " hot head " and " cold feet " are enough to
bring disaster to even a well man.   — *O. Byron Cooper*

There are two kinds of discontent in' this world: The
discontent that works, and the discontent that wrings its
hands. The first gets what it wants, and the second loses
what it has. There's no cure for the first but success; and
there's no cure at all for the second.   — *Gordon Graham*

Fame is a vapor, popularity an accident, riches take
wings. Only one thing endures, and that is character.

— *Horace Greeley*

Material riches are proving inadequate and are de-
preciated. God's love is bestowing sufficient benefits on the
nation and the world, but the benefits are not getting to the
people. Something is intervening, and it is the greed of
people. The only values that are everlasting are spiritual,
and when we lose them we lose everything.

— *Anthony H. Evans, D.D.*

Commerce is a game of skill, which every man can not play, which few men can play well. The right merchant is one who has the just average of faculties we call common-sense; a man of strong affinity for facts, who makes up his decision on what he has seen. He is thoroughly persuaded of the truths of arithmetic. There is always a reason, in the man, for his good or bad fortune; and so, in making money. Men talk as if there were some magic about this, and believe in magic, in all parts of life. He knows that all goes on the old road, pound for pound, cent for cent — for every effect a perfect cause — and that good luck is another name for tenacity of purpose. *— Emerson*

Government is not reason, it is not eloquence — it is force! Like fire it is a dangerous servant and a fearful master; never for a moment should it be left to irresponsible action. *— George Washington*

Touchiness, when it becomes chronic, is a morbid condition of the inward disposition. It is self-love inflamed to the acute point. *— William Drummond*

I rejoice that intelligence rules, that there are thousands and tens of thousands of wide-awake men and women, rich in the understanding of life's meaning, plodding along, singing as they go, doing their work, whether it be uphill or down, with an invincible determination, a simple modesty and a cheerfulness that radiates joy and happiness to all within reach of their influence. *— Louis A. Stremple*

Do not think that what your thoughts dwell upon is of no matter. Your thoughts are making you.
— Bishop Steere

In the world men must be dealt with according to what they are, and not to what they ought to be; and the great art of life is to find out what they are, and act with them accordingly.   — *Charles C. F. Greville*

The intellectual function of trouble is to lead men to think. . . . Depression is a small price to pay if it induces us to think about the cause of the disorder, confusion and insecurity which are the outstanding traits of our social life.
— *John Dewey*

You cannot legislate the human race into heaven.
— *C. H. Parkhurst, D.D.*

Thousands of engineers can design bridges, calculate strains and stresses, and draw up specifications for machines, but the great engineer is the man who can tell whether the bridge or the machine should be built at all, where it should be built, and when.   — *Eugene G. Grace*

Toleration has never been the cause of civil war; while, on the contrary, persecution has covered the earth with blood and carnage.   — *Voltaire*

To insure good health: Eat lightly, breathe deeply, live moderately, cultivate cheerfulness, and maintain an interest in life.   — *William Louden*

Details often kill initiative, but there have been few successful men who weren't good at details. Don't ignore details. Lick them.   — *Wm. B. Given, Jr.*

A man is already of consequence in the world when it is known that we can implicitly rely upon him. Often I have known a man to be preferred in stations of honor and profit because he had this reputation: When he said he knew a thing, he knew it, and when he said he would do a thing, he did it.
— *Bulwer-Lytton*

One very important ingredient of success is *a good, wide-awake, persistent, tireless enemy.* An enemy to an ambitious man is like the rhinoceros bird to the rhinoceros. When the enemy comes the rhinoceros bird tells about it. When a successful man is making mistakes the enemy immediately calls attention and warns the man. Get for yourself a first class enemy, cultivate him as an enemy, and when you achieve success, thank him.
— *Colonel Frank B. Shutts*

Do we know that truth is life and falsehood spiritual death? Do we know that beauty is joy and ugliness sin? Do we know that justice is the condition of well-being and happiness, while injustice of any kind is defeat? In a universe of uncertainties these values alone are certain. They give order and design to living.
— *Sydney Bruce Snow, D.D.*

Any man worth his salt will stick up for what he believes right, but it takes a slightly bigger man to acknowledge instantly and without reservation that he is in error.
— *Gen. Peyton C. March*

Our great problem of the new post-war age will be not how to produce, but how to use; not how to create, but how to co-operate; not how to maim and to kill, but how to *live.*
— *Robert A. Millikan*

A man's character is the reliability of himself. His
reputation is the opinion others have formed of him. Character is in him; reputation is from other people.
— *Henry Ward Beecher*

A judicious silence is always better than truth spoken
without charity.   — *De Sales*

Independency may be found in comparative as well as in
absolute abundance; I mean where a person contracts his
desires within the limits of his fortune.   — *Shenstone*

Clocks will go as they are set; but man, irregular man,
is never constant, never certain.   — *Otway*

In times of great stress, in times of depression, the public
mind loses its balance and becomes the victim of the
catchword.   — *Sir Henry Thornton*

Abolish lashing ambition. Stifle stinging jealousy.
Wreck remorse's whip. Regret no yesterdays. Hobble
feverish hurry. Trust serenely. Choke complaints with
commendation. Make " Smile and Push " your motto.
— *Christian F. Reisner, D.D.*

The only worthwhile things that have come to us in this
life have come through work that was almost always hard,
and often bitter. We believe that this has always been true
of mankind and that it will always be true. We believe not
in how little work, but how much; not in how few hours,
but how many. *America must not grow soft!*
— *J. Kindleberger*

Nothing is lost upon a man who is bent upon growth; nothing wasted on one who is always preparing for his work and his life by keeping eyes, mind, and heart open to nature, men, books, experience. Such a man finds ministers to his education on all sides; everything co-operates with his passion for growth. And what he gathers serves him at unexpected moments in unforeseen ways.

— Hamilton Wright Mabie

It is where a man spends his money that shows where his heart lies. *— A. Edwin Keigwin, D.D.*

I don't want to do business with those who don't make a profit, because they can't give the best service.

— Lee Bristol

He that loveth a book will never want a faithful friend, a wholesome counselor, a cheerful companion, an effectual comforter. By study, by reading, by thinking, one may innocently divert and pleasantly entertain himself, as in all weathers, as in all fortunes. *— Barrow*

What needs to be cultivated among men interested in social relationships whether as owner, manager or employee, producer or consumer, seller or buyer, partner or competitor, is self-control, refraining from unfair advantage, determination to give value as well as to take it; the appreciation that immediate gain is not the principal consideration; that one group can not continue to profit at the expense of another without eventual loss to both; that all classes of men are mutually dependent on the services of each other; that the best service yields the greatest profit.

— Preston S. Arkwright

The Government can destroy wealth but it cannot create wealth, which is the product of labor and management working with creation. — *" Alfalfa Bill " Murray*

People will sit up and take notice of you if you will sit up and take notice of what makes them sit up and take notice.
— *Frank Romer*

Only a life built into God's place can succeed. Half of our discouragements are due to the fact that we are not in tune with the infinite harmony of the Great Power. We should be helpers in building the city of God — a city that will endure when all earthly cities crumble to dust.
— *Bishop Herbert E. Welch*

Things that I felt absolutely sure of but a few years ago, I do not believe now; and this thought makes me see more clearly how foolish it would be to expect all men to agree with me. — *F. D. Van Amburgh*

Higher education must lead the march back to the fundamentals of human relationships, to the old discovery that is ever new, that man does not live by bread alone.
— *John A. Hannah*

Truth lives in the cellar: error on the doorstep.
— *Austin O'Malley*

I have ever held that the rod with which popular fancy invests criticism is properly the rod of divination: a hazel switch for the discovery of buried treasure, not a birch twig for the castigation of offenders. — *Arthur Symons*

Joy is spiritual prosperity. That motto above your desk — " Smile! " How did that ever get into so many business offices? Does a smile help business? Try it. Joy makes the face shine, and he that hath a merry heart hath a continual feast. — *W. C. Isett*

Some thoughts always find us young, and keep us so. Such a thought is the love of the universal and eternal beauty. — *Emerson*

The very helpfulness of the world today is in itself a repudiation of that self-sufficient and self-confident view of life that the world in its progressive development has out-grown the need of religion. It is religion which gives the world what it most needs, a standard of right living, a cause to maintain and defend, a leader to follow and a law to obey. — *John Grier Hibben*

It is a general error to suppose the loudest complainers for the public to be the most anxious for the welfare. — *Burke*

Have patience. All things are difficult before they be-come easy. — *Saadi*

A slender acquaintance with the world must convince every man that actions, not words, are the true criterion of the attachment of friends. — *George Washington*

If men could learn from history, what lessons it might teach us! But passion and party blind our eyes, and the light which experience gives us is a lantern on the stern which shines only on the waves behind us. — *Coleridge*

Don't push out, or to use a slang expression, don't be on the make. Don't play the braggart. Don't be conceited. Don't have bad manners. Don't be on the lookout for number one. Don't lose your temper. Don't be resentful of slights. Don't get malicious satisfaction out of the sins of others.   *— Frank S. Gavin, D.D.*

Life is the continuous adjustment of internal relations to external relations.   *— Herbert Spencer*

Unlimited power is worse for the average person than unlimited alcohol; and the resulting intoxication is more damaging for others. Very few have not deteriorated when given absolute dominion. It is worse for the governor than for the governed.   *— William Lyon Phelps*

Whoever yields to temptation debases himself with a debasement from which he can never rise. A man can be wronged and live; but the unrestricted, unchecked impulse to do wrong is the first and second death.
                                           — Horace Mann

There are two insults no human will endure: the assertion that he has no sense of humor and the doubly impertinent assertion that he has never known trouble.
                                           — Sinclair Lewis

Practise in life whatever you pray for, and God will give it to you more abundantly.   *— Pusey*

" One soweth and another reapeth " is a verity that applies to evil as well as good.   *— George Eliot*

The Christian faith is not one of cold intellect; rather it is full of love, grace and humanity. It has the strength and compassion with which Christ was able to change the course of human life from evil to good, from selfishness to service, from despair to faith in the highest.

— *William T. Manning, D.D.*

I never knew an early-rising, hard-working, prudent man, careful of his earnings and strictly honest, who complained of hard luck. A good character, good habits and iron industry are impregnable to the assaults of all ill-luck that fools ever dreamed. — *Addison*

No person was ever honored for what he received. Honor has been the reward for what he gave.

— *Calvin Coolidge*

Show me the business man or institution not guided by sentiment and service; by the idea that " he profits most who serves best " and I will show you a man or an outfit that is dead or dying. — *B. F. Harris*

The speciously clever people who have been running things and us, calling themselves benefactors, bidding all men admire their sagacity, telling the church to rise up and bless them, appear more and more in their true light, as poor ignorant souls who in a strange madness for power and money have overlooked the beauty and the worth of God's great common people.

— *Bernard Iddings Bell, D.D.*

Drop the hammer and pick up the shovel.

— *J. A. Dever*

Fear is like fire: If controlled it will help you; if uncontrolled, it will rise up and destroy you. Men's actions depend to a great extent upon fear. We do things either because we enjoy doing them or because we are afraid not to do them. This sort of fear has no relation to physical or moral courage. It is inspired by the knowledge that we are not adequately prepared to face the future and the events it may bring — poverty perhaps, or injury, or death.   — *John F. Milburn*

It's the men behind who " make " the man ahead.
                                        — *Merle Crowell*

It is impossible to win the great prizes of life without running risks, and the greatest of all prizes are those connected with the home. No father and mother can hope to escape sorrow and anxiety, and there are dreadful moments when death comes very near to those we love, even if for the time being it passes by. But life is a great adventure, and the worst of all fears is the fear of living. There are many forms of success, many forms of triumph. But there is no other success that in any shape or way approaches that which is open to most of the many men and women who have the right ideals. These are the men and women who see that it is the intimate and homely things that count most. They are the men and women who have the courage to strive for the happiness which comes only with labor and effort and self-sacrifice, and those whose joy in life springs in part from power of work and sense of duty.   — *Theodore Roosevelt*

Liberty has never come from Government. Liberty has always come from the subjects of it. The history of liberty is a history of resistance. The history of liberty is a history of limitations of governmental power, not the increase of it.   — *Woodrow Wilson*

There are safe and unsafe ways of doing nearly anything. The knowledge or the knack of doing things safely is gained by experience, properly directed.

— *Ralph Budd*

Christ didn't waste His time-trying to change the social order. Christ spent all His time fighting sin. Therefore it behooves the witnesses of Christ to say that we do not have to abolish capitalism and establish socialism or communism, that sin can flourish under those systems as well. Christianity is not opposed to any social order, but to sin.

— *John H. McComb, D.D.*

The law of harvest is to reap more than you sow. Sow an act, and you reap a habit; sow a habit, and you reap a character; sow a character and you reap a destiny.

— *G. D. Boardman*

Ideas lose themselves as quickly as quail, and one must wing them the minute they rise out of the grass — or they are gone.

— *Thomas F. Kennedy*

Truth, when not sought after, rarely comes to light.

— *Holmes*

Think of the ills from which you are exempt.

— *Joubert*

Why fools are endowed by Nature with voices so much louder than sensible people possess is a mystery. It is a fact emphasized throughout history.

— *Hertzler*

If you expect perfection from people your whole life is a series of disappointments, grumblings and complaints. If, on the contrary, you pitch your expectations low, taking folks as the inefficient creatures which they are, you are frequently surprised by having them perform better than you had hoped.   — *Bruce Barton*

The present is big with the future.   — *Leibnitz*

God gave man an upright countenance to survey the heavens, and to look upward to the stars.   — *Ovid*

If a man hears our system attacked, and doesn't understand it well enough to pick out the flaws and the phonies in the argument, he is a likely candidate for the pinks and reds.   — *Charles G. Mortimer*

There is no better ballast for keeping the mind steady on its keel, and saving it from all risk of crankiness, than business.   — *Lowell*

There will be no peace so long as God remains unseated at the conference table.   — *William M. Peck*

Luxury is the first, second and third cause of the ruin of republics. It is the vampire which soothes us into a fatal slumber while it sucks the life-blood of our veins.

— *Payson*

Harsh counsels have no effect; they are like hammers which are always repulsed by the anvil.   — *Helvetius*

A Creed

To be so strong that nothing can disturb your peace of mind; to talk health, happiness and prosperity; to make your friends feel that there is something in them; to look on the sunny side of everything; to think only of the best; to be just as enthusiastic about the success of others as you are about your own; to forget the mistakes of the past and profit by them; to wear a cheerful countenance and give a smile to everyone you meet; to be too large for worry, too noble for anger, too strong for fear, and too happy to permit the presence of trouble. — *Christian D. Larson*

It is a thing of no great difficulty to raise objections against another man's oration — nay, it is very easy; but to produce a better in its place is a work extremely troublesome. — *Plutarch*

The longer I live, the more I have come to value the gift of eloquence. Every American youth, if he desires for any purpose to get influence over his countrymen in an honorable way, will seek to become a good public speaker. — *George F. Hoar*

Ten Commandments

1. Never put off till to-morrow what you can do to-day.
2. Never trouble another for what you can do yourself.
3. Never spend your money before you have earned it.
4. Never buy what you do not want because it is cheap.
5. Pride costs more than hunger, thirst and cold.
6. We seldom report of having eaten too little.
7. Nothing is troublesome that we do willingly.
8. How much pain evils have cost us that have never happened!
9. Take things always by the smooth handle.
10. When angry, count ten before you speak, if very angry, count a hundred. — *Thomas Jefferson*

ANOTHER TACK

When you suspect you're going wrong,
Or lack the strength to move along
With placid poise among your peers,
Because of haunting doubts or fears:
It's time for you to shift your pack,
And steer upon another tack!

When wind and waves assail your ship,
And anchors from the bottom slip;
When clouds of mist obscure your sun,
And foaming waters madly run:
It's time for you to change your plan
And make a port while yet you can!

When men laugh at your woeful plight,
And seek your old repute to blight;
When all the world bestows a frown,
While you are sliding swiftly down:
It's time for you to show your grit.
And let the scoffers know you're fit!

When Failure opes your luckless door,
And struts across the creaking floor;
When Fortune flees and leaves you bare,
And former friends but coldly stare:
It's time for you to take a tack,
And show the world you're " coming back! "
     — *Lilburn Harwood Townsend*

Advertising gives industry an opportunity to keep its
clean hands before the public. If industry is clean and has
no dirty hands to hide, it should be proud to display its
purity.   — *Robert W. Sparks*

True prosperity is the result of well placed confidence
in ourselves and our fellow man.   — *Burt*

Magic Medicine

There's a heap o' consolation
  In the handclasp o' a friend;
It can wipe out desolation,
  An' bring heartaches to an end;
It can soothe a troubled spirit
  Like no magic in the land;
Heaven? You are pretty near it —
  When a good friend grips your hand!

There's a heap o' satisfaction
  In a friendly shoulder pat;
It's a simple little action —
  But a mighty one, at that!
When firm fingers grip your shoulder,
  When you sort o' need a brace,
Makes you stronger, braver, bolder,
  An' more fit to run the race!

When you're full o' worry pizen,
  An' the world is lookin' drear,
There's a heap o' energizin'
  In a little pill o' cheer!
When some little frets distress you,
  They put nectar in your cup —
Little phrases like " God bless you! "
  An' the other one, " Cheer up! "

          — *James Edward Hungerford*

    It is a prime objective of civilized society to raise the
plane of living of all people, not to some single type, level
or standard, but according to their respective needs and
preferences, in such ways as will make for harmonious relations within and among nations. If nations will devote to
this objective even a sizable fraction of the intelligence,
human energies and material resources that total war brings
forth, progressive success can be confidently expected.

          — *Joseph S. Davis*

I am persuaded that every time a man smiles — but much more so when he laughs — it adds something to this fragment of life.   — *Sterne*

No man is worthy the honored name of a statesman who does not include the highest practicable education of the people in all his plans of administration. He may have eloquence, he may have a knowledge of all history, diplomacy, jurisprudence; and by these he might claim, in other countries, the elevated rank of a statesman; but, unless he speaks, plans, labors, at all times and in all places, for the culture and edification of the whole people, he is not, he cannot be, an American statesman.   — *Horace Mann*

They that govern the most make the least noise.
                                    — *Selden*

Honor is like the eye, which cannot suffer the least injury without damage; it is a precious stone, the price of which is lessened by the least flaw.   — *Boussuet*

Lack of proper humility, which is the fundamental aspect of Christianity, is the reason many men fail to display the courage and foresight that comes through complete faith in God.   — *Adam W. Burnett, D.D.*

Keep true to the dreams of thy youth.   — *Schiller*

A true history of human events would show that a far larger proportion of our acts are the results of sudden impulses and accident, than of that reason of which we so much boast.   — *Cooper*

How difficult it is to persuade a man to reason against his interest; though he is convinced that equity is against him. *— Trusler*

There is no advancement to him who stands trembling because he cannot see the end from the beginning.

— E. J. Klemme

The church may have seen its duty imperfectly, for it is made up of fallible human beings, but when all is said it has been the one power through nearly two thousand years which has stood for peace, for brotherhood, for the cause of the poor and distressed. *— Ernest F. Scott, D.D.*

Keep out of the suction caused by those who drift backwards. *— E. K. Piper*

The time is undoubtedly coming when it will be a confession of inferiority to overstate or distort the merits and special uses of any commodity, just as any boaster is self-branded a lightweight rather than a man of parts.

— Dr. Harvey W. Wiley

Utmost decency, in all our dealings with the OTHER FELLOW, is the greatest need of the hour. Isn't he just you and me? Besides, being the proper thing, in the long run, it pays handsome dividends. *— Albert B. Lord*

Duty is the sublimest word in the language; you can never do more than your duty; you shall never wish to do less.

— Robert E. Lee

The whole world is learning that treaties, constitutions, ordinances and bonds are good only to the extent that they are made coincident with basic human relationships which have the approval of that sensitive, quick acting and dominant power, the public opinion of the world.

— Owen D. Young

Nobody's problem is ideal. Nobody has things just as he would like them. The thing to do is to make a success with what material I have. It is sheer waste of time and soul-power to imagine what I would do if things were different. They are not different.　　*— Dr. Frank Crane*

The harder the conflict, the more glorious the triumph. What we obtain too cheap, we esteem too lightly; 'tis dearness only that gives everything its value. I love the man that can smile in trouble, that can gather strength from distress, and grow brave by reflection. 'Tis the business of little minds to shrink; but he whose heart is firm, and whose conscience approves his conduct, will pursue his principles until death.　　*— Thomas Paine*

A self-contained nation is a backward nation, with large numbers of people either permanently out of work, or very poorly paid in purchasing power. A nation which trades freely with all the world, selling to others those commodities which it can best produce, and buying from others those commodities which others can best produce, is by far the best conditioned nation for all practical purposes.

— Walter Parker

False happiness renders men stern and proud, and that happiness is never communicated. True happiness renders them kind and sensible, and that happiness is always shared.

— Montesquieu

The soul of the individual was " established " nineteen hundred years ago, while only today are we beginning to see beyond that into the soul world of organization. We are realizing that an organization is not merely a collection of individuals, but is a super-individual with like qualities, only larger. It should be as much more powerful spiritually than a single individual, as it is more powerful materially than a single individual. Everywhere men are recognizing that organizations should have souls. The meaning of this is overwhelming when one considers that the term " organization " covers not only the multitude of business and social societies, but countries, nations, and even international associations. — *Alva Konkle*

You must regulate your life by the standards you admire when you are at your best. — *John M. Thomas*

The birthplace of Christianity was the tomb. The birthplace of splendor is desolation. Spring is conceived in the dark womb of Winter. And light is inevitably the offspring of darkness. For four dreary years and more the world writhed under the cruel thumb of economic disaster. Many thought that happiness had forever fled the earth. All this heaviness of night is surely but the prelude to a better dawn. The voice of God and the voice of Nature proclaim that the best is yet to be — always, the best is yet to be. — *Robert Cromie*

There is danger when a man throws his tongue into high gear before he gets his brain a-going. — *C. C. Phelps*

Faith in the ability of a leader is of slight service unless it be united with faith in his justice.
— *George W. Goethals*

The saying that knowledge is power is not quite true.
Used knowledge is power, and more than power. It is
money, and service, and better living for our fellowmen,
and a hundred other good things. But mere knowledge,
left unused, has not power in it. — *Dr. Edward E. Free*

Goodwill to others is constructive thought. It helps
build us up. It is good for your body. It makes your blood
purer, your muscles stronger, and your whole form more
symmetrical in shape. It is the real elixir of life. The more
such thought you attract to you, the more life you will have.
— *Prentice Mulford*

There is no man in any rank who is always at liberty to
act as he would incline. In some quarter or other he is
limited by circumstances. — *Blair*

A Creed

I would be true,
For there are those who trust me;
I would be pure,
For there are those who care;
I would be strong,
For there is much to suffer;
I would be brave,
For there is much to dare;
I would be friend to all —
The foe — the friendless;
I would be giving,
And forget the gift;
I would be humble,
For I know my weakness;
I would look up —
And laugh — and love — and lift.
— *Howard A. Wheeler*

Many imagine that the higher you go, the easier the climbing. Don't be governed by that theory unless you have a soft place to fall back into. — *J. L. Boggus*

It is the hardest thing in the world to be a good thinker without being a good self-examiner. — *Shaftesbury*

Science is but a mere heap of facts, not a gold chain of truths, if we refuse to link it to the throne of God.
— *F. P. Cobbe*

Times of general calamity and confusion have ever been productive of the greatest minds. The purest ore is produced from the hottest furnace, and the brightest thunderbolt is elicited from the darkest storms. — *Colton*

How little do they see what really is, who frame their hasty judgment upon that which seems. — *Southey*

Justice is the insurance we have on our lives, and obedience is the premium we pay for it. — *William Penn*

In matters of conscience, first thoughts are best; in matters of prudence, last thoughts are best.
— *Robert Hall*

Life is the acceptance of responsibilities or their evasion; it is a business of meeting obligations or avoiding them. To every man the choice is continually being offered, and by the manner of his choosing you may fairly measure him.
— *Ben Ames Williams*

Before I started on my trip around the world, someone gave me one of the most valuable hints I have ever had. It consists merely in shutting your eyes when you are in the midst of a great moment, or close to some marvel of time or space, and convincing yourself that you are at home again with the experience over and past; and what would you wish most to have examined or done if you could turn time and space back again.   *— William Beebe*

Christians are supposed not merely to endure change, nor even to profit by it, but to cause it.

— Harry Emerson Fosdick, D.D.

Given three requisites — means of existence, reasonable health, and an absorbing interest — those years beyond sixty can be the happiest and most satisfying of a lifetime.

— Earnest Elmo Calkins

Money is a stupid measure of achievement but unfortunately it is the only universal measure we have.

— Charles P. Steinmetz

If I had the opportunity to say a final word to all the young people of America, it would be this: Don't think too much about yourself. Try to cultivate the habit of thinking of others; this will reward you. Selfishness always brings its own revenge. It cannot be escaped. Be unselfish. That is the first and final commandment for those who would be useful and happy in their usefulness.

— Charles W. Eliot

It is the calling of great men, not so much to preach new truths, as to rescue from oblivion those old truths which it is our wisdom to remember and our weakness to forget.   *— Sidney Smith*

As you think, you travel; and as you love, you attract. You are today where your thoughts have brought you; you will be tomorrow where your thoughts take you. You cannot escape the result of your thoughts, but you can endure and learn, can accept and be glad. You will realize the vision (not the idle wish), of your heart, be it base or beautiful, or a mixture of both, for you will always gravitate towards that which you, secretly, most love. Into your hands will be placed the exact results of your thoughts; you will receive that which you earn; no more, no less. Whatever your present environment may be, you will fall, remain or rise with your thoughts, your vision, your ideal. You will become as small as your controlling desire; as great as your dominant aspiration.　　—*James Allen*

The eyes of America are on the future; but what use is that if those eyes are blinded? Unless we build our social structure to-day upon a more permanent foundation than the past it will not last beyond the lifetime of those who founded it. Charity, the realization of our brotherhood in God, is the only enduring foundation.
　　　　　　—*Robert E. Woods, D.D.*

The six laws of work are:

1. A man must drive his energy, not be driven by it.

2. A man must be master of his hours and days, not their servant.

3. The way to push things through to a finish effectively must be learned.

4. A man must earnestly want.

5. Never permit failure to become a habit.

6. Learn to adust yourself to the conditions you have to endure, but make a point of trying to alter or correct conditions so that they are most favorable to you.
　　　　　　—*William Frederick Book*

All experience hath shown that mankind are more disposed to suffer, while evils are sufferable, than to right themselves by abolishing the forms to which they are accustomed.   — *Thomas Jefferson*

To-day's pioneers are building to-morrow's progress.
— *Thomas J. Watson*

We would rather have one man or woman working with us than three merely working for us.   — *J. Dabney Day*

As we look at the oppressed lands we are forced to the conclusion that many of the evils which confront them, and indeed us, today derive directly from man's service to Mammon. The creation of godless ideals, the setting up of wealth, power and personal success as the chief aims of life, has contributed more than any other single factor to precipitate the moral and economic crisis with which these lands are faced today and which at present is even overshadowing and threatening the demoralization of our own country.
— *William T. Green, D.D.*

There is scarcely anything more harmless than political or party malice. It is best to leave it to itself. Opposition and contradiction are the only means of giving it life or duration.   — *Witherspoon*

The highest function of conservation is to keep what progressiveness has accomplished.   — *R. H. Fulton*

Sorrow's best antidote is employment.   — *Young*

The most substantial glory of a country is in its virtuous great men. Its prosperity will depend on its docility to learn from their example.   *— Fisher Ames*

The surest way to establish your credit is to work yourself into the position of not needing any.   *— Switzer*

The major problem confronting the world today is: Shall the people govern or be governed?
   — Dr. John A. Ross, Jr.

Let the people know the truth and the country is safe.
   — Abraham Lincoln

The grand essentials of happiness are: something to do, something to love, and something to hope for.
   — Chalmers

Be friends with everybody. When you have friends you will know there is somebody who will stand by you. You know the old saying, that if you have a single enemy you will find him everywhere. It doesn't pay to make enemies. Lead the life that will make you kindly and friendly to every one about you, and you will be surprised what a happy life you will live.   *— Charles M. Schwab*

Research is an organized method of trying to find out what you are going to do after you cannot do what you are doing now. It may also be said to be the method of keeping a customer reasonably dissatisfied with what he has. That means constant improvement and change so that the customer will be stimulated to desire the new product enough to buy it to replace the one he has.   *— Charles F. Kettering*

A man may fight fiercely to hold his own in business; but he does not need to fight to get ahead of someone in the elevator, or up the car steps, or at the postoffice window. And no matter how strong competition is, business and personal courtesy make it easier and pleasanter for everybody.   — *William H. Hamby*

No international Eighteenth Amendment will get rid of war or the instruments of war until civilization finds a way for accomplishing what war has done in the past. Simply to prohibit war is not going to get rid of it. Wars must be anticipated and the causes got rid of by a readiness to accept peaceful means of settlement.
                                        — *Dr. James T. Shotwell*

During a very busy life I have often been asked, " How did you manage to do it all? " The answer is very simple: It is because I did everything *promptly.*
                                        — *Sir Richard Tangye*

Sharing is the great and imperative need of our time. An unshared life is not living. He who shares does not lessen but greatens his life, especially if sharing be done not formally nor conventionally, but with such heartiness as springs out of an understanding of the meaning of the religion of sharing.   — *Rabbi Stephen S. Wise*

The big work of man is neither masonry, manufacturing nor merchandising. It is life itself. Incidentally, there are bricks to be laid, wood to be shaped and goods to be sold; but these are only jots and tittles in the scheme of individual existence. The main thing is life itself.
                                        — *Richard Wightman*

I've never met a person, I don't care what his condition, in whom I could not see possibilities. I don't care how much a man may consider himself a failure, I believe in him, for he can change the thing that is wrong in his life anytime he is prepared and ready to do it. Whenever he develops the desire, he can take away from his life the thing that is defeating it. The capacity for reformation and change lies within.
— *Preston Bradley*

Getting an idea should be like sitting down on a pin; it should make you jump up and do something.
— *E. L. Simpson*

A crowd of troubles passed him by
   As he with courage waited;
He said, " Where do you troubles fly
   When you are thus belated? "
" We go," they say, " to those who mope,
   Who look on life dejected,
Who meekly say ' good-bye ' to hope,
   We go where we're expected."
— *Francis J. Allison*

Better shun the bait than struggle in the snare.
— *John Dryden*

Thrift and prosperity have gone hand in hand since Abraham's flocks grew and multiplied. Thrift is not, as many suppose, a self repression. It is self expression, the demonstration of a will and ability to raise one's self to a higher plane of living. No depression was ever caused by people having too much money in reserve. No human being ever became a social drifter through the practice of sensible thrift.
— *Harvey A. Blodgett*

There are two worlds: the world that we can measure with line and rule, and the world that we feel with our hearts and imagination.   — *Leigh Hunt*

Our civilization demands love and justice more than any other civilization ever has. The whole technical mechanics of our era demands that we live as brothers. When we try, we realize how stubborn we are in resistance to God. We may go down to perdition before we are willing to live as brothers. The way we maintain our self-respect is to hold someone else in contempt.   — *Reinhold Niebur, D.D.*

Speeches that are measured by the hour will die with the hour.   — *Thomas Jefferson*

The real problem with which modern government has to deal is how to protect the citizen against the encroachment upon his rights and liberties by his own government, how to save him from the repressive schemes born of the egotism of public office.   — *William E. Borah*

Every one comes between men's souls and God, either as a brick wall or as a bridge. Either you are leading men to God or you are driving them away.
                                         — *Canon Lindsay Dewar, D.D.*

He that will not apply new remedies must expect new evils.   — *Bacon*

No man has a right to do as he pleases except when he pleases to do right.   — *G. Simmons*

I have about concluded that wealth is a state of mind, and that anyone can acquire a wealthy state of mind by thinking rich thoughts. — *Young*

Half the work that is done in this world is to make things appear what they are not. — *E. R. Beadle*

He is incapable of a truly good action who finds not a pleasure in contemplating the good actions of others.
— *Lavater*

Talents are best nurtured in solitude; character is best formed in the stormy billows of the world. — *Goethe*

If thou art a master, sometimes be blind; if a servant, sometimes be deaf. — *Fuller*

The dole is utterly demoralizing; its chief effect is to turn the unemployed into the unemployable.
— *Dean Inge*

We seem to want mass production, but we must remember that men are individuals not to be satisfactorily dealt with in masses, and the making of men is more important than the production of things. — *Ralph W. Sockman, D.D.*

If you believe in fate, believe in it, at least, for your good. — *Emerson*

Sometimes the best gain is to lose. — *Herbert*

I received a letter from a lad asking me for an easy berth. To this I replied: " You cannot be an editor; do not try the law; do not think of the ministry; let alone all ships and merchandise; abhor politics; don't practice medicine; be not a farmer or a soldier or a sailor; don't study, don't think. None of these are easy. O, my son, you have come into a hard world. I know of only one easy place in it, and that is the grave! "   — *Henry Ward Beecher*

If you cannot make money on one dollar — if you do not coax one dollar to work hard for you, you won't know how to make money out of one hundred thousand dollars.
                              — *E. S. Kinnear*

He who freely magnifies what hath been nobly done, and fears not to declare as freely what might be done better, gives ye the best covenant of his fidelity.   — *John Milton*

You are not very good if you are not better than your best friends imagine you to be.   — *Lavater*

Competition, as the " life " of trade, surely is a tremendous spur to progress. Is it not the pursued man or business that advances through persistent effort to keep ahead? The constant striving to maintain leadership ever involves new ways and means of accomplishing more efficiently and thus it is the " pursued is the progressive man." Put your pursuers on the pay roll.   — *W. D. Toland*

The right use of leisure is no doubt a harder problem than the right use of our working hours. The soul is dyed the color of its leisure thoughts. As a man thinketh in his heart so is he.   — *Dean Inge*

Whoever claims a right for himself must respect the like right in another. Whoever wishes to assert his will as a member of a community must not only consent to obey the will of the community but bear his share in serving it. As he is to profit by the safety and prosperity the community provides, so he must seek its good and place his personal will at its disposal. Benefit and burden, power and responsibility go together. *—James Bryce*

Zeal is very blind, or badly regulated, when it encroaches upon the rights of others. *— Quesnel*

What our deepest self craves is not mere enjoyment, but some supreme purpose that will enlist all our powers and will give unity and direction to our life. We can never know the profoundest joy without a conviction that our life is significant — not a meaningless episode. The loftiest aim of human life is the ethical perfecting of mankind — the transfiguration of humanity. *— Henry J. Golding*

Youth is not a time of life; it is a state of mind. People grow old only by deserting their ideals and by outgrowing the consciousness of youth. Years wrinkle the skin, but to give up enthusiasm wrinkles the soul. . . . You are as old as your doubt, your fear, your despair. The way to keep young is to keep your faith young. Keep your self-confidence young. Keep your hope young.
  — Dr. L. F. Phelan

All of the things now enjoyed by civilization have been created by some man and sold by another man before anybody really enjoyed the benefits of them.
  —James G. Daly

A great business success was probably never attained by chasing the dollar, but is due to pride in one's work — the pride that makes business an art.   *— Henry L. Doherty*

Men who pay whole-hearted attention to business, who train themselves, who develop every power to the full, are favored by the ill-training of the average man. Despite our boasted institutions of learning, most men are only half-educated, have no clear purpose in life or little real ambition, and are not honest in the highest meaning of the word. The only wonder is that well-trained, honest, ambitious, creative men do not forge to the front more rapidly.   *— Darwin P. Kingsley*

The best kind of citizen and the solidest kind of enterprise is one that can look the whole world in the face.
          — M. E. Tracy

Felicity, not fluency of language, is a merit.
          — E. P. Whipple

Faults of the head are punished in this world; those of the heart in another; but as most of our vices are compound, so is their punishment.   *— Colton*

Jails and prisons are the complement of schools; so many less as you have of the latter, so many more you must have of the former.   *— Horace Mann*

Some men go in for big game hunting or Old Masters or postage stamps, but my hobby happens to be my country.
          — Samuel B. Pettengill

I count him braver who overcomes his desires than him who conquers his enemies; for the hardest victory is the victory over self.

— *Aristotle*

Don't foul, don't flinch — hit the line hard.

— *Theodore Roosevelt*

That charity is bad which takes from independence its proper pride, and from mendicity its proper shame.

— *Southey*

When the Norsemen discovered America, they had no compass. Yet the compass had been invented by the Chinese thousands of years before. When, however, Mme. Curie discovered radium, the knowledge of her achievement was spread throughout the world as rapidly as cables and wires could carry it. Mme. Curie's work could have been of no value to the world if her discovery had been known to her alone.

— *Ivy L. Lee*

You have a shilling. I have a shilling. We swap. You have my shilling and I have yours. We are no better off. But suppose you have an idea and I have an idea. We swap. Now you have two ideas and I have two ideas. We have increased our stock of ideas 100 per cent.

— *A. S. Gregg*

The delusive idea that men merely toil and work for the sake of preserving their bodies, and procuring for themselves bread, houses, clothes, is degrading and not to be encouraged. The true origin of man's activity and creativeness lies in his unceasing impulse to embody outside himself the divine and spiritual element within.

— *Froebel*

To find one's work in the world and do it honorably, to
keep one's record clean so that nothing clandestine, furtive,
surreptitious can ever leap out upon one from ambush and
spoil one's life, to be able, therefore, unafraid to look the
world in the face, to live honorably also with one's own
soul because one keeps there no secret place like the bloody
closet in Bluebeard's palace where the dead things hang,
to walk life's journey unhaunted by the ghosts of people
from whose ruin one has stolen pleasure, and so at last to
be a gentleman, one, that is, who puts a little more into life
than one takes out — gather up the significance of such
character, forty years old, sixty years old, eighty years old
— one may well celebrate the solid satisfactions of such a
life.   *— Harry Emerson Fosdick, D.D.*

I pity that man who wants a coat so cheap that the man
or woman who produces the cloth shall starve in the process.
— Benjamin Harrison

Capacity never lacks opportunity. It cannot remain undiscovered because it is sought by too many anxious to use it.
— Cochran

Government can be bigger than any of the players on the
field as a referee, but it has no right to become one of the
players.   *— Austin Igleheart*

You can legislate many conditions — but you cannot
legislate harmony into the hearts of men. To attain industrial peace, we need more than by-laws and compulsory
rules.   *— Clarence Francis*

Obstinacy and vehemency in opinion are the surest proof
of stupidity.   *— Bernard Barton*

The ascending spiral of greatness in America has risen because industry has produced wealth, which in turn has supported educational institutions, which in turn have supplied
leadership to industry in order that with each succeeding
generation it might produce more wealth.

— *Wallace F. Bennett*

He who has health, has hope; and he who has hope, has
everything. — *Arabian Proverb*

Every human life involves an unfathomable mystery, for
man is the riddle of the universe, and the riddle of man in
his endowment with personal capacities. The stars are not
so strange as the mind that studies them, analyzes their
light, and measures their distance.

— *Harry Emerson Fosdick, D.D.*

There are no warlike peoples — just warlike leaders.
— *Ralph J. Bunche*

There is a time in every man's education when he arrives
at the conviction that envy is ignorance; that imitation is
suicide; that he must take himself for better, for worse, as
his portion; that though the wide universe is full of good,
no kernel of nourishing corn can come to him but through
his toil bestowed on that plot of ground which is given to
him to till. — *Ralph Waldo Emerson*

There is nothing in the way of amelioration of the conditions of life, of politics, of social and ethical matters, that
may not be affected through the skilful application of those
principles of advertising that, in business, have proved to
be so wonderfully effective. — *George French*

Often our work seems insignificant and unimportant
when we compare ourselves with the immensity of time and
the universe, but God gave us our moment on earth to be
used in the best possible way.

— *J. V. Moldenhawer, D.D.*

Tell the truth and shame the Devil.   — *Rabelais*

If peace is to come, it must be peace within your own
mind and heart. If hatred is to die, you must scotch it
within yourself. If intelligence is to triumph, you must be
intelligent. There is no other pathway, no other salvation.

— *Henry M. Wriston*

If we could all agree that the world belongs to God we
would see the world as a co-operative fellowship. We of the
human race are so bound together and so interdependent
that it behooves us all to live for the good of the whole.

— *W. Earl Waldrop, D.D.*

New occasions teach new duties.

— *James Russell Lowell*

I set myself on fire and people come to watch me burn.

— *John Wesley*

The Christian in whatever weather and under whatever
skies, commits his life to God, is humble in spirit and is
sure that God will vindicate those who trust Him. He
frees himself in days of uncertainty from overanxious fear.

— *G. Morris Smith, D.D.*

It is worth remembering that output per man in this country has increased on the average about two per cent a year during this century. Mere continuation of this trend will mean a future full of better things for more people. But it is my own feeling that the tremendous gains which have been achieved by machine techniques may be substantially matched when we learn to make better use of ourselves as people. — *Henry Ford, II*

RESOLUTION

Whereas the Supreme Power of the universe has deemed it natural to create human beings of various colors, races, and creeds; and

Whereas in His sight they all are His equally beloved children;

Therefore be it resolved that there is no superior race or group of peoples and that all men are brothers of equal rank; and be it further resolved that we know this and believe it now and forever! — *M. Newman*

In making our decisions, we must use the brains that God has given us. But we must also use our hearts which He also gave us. — *Fulton Oursler*

How many people ever consider that the lack of certain qualities — such as balance, common sense, tranquility — affect the physical state of the human body? . . . Did you ever hear of people being sick because they hated someone? This is not uncommon. — *Bishop Westcott*

Whether we wish to begin a program of job simplification, or to improve the economic outlook of our people we must first be sure that the atmosphere is right. New ideas do not thrive in an atmosphere of suspicion, jealousy, fear or antagonism. — *Melvin J. Evans*

" It's becoming increasingly difficult to reach the down-trodden masses in America," a comrade wrote to his superior. " In the spring they're forever polishing their cars. In the summer they take vacations. In the fall they go to the world series and football games. And in the winter you can't get them away from their television sets. Please give me suggestions on how to let them know how oppressed they are."   — *Prof. Dexter Williams*

A Business Man's Prayer

Help me, O Lord, to remember that three feet make one yard, sixteen ounces one pound, four quarts one gallon and sixty minutes one hour. Help me to do business on the square. Make me sympathetic with the fellow who has broken in the struggle. Keep me from taking an unfair advantage of the weak, or from selling my self-respect for a profit. Blind my eyes to the petty faults of others, but reveal to me my own. Deafen my ears to the rustle of unholy skirts, and help me to live, day by day, in such a way that I shall be able to look across the table at my wife, who has been such a blessing to me, and have nothing to conceal.

And when comes the sound of low music, the scent of sweet flowers, and the crunch of footsteps on the gravel, make the ceremony short, and the epitaph simple — " Here lies a man . . . one who was of service to others."

       — *A. A. Larsen*

It's a pity so many of us persist in regarding politeness as being merely a superficial social grace instead of what it really is, namely one of the necessities of life. Quite apart from politeness for its own sake, and as a matter of plain justice, it is invaluable as a sort of cushion or buffer to hold off the jolt that would otherwise disrupt the harmony of things.   — *Zealandia*

Hell begins on the day when God grants us a clear vision of all that we might have achieved, of all the gifts which we have wasted, of all that we might have done which we did not do. — *Gian-Carlo Menotti*

Speech is the gift of all, but thought of few. — *Cato*

Character is that which reveals moral purpose, exposing the class of things a man chooses or avoids. — *Aristotle*

Greatness is a two-faced coin — and its reverse is humility. — *Marguerite Steen*

A man's true wealth is the good he does in this world. — *Mohammed*

If we command our wealth, we shall be rich and free; if our wealth commands us, we are poor indeed. — *Burke*

A lie leads a man from a grove into a jungle. — *Marcelene Cox*

We still have it in our power to rise above the fears, imagined and real, and to shoulder the great burdens which destiny has placed upon us, not for our country alone, but for the benefit of all the world. That is the only destiny worthy of America. — *Helen Keller*

Human society is based on want. Life is based on want. Wild-eyed visionaries may dream of a world without need. Cloud-cuckoo-land. It can't be done. — *H. G. Wells*

There is nothing that solidifies and strengthens a nation like reading of the nation's own history, whether that history is recorded in books or embodied in customs, institutions and monuments.   — *Joseph Anderson*

Originality does not consist of inventing a new language, but in expressing in the accepted language all possible new and personal thoughts.   — *René Dumesnil*

Goodwill is no easy symbol of good wishes. It is an immeasurable and tremendous energy, the atomic energy of the spirit.   — *Eleanor B. Stock*

If you have not often felt the joy of doing a kind act, you have neglected much, and most of all yourself.
— *A. Neilen*

Research is the reconnaissance party of industry, roving the unknown territories ahead independently, yet not without purpose, seeing for the first time what all the following world will see a few years hence.   — *S. M. Kinter*

America must remain, at any cost, the custodian of freedom, human dignity and economic security. The United States must be strong, so that no nation may dare attack.
— *Louis B. Mayer*

How beautifully is it ordered, that as many thousands work for one, so must every individual bring his labor to make the whole. The highest is not to despise the lowest, nor the lowest to envy the highest; each must live in all and by all.   — *G. A. Sala*

Let us always have in mind that every attempt in the history of the world to establish a loafer's paradise has wound up in a dictator's hell-hole.   — *Harold E. Stassen*

Though I have been among paralytics, to me the worst physical affliction is blindness. But spiritual blindness is worse.   — *Francis F. Fisher, D.D.*

We have inherited new difficulties because we have inherited more privileges.   — *Dr. Abram Sacher*

The sunrise never failed us yet.   — *Celia Baxter*

The testimony of every scientist is that the frontiers that are opening out ahead of us now are far wider and more spectacular than any frontier of America in the past. Our horizons are not closed. We are going to write a greater development in America than has ever been conceived.
                                   — *Eric Johnston*

It is the duty of government to make it difficult for people to do wrong, easy to do right.   — *William E. Gladstone*

Life, if properly viewed in any aspect, is great, but mainly great when viewed in its relation to the world to come.
                                   — *Albert Barnes*

Wise men ne'er sit and wail their loss, but cheerily seek how to redress their harms.   — *Shakespeare*

It is not being out at heels that makes a man discontented,
it is being out at heart. To be contented is to be good
friends with yourself.   — *Bliss Carman*

There is work that is work and there is play that is play;
there is play that is work and work that is play. And in
only one of these lies happiness.   — *Gelett Burgess*

The man who wears injustice by his side, though powerful
millions followed him to war, combats against the odds —
against high heaven.   — *Havard*

If honesty did not exist, we ought to invent it as the best
means of getting rich.   — *Mirabeau*

No small part of the cruelty, oppression, miscalculation,
and general mismanagement of human relations is due to
the fact that in our dealings with others we do not see them
as persons at all, but only as specimens or representatives
of some type or other. . . . We react to the sample instead
of to the rea' person.   — *Robert J. MacIver*

The real problem in the years ahead is one of making
the most efficient use of all our national resources — and
not the least of these resources is our intelligent youth.
                                           — *George A. Sloan*

One ship drives east and another west
    While the self-same breezes blow:
'Tis the set of the sail and not the gale
    That bids them where to go.
                                           — *Ella Wheeler Wilcox*

Economic nationalism is a tenacious and potent enemy of world order. To combat this foe, world citizens must become more active. . . . To secure better legislation, the best informed citizens should be the most vocal in their own communities in demanding that measures of dubious sectional short-run benefit give way to policies better calculated to advance the interests of a free, democratic world civilization with material abundance for all of Adam's children.
— *Robert L. Gulick, Jr.*

All are not just because they do no wrong; but he who will not wrong me when he may, he is truly just.
— *Cumberland*

Men are more important than tools. If you don't believe so, put a good tool into the hands of a poor workman.
— *John J. Bernet*

We never think of the main business of life till a vain repentance minds us of it at the wrong end.
— *L'Estrange*

Opportunity rarely knocks until you are ready. And few people have ever been really ready without receiving opportunity's call.
— *Channing Pollock*

Little progress can be made by merely attempting to repress what is evil; our great hope lies in developing what is good.
— *Calvin Coolidge*

This generation has learned all over again that there are great differences between a social order that is fundamentally bad and one that is essentially good.

— *Harry Woodburn Chase*

The Japanese boy is trained to go to a place, stay there, fight and die. We train our men to go to a place, to fight, to win and to live. I can assure you, it is a better theory.

— *Major General Vandegrift*

Does anyone believe for one moment that the progress we have made would have been possible under bureaucratic control of any government. This country was founded upon the principle of the regulation of private effort, of making rules for the game, and under that system alone can we look for the same success in the future which has been ours in the past. Our position today is the direct result of the free play among our people of private competitive effort.

— *Roger Babson*

God grants liberty only to those who love it and are always ready to guard and defend it. Let our object be our country. And, by the blessing of God, may that country itself become a vast and splendid monument, not of oppression and terror, but of wisdom, of peace, and of liberty, upon which the world may gaze with admiration forever!

— *Daniel Webster*

The smallest actual good is better than the most magnificent promise of impossibilities. — *Macaulay*

There is no twilight zone of honesty in business — a thing is right or it's wrong — it's black or it's white.

— *John F. Dodge*

Life is for everybody, just as sunshine is for everybody. To assert that you live your own life is like asserting that the sun sends out special rays for your own private benefit.

— *Franc-Nohair*

Charm strikes the sight, but merit wins the soul.

— *Pope*

Produce great men, the rest follows.

— *Walt Whitman*

Our success in war and peace depends not on luck, or rhetoric, or the intervention of mythical gods; it depends on human character and modern scientific creations, and on respect for the meaning and methods of science. . . . It is not luck but logic which in the present and future will win — the careful and logical consideration of what effects come from specific causes, what are the natural reasons behind events, what are the processes required to adapt nature to the material and spiritual advantages of mankind.

— *Harlow Shapley*

Mistakes remembered are not faults forgot.

— *B. H. Newell*

Majorities must recognize that minorities have rights which ought not to be extinguished and they must remember that history can be written as the record of the follies of the majority. — *Lindsay Rogers*

Doubly rich is the man still boyish enough to play, laugh and sing as he carries and emanates sunshine along a friendly road. — *Charles R. Wiers*

In order to have an enemy, one must be somebody. One must be a force before he can be resisted by another force. A malicious enemy is better than a clumsy friend.
— *Madame Swetchine*

Almost all of our sorrows spring out of our relations with other people. — *Schopenhauer*

The moment our democracy ceases to respect God it will cease to respect your value as an individual. The moment it ceases to respect your value as an individual it ceases to be democracy. — *Thomas J. Curran*

The force of selfishness is as inevitable and as calculable as the force of gravitation. — *Hailliard*

It is the greatest good to the greatest number which is the measure of right and wrong. — *Jeremy Bentham*

Concentrate on finding your goal, then concentrate on reaching it. — *Col. Michael Friedsam*

The average person puts only 25% of his energy and ability into his work. The world takes off its hat to those who put in more than 50% of their capacity, and stands on its head for those few and far between souls who devote 100%. — *Andrew Carnegie*

Win hearts, and you have all men's hands and purses.
— *Burleigh*

Democracy does not contain any force which will check the constant tendency to put more and more on the public payroll. The state is like a hive of bees in which the drones display, multiply and starve the workers so the idlers will consume the food and the workers will perish. — *Plato*

When we know how to read our own hearts, we acquire wisdom of the hearts of others. — *Denis Diderot*

We can believe almost anything if it be necessary to protect our pride. — *Dr. Douglas A. Thom*

Education is the indispensable means by which the ideas of the men who founded the American Republic can be disseminated and perpetuated. Only through education can the people be kept from becoming greedy and ignorant, from degenerating into a populace incapable of self-government. It is only by education, religion, and morality that the people can save themselves from becoming a willing instrument of their own debasement and ruin. The American Republic will endure only as long as the ideas of the men who founded it continue dominant.
— *Daniel L. Marsh*

Many receive advice, only the wise profit by it.
— *Syrus*

History makes some amends for the shortness of life.
— *Skelton*

They are happy men whose natures sort with their vocations. — *Bacon*

We must lift the level of understanding both at home and abroad of what the free enterprise system is, what it is not, and how it benefits the people who live under it. We must somehow get these elementary truths across, not only to the people of other lands but to millions here at home who do not understand it, if we are to generate a powerful demand and desire for its retention.   — *Philip D. Reed*

The Christian State proclaims human personality to be supreme; the servile State denies it. Every compromise with the infinite value of the human soul leads straight back to savagery and to the jungle.   — *Baldwin*

The height of human wisdom is to bring our tempers down to our circumstances, and to make a calm within, under the weight of the greatest storm without.

— *DeFoe*

When you know men and you know how to handle men, you've licked the problem of running a business. The executive's job is to provide leadership, the kind of leadership that develops the best efforts of the men under him. He can't do that if he shuts himself up in his office. He has to get out and get acquainted with his men.

— *Roy W. Moore*

Do not spill thy soul in running hither and yon, grieving over the mistakes and the vices of others. The one person whom it is most necessary to reform is yourself.

— *Emerson*

Great minds have purposes, others have wishes.

— *Washington Irving*

I am one of those people optimistic enough to believe in the future of democracy. No matter how widely we may have departed from the practice of democracy, no matter how many failures we may have had as a nation, it is a conviction to me that it is something too precious to make it a matter of any light moment that those things should be discarded. — *Harry Woodburn Chase*

Dreamers and doers — the world generally divides men into those two general classifications, but the world is often wrong. There are men who win the admiration and respect of their fellowmen. They are the men worth while. Dreaming is just another name for thinking, planning, devising — another way of saying that a man exercises his soul. A steadfast soul, holding steadily to a dream ideal, plus a sturdy will determined to succeed in any venture, can make any dream come true. Use your mind and your will. They work together for you beautifully if you'll only give them a chance. — *B. N. Mills*

Quality isn't something that can be argued into an article or promised into it. It must be put there. If it isn't put there, the finest sales talk in the world won't act as a substitute. — *C. G. Campbell*

The man who lives for himself is a failure. Even if he gains much wealth, position or power he still is a failure. The man who lives for others has achieved true success. A rich man who consecrates his wealth and his position to the good of humanity is a success. A poor man who gives of his service and his sympathy to others has achieved true success even though material prosperity or outward honors never come to him. — *Norman Vincent Peale, D.D.*

We cannot define God or any of the real values of life. What is the vague thing called forth that is worth living and dying' for? Beauty, truth, friendship, love, creation — these are the great values of life. We can't prove them, or explain them, yet they are the most stable things in our lives. — *Dr. Jesse Herman Holmes*

When young men are beginning life, the most important period, it is often said, is that in which their habits are formed. That is a very important period. But the period in which the ideas of the young are formed and adopted is more important still. For the ideal with which you go forward to measure things determines the nature, so far as you are concerned, of everything you meet.

— *Henry Ward Beecher*

With the proper flow of commerce across the borders of all countries it is unnecessary for soldiers to march across those borders. — *Thomas J. Watson*

There ought to be a system of manners in every nation which a well-formed mind would be disposed to relish. To make us love our country, our country ought to be lovely. — *Burke*

Our business in life is not to get ahead of others, but to get ahead of ourselves — to break our own records, to outstrip our yesterday by our today, to do our work with more force than ever before. — *Stewart B. Johnson*

Deliberate with caution, but act with decision; and yield with graciousness, or oppose with firmness.

— *Charles Hole*

If we would stick to our knitting and do all the things we know we should do in carrying out the full intent and purpose of all of our old, tried, and found-true ideas and methods, we wouldn't have very much time to be dreaming about the new idea that so many people seem to think will be the savior of business. — *E. V. Walsh*

Under normal periods, any man's success hinges about 5 per cent. on what *others* do for him and 95 per cent. on what *he* does, with emphasis on the *does*. The years that lie ahead will be no bed of roses for any business man. No matter how high the tide of prosperity may rise, no business man will share therein who does not gear himself and his business to a new tempo to meet changing conditions and the problems and difficulties that await our solution. — *James A. Worsham*

To-day a reader, to-morrow a leader. — *W. Fusselman*

Every man has some peculiar train of thought which he falls back upon when he is alone. This, to a great degree, moulds the man. — *Dugald Stewart*

Some people grow under responsibility, others merely swell. — *Hubbell*

It is not the variegated colors, the cheerful sounds, and the warm breezes which enliven us so much in Spring; it is the quiet prophetic spirit of endless hope, a presentiment of many happy days, the anticipation of higher everlasting blossoms and fruits, and the secret sympathy with the world that is developing itself. — *Martin Opitz*

The Good New Day

None but the futile mourn the past,
   Or waste their hours in vain berating;
Each day is richer than the last;
   There are new worlds to conquer waiting!

Though somber sunsets lend a wan
   Regret to pleasant days gone from us,
The pilgrim stars go wheeling on,
   And dawns bring new demesnes of promise!

The path that yesterday we trod
   Was bright with blossom, sweet with clover;
Yet there must be a richer sod
   Where the horizon trail dips over.

Onward and upward, mile on mile;
   Deaf to the jibes, the mocker's chorus;
Facing each hazard with a smile —
   Till a new world lies wide before us!

There is no going back. Why bind
   Your swift pace with a phantom fetter?
Forget the good old days behind.
   Go on — and make the new ones better!

                               — *Ted Olsen*

It is indeed a desirable thing to be well descended, but
the glory belongs to our ancestors.   — *Plutarch*

Don't get up from the feast of life without paying for
your share of it.   — *W. R. Inge*

Character is not made in a crisis — it is only exhibited.
                            — *Dr. Robert Freeman*

The continual tendency toward shorter hours is certainly connected with the modern development of industry, for with the use of power, mechanical devices and quicker methods the amount of effort to do the world's work is constantly being reduced. This tendency must be beneficial to the human race, for its more leisure time, and contributes to the joy of life. — *Lammot du Pont*

A state, in which the citizens are compelled or actuated by means of a dictator to obey even the best laws, might be a tranquil, peaceable, prosperous State; but it would always seem to me a multitude of well-cared-for slaves, rather than a nation of free and independent men with no restraint save such as was required to prevent any infringement on right. — *Wilhelm von Humboldt*

When a man says money can do anything, that settles it: he hasn't any. — *Ed. Howe*

We must believe in a Being, a divine will, or in an intelligent purpose behind the world. And we must live as if the world had sense, not as if the world were meaningless. Cold, cynical people are not only unhappy, but are dead to the spiritual values that make life. Only the positive attitude in acts of kindness and peace will give the joyous life. — *Dr. Charles Reynolds Brown*

Sympathy is a thing to be encouraged apart from humane considerations, because it supplies us with the materials for wisdom. — *R. L. Stevenson*

Do you know what is more hard to bear than the reverses of fortune? It is the baseness, the hideous ingratitude of man. — *Napoleon*

What is an individual? Just a bit of life shot off from
the one Life in the universe — just a bit of love and truth
dropped on this globe, just as the globe itself was once a
bit of light and heat dropped from the sun.

— C. W. Barron

External things and opportunities so abound in American
life that, instead of nurturing the true source of happiness,
we tend to make it a direct aim. So we end in looking for
happiness in possession of the external — in money, a good
time, somebody to lean on, and so on. We are impatient,
hurried and fretful because we do not find happiness where
we look for it.   *— John Dewey*

Contemplation is necessary to generate an object, but
action must propagate it.   *— Feltham*

Business is always a struggle. There are always obstacles and competitors. There is never an open road,
except the wide road that leads to failure. Every great
success has always been achieved by fight. Every winner
has scars. . . . The men who succeed are the efficient
few. They are the few who have the ambition and will-
power to develop themselves.   *— Herbert N. Casson*

Worry, whatever its source, weakens, takes away courage,
and shortens life.   *— John Lancaster Spalding*

What religion needs today is not more flying with God,
or leaping with God, or jumping up and down with God,
or going into spasms and convulsions and epileptic fits with
God. What religion needs today is more walking with
God.   *— Milo H. Gates, D.D.*

I do not want anybody to convince my son that some one will guarantee him a living. I want him rather to realize that there is plenty of opportunity in this country for him to achieve success, but whether he wins or loses depends entirely on his own character, perseverance, thrift, intelligence and capacity for hard work.

— Major John L. Griffith

Goodwill for a business is built by good goods, service and truthful advertising.   *— E. R. Waite*

All worthwhile men have good thoughts, good ideas and good intentions — but precious few of them ever translate those into action.   *— John Hancock Field*

It is the surmounting of difficulties that makes heroes.

— Kossuth

Like swimming, riding, writing or playing golf, happiness can be learned.   *— Dr. Boris Sokoloff*

Nothing can lift the heart of man like manhood in a fellow man.   *— Herman Melville*

Were I to pray for a taste which should stand me in good stead under every variety of circumstances and be a source of happiness and a cheerfulness to me during life and a shield against its ills, however things might go amiss and the world frown upon me, it would be a taste for reading.

— Sir John Herschel

To be honest, to be kind — to earn a little and spend a little less, to make upon the whole a family happier for his presence, to renounce when that shall be necessary and not be embittered, to keep a few friends, but these without capitulation — above all, on the same grim condition, to keep friends with himself — here is a task for all that a man has of fortitude and delicacy.

— Robert Louis Stevenson

Greatness, in the last analysis, is largely bravery — courage in escaping from old ideas and old standards and respectable ways of doing things. This is one of the chief elements in what we vaguely call capacity. If you do not dare differ from your associates and teachers you will never be great or your life sublime. You may be the happier as a result, or you may be miserable. Each of us is great insofar as we perceive and act on the infinite possibilities which lie undiscovered and unrecognized about us.

— James Harvey Robinson

My message to you is: Be courageous! I have lived a long time. I have seen history repeat itself again and again. I have seen many depressions in business. Always America has come out stronger and more prosperous. Be as brave as your fathers before you. Have faith! Go forward.

— Thomas A. Edison's
last public message.

And in the end, through the long ages of our quest for light, it will be found that truth is still mightier than the sword. For out of the welter of human carnage and human sorrow and human weal the indestructible thing that will always live is a sound idea.   *— Gen. Douglas MacArthur*

INDEX